Beckett Translating/Translating Beckett

Beckett Translating /
/ Translating Beckett

Edited by
Alan Warren Friedman
Charles Rossman
Dina Sherzer

THE PENNSYLVANIA STATE UNIVERSITY PRESS
University Park and London

Library of Congress Cataloging-in-Publication Data

Beckett translating/translating Beckett.

Bibliography: p.
1. Beckett, Samuel, 1906–   —Criticism and
interpretation. 2. Literature—Translating.
3. Literature—Adaptations.
I. Friedman, Alan Warren. II. Rossman, Charles.
III. Sherzer, Dina.
PR6003.E282Z5724 1986   848'.91409   86–43032
ISBN 0-271-00480-0

This book is dedicated to the memory of Alan Schneider, Beckett's friend and director for two decades. Alan first began to "translate" Beckett in 1956, when, as the American director of *Waiting for Godot,* he gave Beckett's potent text its life on the stage. Since then, he has transmuted many silent Beckett scripts into dynamic performance. We include Ruby Cohn's homage to Alan Schneider, "Inexhaustible Alan," as an Afterword.

Contents

Introduction

Samuel Beckett won the Nobel Prize for literature in 1969 for his achievement as both playwright and novelist. Before and since, he has had an enormous impact on twentieth-century art. Up to now, Beckett has been regarded largely as a commentator on the human condition—as one of the most penetrating and subtle registrars of the angst of our time—and as a writer who undermines and manipulates the metaphysical conventions that underlie both the verbal representation of "reality" and language itself.

This book offers a new perspective. It emphasizes three significant aspects of Beckett's art that have received insufficient consideration. First, Beckett is a translator, an experimenter in two languages simultaneously whose unique achievements result, to a large extent, from his bilinguality. Second, Beckett's creativity explores several verbal, kinetic, and visual media. And third, because of the experimental and innovative qualities of Beckett's work, he has inspired creative experimentation in many other artists.

Because of Beckett's achievement and influence, the notion of translation is of preeminent significance. This book regards translation not as a secondary production but rather as a fundamental, dynamic process that involves interpretation, adaptation, transformation, and transposition—activities requiring strategies and techniques for transcoding on the part of the translator. Consequently, a double line of inquiry informs this book: it examines not only *what* is translated but *how* it is translated and thus raises a new set of questions about Beckett's works.

Beckett is a translator who puts what he has written in English or French into the other language. How does he translate from one language to another? How does the second version both repeat and change the original? Like any writer, Beckett transmutes his experiences, his feelings, and his sensibilities, through language, into art. What devices does he use? What metaphors does he invent? Do other creators share his methods? If so, in what ways? Beckett experiments with literary genres and conventions. How does he adopt, transform, and translate inherited genres and conventions into his own terms? Other creators have, in turn, translated, transformed, and interpreted Beckett's works through directing Beckett's plays, writing their own, or illustrating his texts. How have they translated his language, his tones, his moods, and his concepts in shaping their own representations?

Confronting these various transmutations and questions, this book both constitutes a new phase in Beckett scholarship and contributes to contemporary critical thought. In discussing various forms and techniques of translation, it emphasizes the artist's strategies of signification and representation, an issue of central concern to modern criticism and semiotics.

Part 1, "Translations: French/English, English/French," discusses Beckett's bilingualism and his unique activity as self-translator. It offers reflections on the status of the translated text and on the differences between the original and the translation. This section underscores the complexities, refinements, and genius of Beckett's translations, as well as the sociolinguistic and cultural awareness that they imply. In specific cases, the original and the translation form complementary texts in which the translation is, in fact, a kind of interpretation of the original; recently translated texts are uncanny spaces that allow the reemergence of images and motifs that Beckett had earlier suppressed. Complementing these presentations of Beckett manipulating, exploring, and exploiting two languages, a discussion of the characteristics of Beckett's linguistic personality demonstrates how his techniques express an acute awareness of what language is, and of what it is not.

Part 2, "Conceptual Transmutations," focuses on how Beckett expresses his central themes. It discusses Beckett's invention of specific metaphors to translate metaphysical concepts, perhaps the core of his vision. In addition, it shows how Beckett translates not only the metaphysical but also the political world of the twentieth century into powerful tragic images; how Beckett's early comic texts are fictional and dramatic reenactments of the theories of such thinkers as Freud, Burke, Kris, and Frankl, who thought of comedy as a form of wisdom and a way of mastering an art of living; and how Beckett and Duchamp employ similar techniques of translating their ironic negativity concerning life and art.

Part 3, "Genre Transformations," treats an important feature of Beckett's aesthetic orientation: his contesting of genre conventions and his acute distrust of conventional art, which lead him to manipulate and transform genres and traditions. The reflections in this section offer insights into the forms of Beckett's antiformality: how Beckett manipulates conventions of autobiography, of the pastoral, and of drama; how he translates myths for his own purposes; and how, in recent texts, he changes the relationship between sound patterns and thematic structure.

Part 4, "Transpositions for Stage and Screen," examines one of Beckett's favorite mediums: his plays for theater and television. It analyzes the nature and the process of Beckett's transpositions for television and his impact on the American stage, both in the Mabou Mines' translations of his texts and in

Sam Shepard's adaptation of Beckett's techniques and metaphysics into an American medium.

Part 5, "Transcreations: Language to Paintings," documents yet another aspect of Beckett's influence on the artistic life of our time. Beckett has not only influenced directors and playwrights, he has also stimulated well-known artists to illustrate his works, thereby performing transcreations—translations that are also creations. Avigdor Arikha and Jasper Johns are well-known painters who have been compelled by Beckett's works, as have Max Ernst and H. M. Erhardt, who have created illustrations that are visual signs to be read both in their own terms and as commentary on Beckett's writing. It is shown here that Ernst and Erhardt performed transcreations that enlarge our sense of the meaning inherent in image and text.

We have always known that Beckett is a complex writer. This book helps us to understand exactly *how* he is complex. It emphasizes the need to take seriously, after their initial creation, Beckett's various activities vis à vis his texts. His translations from one language to another and his adaptations for the screen are significant transcreations that both comment on the original work and offer insights into Beckett's own thinking. Beckett not only writes novels and stages his plays, he also invents twin creations in two languages, as well as multiple verbal and visual forms. He is an intermedia creator par excellence.

Several other facets of Beckett's creativity, largely unrecognized until now, also emerge in this book. Previously, critics have tended to consider Beckett as an aloof metaphysician, one who refuses to partake of the world that he perforce inhabits. Now it is possible to say that his metaphysics derives from and responds to the most urgent social and political issues. Similarly, Beckett is often considered a skeptic who undermines language. But his particular works as examined here challenge that interpretation: Beckett uses language in his own idiosyncratic ways, not merely to undermine but to create.

Our purpose is to demonstrate how and why Beckett manipulates traditional genres, literary and dramatic conventions, and his verbal medium. Beckett's response to conventional forms, like the innovations of Marcel Duchamp, Ernst, and other modernists, is indicative of an iconoclastic spirit that refuses simple categorization. Beckett's incessant questioning and experimentation have inspired a like questioning and experimentation in others. Beckett's work has changed our idea of what is possible—and in fact has changed the very notion of *limits* on what is possible.

PART 1

Translations:
French/English, English/French

RAYMOND FEDERMAN

The Writer as Self-Translator

Like all those who get involved with Beckett's work, initially I wanted to know what that work means. And so I devoted a lot of time and effort to the "pursuit of meaning" in the Beckett landscape. Gradually, this pursuit of meaning became less and less important, less and less interesting to me. Perhaps because I had no more to say (if I ever had anything to say) to my own satisfaction, and perhaps also because what was being said was being said over and over again.

In any event, having freed myself of this need for understanding the meaning of Beckett's work, I found a new enjoyment in returning to his books. I found myself pausing for long periods of time simply to admire the beauty, and especially the shape, of Beckett's sentences, both in French and in English. And it occurred to me, as I spent more and more time with Beckett's language rather than with the meaning, that little critical attention has been paid to Beckett's bilingualism and his unique activity as a self-translator. The bibliography of Beckett that John Fletcher and I put together fourteen years ago contains no entry in the index for bilingualism and/or self-translating. A gross omission on our part.

And it is still true today that very little has been written on this crucial, fundamental aspect of Beckett's work. In the 1985 PMLA bibliography, only three or four entries are devoted to it. I also consulted the tables of contents and indexes of all the books on Beckett in my personal library (and after all these years of fooling around with Beckett, it is quite a nice collection). And yet though Beckett's bilingualism and his activity as self-translator are mentioned here and there, and references are made, en passant, to the French and English texts, in most instances these are dealt with superficially or impressionistically.

There is, of course, the chapter in Ruby Cohn's book *The Comic Gamut*, a book which remains one of the standard and essential studies of Beckett. It is indeed surprising that, though Cohn's first book has been a model and an inspiration for many subsequent studies, so few Beckett critics have explored this question of bilingualism and self-translating beyond what Cohn had already done back in 1962.

John Fletcher, another early pioneer of Beckett studies, also touches on these questions in his first book, *The Novels of Samuel Beckett*, and though the index of that book contains entries for "style," "bilingualism," and "self-translating," these send us back to only a few pages here and there in the text. Fletcher does, however, devote a nine-page chapter to bilingualism in his *Samuel Beckett's Art*, and he also contributes an essay entitled "L'Ecrivain bilingue" in *Cahier de l'Herne: Samuel Beckett*.

Beyond that, in all the books I consulted, there are no chapters, no long sections, no index entries for bilingualism and/or self-translating. Even more interesting—or perhaps one should say appalling—the index of *the* Beckett biography (authorized or unauthorized as it may be) does not even contain the words *bilingual* or *bilingualism*, *translating*, or *self-translating*. How can one write a biography of Samuel Beckett and totally ignore these fundamental aspects? This baffles me.

As for the French critics—except for Ludovic Janvier, who was to some extent involved with the French translation of *Watt* and wrote about that experience—there is nothing in their work about Beckett's bilingualism. Perhaps the French are too chauvinistic to admit that Beckett even writes in a language other than French.

No, let me correct myself. I did find, while consulting the books in my library, one very interesting essay by Harry Cockerham, entitled "Bilingual Playwright," published in *Beckett the Shape Changer* (edited by Katharine Worth). It is a fine and thorough essay. Of course, there may be others on the same subject with which I am not familiar: it has been a long time since I gave up being a Beckett bibliographer.

Cockerham's essay raises important questions about Beckett's bilingualism, even though he deals only with the theater; questions which are not entirely new but nonetheless are essential. For instance: Is Beckett's French simpler than his English? Is Beckett funnier in French than in English? Is he more poetic in English than in French? Is Beckett more vulgar, more scatological, more blasphemous in French than in English? Are there more cultural and literary references in English than in French? And what happens to these references, allusions, quotations, misquotations, when they pass from one language to the other? Is Beckett's French more slangish than his English?

Here are a few examples:

Nous les avons bazardés. / We got rid of them.
Qui t'a esquinté? / Who beat you?

"Pour jeter le doute, à toi le pompon," says Estragon in *Godot*, which becomes in English the rather flat: "Nothing is certain when you're about." It is certainly interesting and even fun to compare these lines, but that does not get us very far. Perhaps it simply shows that English is not as rich or as funny as French.

Ruby Cohn, in her first book, had already raised some of these questions, but Cockerham's essay deserves to be read because of the well-chosen examples he offers to illustrate his investigation.

So more than twenty years after the first book in English on Beckett was published—by now these books must number in the hundreds, while the articles must number in the thousands—little has been done in terms of Beckett's bilingualism and his self-translating activity.

Usually one studies the Beckett twin-texts to observe if the meaning has changed as the text passes from one language to the other, or to note omissions, deletions, or additions, to delight in the way Beckett translates his own puns or renders a typical Beckettian play-on-words. But nothing much beyond that.

In other words, an urgent need exists for a solid, thorough, definitive study of Beckett's bilingualism and his activity as a self-translator. But not merely to compare passages in the twin-texts, not merely to note differences or variants, but to arrive at an *aesthetic* of bilingualism and self-translating, or better yet to arrive at a *poetics* of such activities (to use Lori Chamberlain's term). An important chapter in that book would have to be devoted to meaning, to the transformation of meaning in Beckett as the text passes from French into English, or vice versa.

EXAMPLE:

> Tant il est vrai que dans le cylindre le peu possible là où il n'est pas n'est seulement plus et dans le moindre moins le rien tout entier si cette notion est maintenue.

> So true it is that when in the cylinder what little is possible is not so it is merely no longer so and in the least the all of nothing if this notion is maintained.

I have difficulty understanding the exact meaning of this marvelous piece of syntax, for though I think it means the same in both languages, I am not sure it does. There seems to be a curious slippage into nonsense from the French into the English.

Here is another example from *Fin de Partie / Endgame*—that often-quoted exchange about God—where the French and the English seem to be saying the same thing and yet slip away from one another:

> Bernique! Et toi? / Sweet damn all! And you?
> Attends . . . Macache! / Nothing doing.
> Le salaud, il n'existe pas! / The bastard! He doesn't exist!
> Pas encore. / Not yet.

The two passages seem to mean the same thing, to state the nonexistence of God. But do they really?

> Bernique / Sweet damn all
> Macache / Nothing doing
> Le salaud / The bastard

When one looks more closely at each word, something happens. A subtle shift of meaning, a displacement of meaning, occurs. Certainly an important chapter of this book would have to deal with such shifts of meaning, which may be a shift of moral attitude as well as a shift of temperament.

Another chapter of our hypothetical book would have to be devoted to what may appear at first a minor question, but which I find fascinating and still unresolved in Beckett: the way he translates his titles and thus launches the new text in a different direction in the other language.

I am sure many Beckett critics have wondered what amazing title Beckett would invent were he to translate *More Pricks Than Kicks* into French. But there are also:

> *La dernière bande* (for) *Krapp's Last Tape* (where is Krapp? Shouldn't it have been *La dernière bande de Krapp?*)
> *Tous ceux qui tombent* (for) *All That Fall*
> *Oh les beaux jours* (for) *Happy Days* (Oh! . . . what is this little Oh?)
> *Comédie* (for) *Play* (has the humor disappeared in English or merely been replaced by playfulness?)
> *Pas* (for) *Footfall*
> *Berceuse* (for) *Rockaby* (that's a tricky one)
> *Ping* (for) *Bing*—or *Bing* (for) *Ping* (or is it *Ping* for *Hop?*)
> *The Lost Ones* (for) *Le dépeupleur* (where did Lamartine go?)
> *No's Knife* (for) *Têtes-mortes* (an interesting shift of metaphors)
> *Fizzles* (for) *Foirades* (has the rich excremental quality of the French title been lost in the English? Not at all, it has simply been reduced to a silent fart)

And perhaps the most fascinating of them all: *Lessness* (for) *Sans.*

On this question of titles, I would like to quote a short passage from a text by E.-M. Cioran. This is from a piece originally included in *Le Cahier de l'Herne: Samuel Beckett* and which appears in an English translation I did in collaboration with one of my graduate students, first in *Partisan Review* and subsequently in *The Critical Heritage* volume on Beckett which I co-edited with Lawrence Graver. The piece is entitled "Encounters with Beckett." Cioran writes:

> The French text *Sans* is called *Lessness* in English, a word coined by Beckett like its German equivalent *Losigkeit.* Fascinated by this word lessness (as unfathom-

able as Boehme's *Ungrund*), I told Beckett one evening that I would not go to bed before finding an honorable equivalent for it in French. . . . Together we had considered all possible forms suggested by *sans* and *moindre*. None of them seemed to us to come near the inexhaustible *lessness*, a blend of loss and infinitude, and emptiness synonymous with apotheosis. We parted company, somewhat disappointed. Back at home, I kept on turning that poor *sans* over and over in my mind. Just as I was about to give up, the idea came to me that I ought to try some derivation of the Latin *sine*. The next day I wrote to Beckett that *sinéité* seemed to me to be the yearned-for word. He replied that he too had thought of it, perhaps at the same moment. Our lucky find, however, it must be admitted, was not one. We finally agreed that we ought to give up the search, that there was no noun in French capable of expressing absence in itself, pure unadulterated absence, and that we had to resign ourselves to the metaphysical poverty of a preposition.

A most interesting passage, especially in its conclusion: "We had to resign ourselves to the *metaphysical poverty* of a preposition." One can indeed wonder how often in the process of translating himself Beckett had to confront the *poverty* of certain French or English words in comparison with their equivalent in the other language.

In the hypothetical book I am here sketching, a chapter would have to be devoted to this question of *poverty,* or rather to the question of *loss.* One would have to consider to what extent parts of the original text are lost in the process of translation, to what extent, that is, Beckett confronts both the semantic and the metaphysical poverty of one language in relation to the other when he translates himself.

But then one would also have to consider the question of *gain:* to what extent certain words, certain expressions in the other language provide metaphysical or even metaphorical richness. In other words, to what extent the translator, or in this case the self-translator, amplifies, augments, embellishes, enriches the original text—enriches the original not in terms of meaning only but in music, in rhythm, in syntactical movement. For instance, the striking rendition in English of this passage from *Le dépeupleur:*

> Mais la persistance de la double vibration donne à penser que dans ce vieux séjour tout n'est pas encore tout à fait pour le mieux.

> But the persistence of the twofold vibration suggests that in this old abode all is not yet quite for the best.

Here the English gains a poetic quality in rhythm and in inner rhyme as it becomes a perfect syllabic couplet.

This matter of *loss* and *gain* in the process of (self-)translation raises another crucial question: whether the translation of a text is merely a substitute for the original, or if in fact (and especially in Beckett's case) it becomes a continuation, an amplification of the original. In other words, this chapter of our book would have to examine Beckett's twin-texts not as separate but as complementary to one another.

We often admire, and even forgive, the liberties a translator takes with the original text of another writer. A case in point: the marvelous, though greatly unfaithful, translations that Richard Howard recently did of Baudelaire's *Les fleurs du mal.* Yet we expect the bilingual writer who translates himself to remain faithful to his original texts. I speak here with some degree of experience not only because I have on occasion translated works by other writers (from English into French or vice versa), but because as a bilingual writer myself I have also translated some of my own work from one language into the other.

We should certainly allow the writer as self-translator some freedom, some room for play within his own work. And of course Beckett allows himself such moments of playfulness—sometimes simply for the sake of playfulness.

EXAMPLE (from *Mercier et Camier*):

> Ame a trois lettres et une ou une et demie et même jusqu'à deux syllabes.

Which becomes in the English text: Soul: "another four-letter word." There is an obvious loss here in terms of the number of words, in terms of the expansiveness of the French, but not in terms of the playfulness; or rather, a totally different kind of play is at work in each language.

Here is another example (one of my favorites—also from *Mercier et Camier*) even more subtle and playful:

> Que ferions-nous sans les femmes? Nous prendrions un autre pli.

> What would we do without women? We would explore other channels.

In our book, we would have to devote a "serious" chapter to this question of play and playfulness in the process of self-translation, but also another chapter to the question of tone, which is related to the question of play. Undoubtedly, one would have to consider to what extent the tone of the original is altered in the translation.

EXAMPLE:

> Le voyage Mercier et Camier, je peux le raconter si je veux, car j'étais avec eux tout le temps. Ce fut un voyage matériellement assez facile.

> The journey of Mercier and Camier is one I can tell, if I will, for I was with them all the time. Physically it was fairly easy going.

Two radically different tones are established here from the opening of the texts, which are of course carried through the entire books. But beyond this matter of tone, one would also have to consider Beckett's unusual syntax—the shape of his sentences.

EXAMPLE (from *Comment c'est*):

> ici donc première partie comment c'était avant Pim ça suit je cite l'ordre à peu près ma vie dernier état ce qu'il en reste des bribes je l'entends ma vie dans l'ordre plus ou moins je l'apprends je cite un moment donné loin derrière un temps énorme puis à partir de là ce moment-là et suivants quelques-uns l'ordre naturel des temps énormes

which becomes in *How It Is:*

> here then part one how it was before Pim we follow I quote the natural order more or less my life last state last version what remains bits and scraps I hear it my life natural order more or less I learn it I quote a given moment long past vast stretch of time on from there that moment and following not all a selection natural order vast tracts of time

Though the English version appears to follow the same movement, the same syntactical order as the French (except for the transformation of "ça suit" to "we follow"), or perhaps one should say follows the same syntactical disorder as the French, nonetheless it seems more accessible, less distorted, less pulverized than the French, and as such seems to gain a more "natural order," whereas the French text appears and sounds unnatural, at least to a French ear. A close comparison of the twin-texts of *Comment c'est* and *How It Is*, on a purely syntactical level, would certainly yield fascinating results.

But there is more that one would have to study in the chapters of this book-yet-to-be-written: humor, of course, poetics, the play of sonorities, the system of echoes—that is to say, to what extent in the translation the equation of terms or ideas count less than the rhythmic or the aural situation of the word in a phrase. Consequently, one would have to study the rhythmic and phonetic patterns of the two texts, as well as resonances and equivalences. By resonances and equivalences, I mean how certain linguistic elements are transformed in the process of translation, but also how certain cultural, philosophical, and literary allusions, and even quotations, are not simply translated but transposed into a French or an English context to produce a totally different set of cultural, philosophical, or literary connotations.

EXAMPLE (from the poem to Nelly that Mr. Hackett reads in *Watt*):

> Tis well! Tis well! Far, far be it
> Pu-we! Pu-we!
> From me, my tit,
> Such innocent joys to chide.
> Burn, burn with Byrne, from Hyde
> Hide naught—hide naught save what
> Is Greh'n's. IT hide from Hyde, with Byrne burn not.

> C'est bon! C'est bon! Loin loin de moi
> (Loin loin de moi)
> De blâmer, ange,
> D'aussi chastes ébats.
> Donne à Dunn tout, à Denis ne dénie
> Que ce qui appartient à Green. Mais ÇA,
> Le dénie à Denis, à Dunn ne donne mie.

These are some of the problems to be confronted in the book that I am here imagining. But the final chapter would perhaps be the most interesting and the most difficult to write. For it would have to confront the fundamental problem of Beckett's bilingualism and his self-translating activity. It would have to confront the essence of language itself, or what Beckett calls:

> rumeur transmissible à l'infini dans les deux sens
>
> rumour transmissible ad infinitum in either direction

"dans les deux sens . . ." / "in either direction . . . ," and already the difficulty arises. For as Beckett knows so well and has often suggested throughout his work: language both gets us where we want to go and prevents us from getting there.

The final chapter would have to come to terms with this matter of language as an obstacle. That is to say, it would have to deal with the central question of the creative process in Beckett—a process which is essentially the same whether he writes in French or in English; or rather, which is doubly complex because he writes in French and in English.

The original creative act (whether in French or in English) always proceeds in the *dark*—Beckett knows this well—in the dark, and in *ignorance* and *error*. Though the act of translating, and especially of self-translating, is also a creative act, it is performed in the *light* (in the light of the existing original text), it is performed in *knowledge* (in the knowledge of the existing text), and therefore it is performed without error—at least at the start.

In other words, the translation of a text reassures, reasserts knowledge, the knowledge already present in the original text. But perhaps it also corrects the initial errors of that text. As a result, the translation is no longer (especially with Beckett) an approximation of the original, or a duplication, or a substitute, but a continuation of the work, of the workings of the text.

Sometimes the translation amplifies the original, sometimes it diminishes it, corrects it, explains it even (no, not to us, not to the reader, but) to the writer, who always knows that the language he uses (whether French or English) is an obstacle he must overcome again and again.

In the conclusion of our book, we would have to deal then with the distance that invariably exists between the twin-texts. What I have found interesting over the years in reading and re-reading Beckett (in French and in English) is how gradually the distance between the original and its translation seems to increase.

Beckett's early works which he translated, such as the trilogy (in the case of *Molloy*, in collaboration with someone else), are close to one another in tone, in syntax, and in other important aspects. But the more recently written and self-translated texts pull away from one another. It would take another chapter of our hypothetical book to illustrate this, and of course one would also have to account for the time that has elapsed between the creation of the original and its translation. But I would like to close with a specific example—the fabulous rendition of *Watt* in French.

Between the original creation of *Watt* (circa 1941–45)—in the dark, in ignorance and in error, and one should add in the "merdecluse"—and the appearance of the French *Watt* more than twenty-five years later, we confront two totally different books that, nevertheless, form a perfect bilingual tandem.

Between *Watt*/English and *Watt*/French, there is a huge distance in tone, in syntax, in textuality, and perhaps even in meaning. In other words, a difference and a distance in all the elements I have proposed here for the book that still remains to be written on Beckett—an essential book. Certainly, the comparison of these two *Watt*s would be most revealing, most enlightening, for our understanding of Beckett as a bilingual writer and as a self-translator.

I am aware that Ludovic and Agnès Janvier worked with Beckett on the preliminary draft of this translation, but ultimately—as Janvier admits—it was Beckett's work. Ludovic Janvier writes of his collaboration with Beckett: "One does not translate Beckett, one provokes him to translate himself. . . . Our work was less one of translation than one of incitation and resonance."

And so our book should perhaps begin with an examination of *Watt*, not the opening sentence of that novel but rather its final statement: "no symbols where none intended." For years, like most Beckett critics, I am sure, I toyed with this puzzling and yet perfect sentence, trying to find an equivalent in French, before Beckett presented us with his own translation.

> Pas de symboles où il n'y en a pas.
> Pas de symboles où l'intention n'y était pas.
> Pas de symboles sauf où l'intention y était.

In each of my clumsy attempts I confronted the question of tone, I confronted the duplicity, the ambivalence, the maddening fluidity of that sentence, but also its symmetry, or rather its asymmetry, and of course its irony. In other words, I confronted a sentence that constructs itself as it deconstructs itself. And beyond that, I also heard, as I read that sentence, its cultural and literary echoes:

> No pun intended—No pun where none intended.
> No evil where none intended.
> No offense, Sir—None intended, Sir.

That sentence, which abolishes itself in its own ambivalence, haunted me for years, as it must have haunted many Beckett readers. Are there symbols only where they are intended, or where they were intended? I kept asking myself. Or are there no symbols except where I intend them to be? And finally Beckett presented us with his translation of that sentence—a sentence which in English contains, as I hope I have clearly suggested, *all* of Beckett (the English-writing Beckett), and which in French contains *all* of Beckett (the French-writing Beckett).

EXAMPLE:

> honni soit qui symboles y voit.

If the English ("no symbols where none intended") contains all of Beckett, it also contains all of English culture and all of English literature—at least as far back as Chaucer. The French sentence "Honni soit qui symboles y voit" contains all of Beckett again, but also all of French culture and French literature, as far back as François Villon.

That is what it means to be a *writer as self-translator*. It means a total displacement of language from one culture to another. And yet, at the same time, especially in the case of Beckett, it means never stepping outside language. In other words, Beckett, in his bilingual work, allows us to listen to the dialogue which he entertains with himself in two languages, and yet somehow we listen to only half of this dialogue, however *mal vu mal dit* / ill-seen ill-said it may be.

LORI CHAMBERLAIN

"The Same Old Stories": Beckett's Poetics of Translation

The question looks simple enough: Is Samuel Beckett English, or Irish, or French? The very structure of this question, however, forcing us to choose one *or* another, should give us a clue to its undecidability; yet it is the question that any library catalogue department, for example, must face each time a new book by or about Beckett is published. The various answers to that question provide a concrete representation of the challenge Beckett provides to the concepts of language and literary canon that our academic institutions are based on—and cling to. Both the Library of Congress and most departments of literature base their divisions on the principle of linguistic nationalism. This system's logic prescribes that one find Cortázar, for example, in the Argentinian section of the library, and that he be taught in the Latin American literature section of the Spanish Department, despite his clear affiliations with both Anglo and French traditions. Cortázar, born in Brussels (1914), has lived in Paris since 1952, but because he wrote in Spanish, we are not particularly tempted to call him a "French" author. Beckett, however, abandoned not only his native land but his native tongue, only eventually returning to the latter to write ambidextrously in both French and English. There is a tradition which regards such moves as profoundly unnatural, monstrous even, and so we are not sure what species of centaur Beckett is: French, English, or Irish. The Library of Congress seems to have decided to catalogue works written originally in French and their English translations in the French section— and works written originally in English and their French translations in the English section. It is an awkward system, which can become chaotic if the individual library does not have the benefit of Library of Congress cards. One university library, for example, has catalogued *How It Is* in the English section and *Comment c'est* in the French section; another has catalogued only some of the recent books, such as *Mal vu mal dit* in the French section, but keeps such earlier French works as the trilogy in the English section. The problem of cataloging the secondary works under such a system seems insurmountable. What this suggests is that our classification systems, at their most literal levels, do not know what to do with Samuel Beckett.

The root of this confusion, it seems, is the status of translation and our conventional privileging of writing; we tend to regard writing as original, primary, and authoritative, while translation is secondary, derivative, and potentially subversive. If we want to be sure of the author's "original intentions," then we must go to the original text, and for this very reason we are profoundly uncomfortable teaching "literature in translation." Thus, in scholarly articles, for any close textual analysis we conventionally must quote a text in its authorized version—that is, in the *original* language—or quote the text in translation while providing the original in a footnote. Beckett scholars, however, tend to cite Beckett's texts either in original or in translation, depending on audience, for example, or the speaker's own linguistic affiliation. In short, we pretend that there is no "problem" of translation. In a more explicit repression of this problem, some Beckett scholars claim that Beckett's translations are not "really" translations. One critic, for example, suggests that Beckett, being his own translator,

> gives to the English and French translations of his works an authenticity not enjoyed by translations of other authors and raises the question how far his translations are such and how far, since they come from the author himself, they become distinct works of art, fresh treatments of the original subject with their own qualities and characteristics. (Cockerham, 144)

Another critic pushes this line of reasoning one step further, noting how intriguing it is to have "genuinely 'original' versions in two languages" (Friedman, 235). The self-translator, then, is no translator at all; his texts are as "original" and "authentic" as those which preceded them. While I am sympathetic to the intent of such arguments, I believe they sidestep the issues translation raises—both for the somewhat special case of self-translation in Beckett's work and for the broad field of translation and its status in our canon.

It seems ironic, in fact, that Beckett's self-translation has been interpreted as a sign of "originality" and "authenticity," for he systematically denies the possibility of these categories in his work. It would seem just as plausible to argue that we have genuinely "secondary" versions in two languages. Beckett's dual role as writer and translator duplicates the situation of many of Beckett's characters, those curiously anonymous narrators who grudgingly attempt to transcribe the anonymous "voice" of the author. It is a strategy Beckett employs in many of his fictions and articulates in surprisingly similar terms (see *Molloy, The Unnamable, Stories and Texts for Nothing*). *How It Is*, for example, begins by delineating the narrator's relationship to the origin of the story he will tell:

how it was I quote before Pim with Pim after Pim how it is three parts I say it as I hear it. (7)

The narrator "quotes" the story as he hears it from an unnamed voice outside. By pretending to be only a faithful scribe, merely repeating what he has heard, the narrator denies authority for the narrative, placing himself in a secondary position analogous to that of the translator. Also in a repetition of Beckett's oscillation between writing and translation, the work consistently confuses the distinction between saying and hearing, between the voice and the scribe, between teller and told. The basis of this confusion rests finally on linguistic grounds over what words or signs really mean—a confusion doubled in translation. In *How It Is*, for example, the narrator pairs up with Pim and tortures him into speech, thumping Pim's skull, carving letters into his flesh, and rapping on his kidneys with a can opener. Just as the narrator himself must respond to the dictates of another ("I say it as I hear it"), so Pim too is forced to interpret the narrator's cruel code:

table of basic stimuli one sing nails in armpit two speak blade in arse three stop thump on skull four louder pestle on kidney

five softer index in anus six bravo clap athwart arse seven lousy same as three eight encore same as one or two as may be (69)

The narrator has provided us with an allegory of the problem of translation: in this table of equivalences, "louder" will be equivalent to "pestle on kidney." But as soon as the narrator begins the system, it breaks down, so that sign number three ("stop" is equivalent to "thump on skull") is confused with sign number seven. Pim's task, like the translator's, is to distinguish, for example, three from seven, and while there is surely a difference, it cannot be discerned in this system. After delineating this relationship, the narrator then discovers that the principles of it apply to all his relationships. He realizes that Pim is interchangeable with Jim or Tim—Bim or Bom—because they are all only functions in this endless coupling of words, a "rumour transmissible ad infinitum in either direction" (120). The very principle of binary opposition as a structure of meaning—that we know the difference between "cat" and "hat"—is here being undermined and made a principle of Beckett's poetics.

In addition, the sadomasochism implied in the relationship between narrator and voice in *How It Is*, or between the narrator and Pim in the above quotation, also characterizes the relationship between an original and a translated text. Yet Beckett constantly confuses the roles: the narrator will be at one time the victim (as he is of the voice outside) and at another time the torturer (as he is in relation to Pim):

and that linked thus bodily together each one of us is at the same time Bom and
Pim tormentor and tormented pedant and dunce wooer and wooed speechless
and reafflicted with speech in the dark the mud nothing to emend there (140)

Just so Beckett reverses the relationships between languages, now French and
now English being in the position of "original" or "secondary."

At the thematic level of his writing, then, Beckett challenges a conventional
privileging of the "original." But what does this challenge literally imply for
reading Beckett's translation? Beckett is, after all, the author of the original
and the author of the translation. I believe, however, that Beckett's poetic
practice should warn us as critics against taking Beckett's "authority" as a
self-translator too literally. We would have to assume that because he wrote
the original he has perfect access to his intentions, as if everything he did in
the original was both deliberate and conscious. Arguments for the "originality" of the translation rely on a similar assumption—that because Beckett is
the author he will have special insight into the ways the texts *should* be translated. Our institutional confusion over Beckett's linguistic identity testifies to
our need to reexamine the critical categories we use to read both the meaning
of translation and the texts themselves. Perhaps the problem lies with the
very terms "original" and "secondary," whose binary relationship seems to
trap us in a vicious circle. What I propose is a theory of repetition to account
both for the poetic production and for the function of translation in that poetics. The advantage of such a theory is that it can account both for the binary
pair original/secondary and for other binary oppositions which haunt our attempts to deal with translation, specifically difference and similarity. In addition, such a theory can do so without reducing the discussion to one or the
other term.

The most thorough of recent theories of repetition is provided by Gilles
Deleuze in his book *Différence et Répétition*. Deleuze attempts to locate this
pair of terms outside the confines of a theory of representation, outside the
concept of equivalence. Such a theory would reduce repetition to a problem of
generality, identity, and same-ness; it would re-duplicate the very problems
we have already witnessed with translation. He attempts to subvert the
hierarchization implicit in a representational model, where original precedes
copy, with what he calls a philosophy of nomads, wherein "concepts" (he rejects the notion of concepts as understood in traditional philosophy) would
be distributed in nomadic, anarchic fashion. For this reason, Deleuze defines
repetition as "la différence sans concept."

I do not choose Deleuze arbitrarily, for he shares with Beckett a serious interest in Proust; even some of the terms Deleuze uses echo those used by Beckett in his early book on Proust. Initially Deleuze sets up a binary opposition between two kinds of repetition. The first is material and mechanical, a static
repetition of surface elements in a successive or horizontal movement. It re-

peats the "Same" and is governed by "Habit." By contrast, the second type of repetition concerns not the material but the psychical or metaphysical, not surfaces and discrete units but depths and totalities. It repeats the "Different" and is governed by memory. Where the first is static and negative, the second is dynamic and positive. The opposition is similar, in fact, to the one Beckett finds in Proust between voluntary and involuntary memory. The first, governed by Habit, "presents the past in monochrome," says Beckett.

> Its action has been compared by Proust to that of turning the leaves of an album of photographs. The material that it furnishes contains nothing of the past, merely a blurred and uniform projection once removed of our anxiety and opportunism—that is to say, nothing. (*Proust*, 19)

The involuntary memory, on the other hand,

> restores, not merely the past object, but the Lazarus that it charmed or tortured, not merely Lazarus and the object, but more because less, more because it abstracts the useful, the opportune, the accidental, because in its flame it has consumed Habit and all its works, and in its brightness revealed what the mock reality of experience never can and never will reveal—the real. (20)

The two kinds of repetition, then, match these two kinds of memory: one that deals with surfaces and sameness, and the other which deals with depths and the accidental. The two cannot, however, be isolated one from the other, for, as Deleuze says,

> chaque fois la répétition matérielle résulte de la répétition plus profonde, qui s'élabore en épaisseur et la produit comme résultat, comme enveloppe extérieure, telle une coque détachable, mais qui perd tout sens, et toute capacité de se reproduire elle-même, dès qu'elle n'est plus animée de sa cause ou de l'autre répétition. Ainsi, c'est le vêtu qui est sous le nu, et qui le produit, qui l'excrète, comme l'effet de sa sécrétion. C'est la répétition secrète qui s'entoure d'une répétition mécanique et nue, comme d'une dernière barrière qui marque ici ou là le bord extrême des différences qu'elle fait communiquer dans un système mobile. (Deleuze, 370)

Not only does Deleuze confuse the two kinds of repetition, but he inverts their relationship. The second kind of repetition is deeper, more secret, more clothed; but, since the first kind of repetition lacks veils, is in fact "nude," it would seem to be what lies *beneath* the veiled repetition. Paradoxically, "nude" repetition concerns surfaces, veiling while clothing unveils.

But these two ways of seeing repetition, Deleuze would argue, still subordinate the idea of repetition under a theory of representation, where repetition will be judged in terms of the concept of identity. Like translations, repetition is thus seen as a secondary production; the repeated instance is seen as a diminution of the first. Beyond habit and memory, then, Deleuze posits a third term, outside of representation, a kind of repetition which is not merely the return of the same but the production of difference. Indebted to both Freud and Nietzsche, this third repetition has the quietly uncanny appearance of the return of the repressed. Literature, according to Deleuze, calls all three types of repetition into play:

> Peut-être est-ce l'object le plus haut de l'art, de faire jouer simultanément toutes ces répétitions, avec leur différence de nature et de rythme, leur déplacement et leur déguisement respectifs, leur divergence et leur décentrement, de les emboîter les unes dans les autres, et, de l'une à l'autre, de les envelopper dans des illusions dont 'l'effet' varie dans chaque cas. L'art n'imite pas, mais c'est d'abord parce qu'il répète, et répète toutes les répétitions, de par une puissance intérieure (l'imitation est une copie, mais l'art est simulacre, il renverse les copies en simulacres). (Deleuze, 374–75)

Repetition, as simulacra, subverts the dichotomy imposed by a doctrine of originality or representation—and this, I would argue, is precisely what Beckett's poetics also accomplishes.

I can only illustrate the utility of this theory briefly here. I will take, then, a short example from Beckett's residual text *Bing/Ping* and will have to assume the reader's familiarity with that text. Its mechanical repetition of surfaces is the most obvious and overwhelming of the three types of repetition Deleuze outlines. The insistence on repeating the same words has the dulling effect of habit, erasing the force of the words as signifieds, turning them into a background of signifiers, a silent field of play. It acts as a passive rehearsal for memory, as the glimmer of an image appears, "bleu et blanc au vent," and the more startling unblinking eye at the end of the text. But beyond this, the very excessiveness of the repetition serves to erase the meaning of the differences between these same old words, forcing us to examine the blurring of meaning and the production of something new: the same story cannot be the same.

The translation is careful in its repetition as well, giving the initial impression of word-by-word fidelity:

> Corps nu blanc fixe seuls les yeux à peine. Traces fouillis gris pâle presque blanc sur blanc.

> Bare white body fixed only the eyes only just. Traces blurs light grey almost white on white.

But such "exact resemblance" is deceptive; it works as a screen to cover up the imprecision of the relationship between words and things, or, as in this case, between words and words. The translation slips back and forth, now symmetrical in relation to the "original," now asymmetrical. We can see this slippage in the following lines:

> Donné rose à peine corps nu blanc fixe un mètre blanc sur blanc invisible. Lumière chaleur murmures à peine presque jamais toujours les mêmes tous sus. Mains blanches invisibles pendues ouvertes creux face. Corps nu blanc fixe un mètre hop fixe ailleurs.

> Given rose only just bare white body fixed one yard white on white invisible. All white all known murmurs only just almost never always the same all known. Light heat hands hanging palms front white on white invisible. Bare white body fixed ping fixed elsewhere.

As this example illustrates, even where Beckett seems to depart from his French "original," he does so within the possibilities of repetition and permutation established by the text. The additions here—"All white all known" and "white on white"—occur elsewhere in the text many times.

By far the most interesting *difference*, then, between the two texts is that of the title. Beckett has rendered both the words "hop" and "bing" of the French text as "ping" in the English (and he has even added a few extra pings). Thus the English text insists more on "ping" than the French does on "bing"; yet Beckett's conflation of "bing" and "hop" suggests that these words serve similar functions in the text. Though it can be argued that the three words generate a kind of *connotative* field (though not one that could be identified with anything approaching agreement), they do not denote in any familiar way. Critics only seem to agree that the words function as principles of movement in what is otherwise a static text. I would like to argue, in addition, that these words illustrate the very essence of repetition, of Deleuze's third term; the words refer to and repeat themselves—they are indeed the "mots blancs." It is significant that Beckett chooses to substitute the *p* for the *b*, as it is reminiscent of the various transformations of names in *How It Is:* Pim, Bim, Bem, Bom, Krim, Kram ("one syllable m at the end all that matters" [109]). The point that the narrator of *How It Is* makes by virtue of these interchangeable names is that Pim is not so much a unique individual, a character, but a function in the rotating couples: tormentor-tormented. The substitution of *p* for *b* is also strikingly reminiscent of Raymond Roussel's transformation of "billard" into "pillard," which he discusses in *How I Wrote Certain of My Books*. But where Roussel thereby conflates two meaningful words, Beckett conflates semantically meaningless words. He then dares the reader to make a meaning of this difference while pointing out that the place of difference cannot be located.

Traditionally, repetition at the textual level has been seen as a principle of coherence. By identifying repeated words, themes, or structures, we as readers construct an order out of the chaos of the text. Clearly, however, the repetition in *Bing* does not produce coherence; on the contrary, repetition is the very principle of chaos. While Beckett's narrators stave off the mess of existence by repeating sums, in a kind of narrative autism, Beckett the author and translator does so by

> always muttering, the same old mutterings, the same old stories, the same old questions and answers. (*Stories*, 134)

The stories are *not* always the same, of course; yet Beckett seems to be daring us to find the meaning of the difference. The difference, then, is barely audible, and perhaps it is for this reason that we have been troubled, imitating Watt's puzzlings over the incident of the piano tuners, bothered

> that nothing had happened, that a thing that was nothing had happened, with the utmost formal distinctness. (*Watt*, 76)

In the translation of "bing" into "ping," almost nothing happens. Yet the challenge for those wishing to study Beckett's poetics of translation is to formulate the relationship between the excess of repetition and the "meaning only just" it produces in the act of both writing and translating.

BRIAN T. FITCH

The Relationship Between *Compagnie* and *Company*: One Work, Two Texts, Two Fictive Universes

This essay forms part of a larger project[1] that seeks to clarify the status of the second version, whether in French or English, of Beckett's prose texts. The main reason for undertaking such a project is that, contrary to what one might gather in reading the vast majority of critics writing on Beckett, the specificity of his achievement as a writer *has* to be bound up with the bilingual character of his work.

To compare the two versions of a given work and define the relationship between them involves taking into account, at one stage or another, the differences between two language-systems, two literary traditions, two critical traditions, and two cultures, plus the difference between a mother tongue and an acquired second language. One way to begin to clarify this situation is to eliminate from the comparison those differences arising from aspects inherent in the English and French languages. It is for this reason that I have chosen to focus upon the fictive universe that takes on form and substance in the imagination of the reader of each version of the work and to limit myself to its nature or content rather than the manner of its composition.

The work I have selected is *Company/Compagnie*. My hypothesis is that the second version cannot be considered a mere duplication of the first, and that the process and product of so-called self-translation are not the same as the process and product of any other form of translation. Consequently, neither version can be appropriately substituted for the other by the critic: each has to be studied in its own right, together with the precise relationship existing between the two.

The fact that seventeen sentences of the original English text are missing from the French text is already indicative of a certain discrepancy between their respective fictive universes. Let me therefore look first at these most obvious omissions from the French.

The statement "Sole sound in the silence your footfalls" is followed by the qualification: "Rather sole sounds for they vary from one to the next" (*Company*, 18).[2] The latter is missing from the French so that the sound it evokes is single and uniform. The evocation of "somewhere on the Ballyogan Road" is accompanied by the mention of there having been a truck there: "Where no truck any more" (30); the truck is absent from the French version. The list of garments worn by the narrator—top coat, block hat, and quarter boots—is said to be complete: "No other garments if any to be seen" (31); the reader of *Compagnie* is left free to conjure up the rest of the character's apparel. In an enumeration of the five senses—"Taste? The sense of taste in his mouth? Long since dulled. Touch?" (71)—the sense of touch is missing from the French. The image of the narrator and his female companion sitting face to face "With eyes closed and your hands on your pubes" (59) is also absent from the second version. In the same episode, where the narrator imagines his female friend's physical attributes—"A single leg appears"—the specification concerning his angle of vision, "Seen from above" (57–58), is not mentioned in the French. Not only details of objects and situations and their description are missing from the universe of the French text but also events. The movement of the feet finally coming to rest as the narrator halts is commented upon thus: "Stilled when finally as always hitherto they do" (52); no such commentary figures in the French. A number of sentences with a purely adverbial function are also absent—"From time to time" (50), "Now and then" (24), "Till the last bump" (55), and "However roughly" (67)—a lack that alters the nature of the events or actions evoked. Finally, the two most substantial omissions occur in the sentence "Vague distress at the vague thought of his perhaps overhearing a confidence when he hears for example, You are on your back in the dark" (62), a significant sentence in any interpretation of the passage in which it occurs. Also missing is the formulation of a hypothesis concerning the possible existence of a further protagonist, who has no place in the world of the French text: "May not there be another with him in the dark to and of whom the voice is speaking?" (9–10).

There are, moreover, as many omissions *within* sentences as there are of whole sentences. In most cases, they concern details, such as the "crest of the rise" (12) being reduced to "la crête" (*Compagnie*, 12), the image of a woman "propped on her elbows head between her hands" (66) being reduced to "appuyée sur ses coudes," (65) and of the protagonist "once fallen and laying on his face" (78) being merely "une fois prostré" (77). The omission of an epithet such as "cankerous" to describe a character as in "that cankerous other" (9) is, however, clearly of more import. So too is the absence of details concerning events and actions, such as "for the space of 30 seconds" (82); no indication of duration is given in the French. The most significant of the present category of omissions is no doubt the explanation given by the English narrator as to why he opens his eyes: "as you sometimes do to void the fluid" (85).

All the examples of omissions from the French text considered so far constitute elements of the fictive universe of *Company* whether they be characters, objects or their attributes or actions, or events and their characteristics. The fact that these elements are wholly absent from the world of *Compagnie* means that we are here dealing with two different fictive worlds: certain mental images the reader of *Company* experiences—visual, auditive, and so on— never enter the imagination of the reader of *Compagnie*.

The differences between the two worlds become even more marked once we take into account not only elements that disappear from the French but also those, no less numerous, that reappear in a different guise; in other words, those features which are radically transformed in the French so that a person, thing, or event is replaced by another. Thus the "bathing-place" (24) of the English becomes "la terre ferme" (23) of the French, "the Eastern window" (84) becomes "la fenêtre côté mer" (83), "the wash" (75) is reduced to "la mer" (74), "with quickening pulse" (55–56) is replaced by "le coeur battant" (55), and, curiously, "Cloudless May day" (53) becomes "Journée d'avril sans nuage" (52). What is evoked is not the same in each text. "All dead still" (58) is not the same as "Silence" (57), nor is "irrelevant" (67) the same as "à discrétion" (66), or "unadvisedly" (75) the same as "trop vite" (74). Where the English says of a voice "it may change place and tone" (19), the French speaks of its changing "de place et de volume" (19). Where "Rare flickers of reason" are "of no avail" (62), "Rares lueurs de raisonnement" are merely "aussitôt éteintes" (61). When the narrator of *Company* says of his female companion's eyes, "In your dark you look in them again" (66), he evokes the whole inner void of his own mind, which is absent from the French version: "Dans le noir tu y plonges à nouveau" (65).

I have kept the most significant modification to the last. It occurs in the third paragraph of the text and it radically transforms its meaning. The English version reads: "Use of the second person marks the voice. That of the third that cantankerous other. Could he speak to and of whom the voice speaks there would be a first. But he cannot" (9). The logic of this play on personal pronouns is missing in the French, for the third sentence reads: "Si lui pouvait parler à qui et de qui parle la voix il y aurait une *troisième*" (8–9). The substitution of "troisième" for "first" makes sense, it seems to me, only if we read it as referring not to the third person pronoun but to a third *persona*. But in any case, the effect created is quite different.

So far we have seen that many aspects of the constituent parts of the universe of *Company* are either modified or absent in *Compagnie*. It is much less common to find elements that have been added to the world of the French version, but there are some, such as the sentence "Comme aux enfers" (68). To the protagonist's lying in the dark, "Crawls and falls. Lies.

Lies in the dark with closed eyes" (76), is added his heavy breathing: "Rampe et tombe. Gît. *Souffle* les yeux fermés dans le noir" (75). When the narrator's father returns home hoping to find that his wife's labor has finally come to an end, there is, in the French, the added detail of his "préférant y pénétrer par la porte de service" (16).

How are we to reconcile the discrepancies between these two fictive universes both belonging to the same work but each corresponding to a different text? To the extent that the world of *Compagnie* represents a kind of paring down or a process of reduction in relation to that of *Company* through its elimination of certain elements in the original, it could be seen as a kind of *quintessential* fictive universe of *Company/Compagnie*. In this respect, what is evoked by the French-language fiction does not always contradict the sights and sounds, the events and actions, conjured up by the English-language fiction. And that is clearly of prime importance in considering their relationship. The fact that some elements are added to the French version does complicate the picture, for the latter does not only and always constitute a paring down of the original to some kind of essential or basic version. The relationship between the two therefore has to be considered rather as a complementary one. In order to get a complete picture of this fictive heterocosm, we would have to effect a merging of the imaginary worlds of the two versions, for only then would we understand what the author had in mind.

The underlying justification for such a manner of proceeding is obviously related to authorial intentionality: it presupposes the preexistence of the fictive universe, subsequently realized by the text, in some nonlinguistic form antedating the actual writing of the work of which the two merged universes would somehow provide a more adequate representation than either one of them alone. Such a hypothesis, in spite of the indisputable problems it would pose in the context of contemporary literary theory with the latter's rejection of any form of transcendental signified, is not ruled out in the first instance when we take into account another category of discrepancies between the two versions: that of the modifications made in *Compagnie*. In many, if not most, of those cases, the two versions of the world of the work could still be taken to be complementary to one another in that it is not inconceivable to view a *change* of detail as an *addition* of new or further detail. There *are* cases, however, where the detailed evocation of the French version does not so much *modify* as *contradict* the original. To take the most flagrant example, by no stretch of the imagination can "avril" (52) be translated as "May" (53). In the final analysis, then, it is impossible to reconcile the two fictive universes in some coherent overall synthesis, and the problem of their incompatibility remains intact.

The discrepancies between the two texts do not, however, concern only the character and exact composition of the fictive heterocosms but also the manner in which they are perceived by the reader and the nature of the precise relationship he establishes with the characters and events of the fiction. Here I am of course referring to the narrative perspective.

The most frequent shifts of perspective are brought about by changes in verb tenses. The classic example concerns the shift from a past definite in the English, "For some reasons you could never fathom" (13), which situates the circumstance in the past, to a composite past in the French, "Pour une raison que tu n'as jamais pu expliquer" (13), where the past continues into the narrator's present. Or a shift in the opposite direction, as in the change from "What can he have seen then" (25) to "Que pouvait-il bien voir alors" (25). But we also find the present of the English—"wondering . . . if the woes of the world are all they used to be" (61)—changed into the past of the French: "se demandant . . . si les maux du monde étaient toujours ce qu'ils étaient" (60). The two most radical changes of perspective occur at the very beginning and the very end of the text. The English text opens thus: "A voice comes to *one* in the dark. Imagine" (7). In the French this first paragraph is rendered: "Une voix parvient à *quelqu'un* dans le noir. Imaginer" (7). Whereas the English "one" could refer to the speaker, the French "quelqu'un" suggests a third (or second) person other than the speaker. At the very least, the latter creates a distancing effect absent from the original. No less striking and significant is the shift in the fourth and fifth sentences from the end of the text. *Company* gives us "The fable of one with you in the dark. The fable of one fabling of one with you in the dark" (88–89), where the "one" obviously refers to someone other than the speaker, acting reflexively in recounting to himself his situation of sharing the company of the speaker ("you") or else sharing with the speaker the activity of talking to himself. *Compagnie,* however, reads "La fable d'un autre avec toi dans le noir. La fable de toi fabulant d'un autre avec toi dans le noir" (87–88), and here it is the *speaker* who is talking about his being with another in the dark. Such discrepancies are not reconcilable and the perspectives offered by the two versions are distinct, mutually exclusive alternatives. Moreover, their situation at the very beginning and end of the text must give them added significance for any interpretation of their respective texts.

The contents of the narration in the form of the comments proffered by the narrative voice also reveal a number of discrepancies. While these may appear to be of less consequence, they nonetheless serve to characterize the narrator. Here, there are about as many omissions as additions in the French text and almost as many additions as modifications. The omissions consist, for example, of the sentence "Till the last thump" coming after "And assuming a certain lifetime a lifetime" (55), and of the explanation, appearing in the middle of a calculation by the narrator: "assuming height of seat adjustable as in the case of certain piano stools" (57). The additions tend to be briefer intercalations within sentences, such as "pour conclure au passé" (39), "en principe" (70), and "qui sait" (82). One might say that the French narrator tends to be a trifle more verbose than his English counterpart, interjecting idiomatic turns of phrase of a phatic character that add nothing of substance to what is being said but serve to emphasize his presence as narrator and, to a lesser extent, convey something of his character as narrator. This is the case with the modification of "Hope and despair and suchlike barely felt" (62) into "Espoir et désespoir *pour ne nommer que ce vieux tandem* à peine ressentis" (61). More interesting are the examples where a definite change of effect is created, as when "Là rien à redire" (46) replaces "No improving those" (46), or there is a distinct difference of meaning, as when "Vite motus" (83) is substituted for "Quick leave him" (84). Here, once again, the discrepancies between the two versions prove to be irreconcilable. The way the narrator expresses himself is not exactly the same in the two versions, and thus our perception of the narrator cannot be the same either.

In order to clarify the relationship between *Compagnie* and *Company*, I propose to examine a hypothesis that is often encountered in writings on translation theory: the view that the translation constitutes an interpretation of and commentary upon the original, thus enjoying a status analogous to that of the critical commentary. Although this view obviously concerns translations that are the work of somebody other than the author of the original, the examination of *Compagnie* in the light of such a hypothesis could well tell us something about the particular status of this text.

There are many occasions in *Company* when the reader does not readily comprehend the text. Often the syntax causes a momentary hesitation before the meaning can be ascertained: "In dark and silence to close as if to light the eyes and hear a sound" (24). Here the French text does not present the same problem since it eliminates the elliptical expression "as if to light"; thus "dans le silence et le noir fermer les yeux et entendre un bruit" (24). At other times, this ambiguity admits, upon reflection, a second, quite different interpretation, as when we read, "And wonder to himself what in the world such sounds might signify" (70), where "what in the world," instead of being understood as a simple exclamatory interjection, could be felt to be an adverbial expression qualifying the verb "signify." This second possible, if less likely, meaning is absent from the French: "En se demandant ce que mon Dieu de tels bruits peuvent signifier" (69). Another such example is provided by the sentence: "Say changing now for some time past though no tense in the dark in that dim mind" (45–46). Here the connection between "time" and "tense" is found only in the two sentences corresponding to it in the second version: "Supposition que depuis quelque temps elle aille se modifiant. Quoique nul temps de nul verbe dans cette conscience ténébreuse" (45–46). It is almost as though the English were a poor translation of the French.

There are cases where the ambiguity of the English is much more pronounced, as in the example of the word "still" in the sentence "Even still in the timeless dark you find figures a comfort" (55), which could refer either to immobility or to continuity. The French opts for the latter: "Encore maintenant dans le noir hors du temps les chiffres te réconfortent" (54). At times the tortured syntax of the original creates downright perplexity: "In what posture and if or not as hearer in his for good not yet devised" (64). But turning to the French version: "Dans quelle posture et si oui ou non tel l'entendeur dans la sienne une fois pour toutes pas encore arrêté" (63). What exactly are we to make of the statement "So light as let be faintest light no longer perceived than the time it takes the lid to fall" (71)? Such formulations pose a problem of interpretation that is invariably resolved by *Compagnie:* "Si bien que cette lumière telle qu'elle finit par être à peine perçue que le temps d'un demi-clin" (70).

It is, I believe, clear from the preceding examples that *Compagnie* does indeed provide a kind of interpretation of *Company* through the resolution of ambiguities in the latter. Interpretation here consists of opting for a particular reading of the original from among the various alternatives offered. This interpretive function is in keeping with one of the tendencies observed on the level of the constitution of the fictive heterocosm: the paring down of the original to a kind of quintessential basis. In this respect, then, the relationship between the second version and the first would appear to be similar to that obtaining between any translation and its original—were it not for the fact that, as in the case of the fictive universe, the contrary tendency can also be seen to be at work. In other words, there are a few occasions when the English version serves to interpret the obscurities of the French. For example, it is difficult to know what to make of the second of the two sentences: ". . . il s'engage à appeler l'entendeur M tout au moins. . . . Soi-même d'un autre personnage" (58). The English version, however, "Himself some other character" (59), is immediately comprehensible. The same is true of "Ensuite le sermon de ne plus cesser qu'avec l'ouïe" (22), which is interpreted—in advance, as it were—thus: "Next the vow not to cease till hearing cease" (23). Even the ingenious formulation "Imaginant imaginé imaginant le tout pour se tenir compagnie" (63) tends to degenerate into a meaningless jingle beside the clarity of the English: "Devised deviser devising it all for company" (64).

Readers are, however, more likely to read the French version in the light of the English original in order to evaluate its quality as an apparent translation. Nonetheless, in as much as *Compagnie* serves to clarify problems of interpretation in *Company*, it provides an explicative, albeit indirect, commentary on the original. What distinguishes its status as an interpretation from that of any other translation is that it is not just another reading of the original but the author's own reading of his work. Whereas a translation offers a possible *perspective* upon the original, which does not affect the status of the latter in any way and which could be replaced by any number of other perspectives provided by other translations, the existence of *Compagnie* renders *Company* subject to modification: what was originally complete in itself and autonomous (*Company*) is now rendered retroactively incomplete. In this sense, the first version is paradoxically in the dependence of the second, and the classic situation of the translation's relationship to its original has been turned upside down. What better proof of this could there be than the fact that, at times, it is the first version that furnishes an interpretation of the second rather than vice versa. This means that the *dependence* of the translation upon the original has been replaced by an *interdependence* between the two versions of Beckett's work.

Since *Company* and *Compagnie* manifestly cannot be substituted for one another, the sum total of the two texts is necessarily greater than either of them. What is more, the result of bringing the two together to study the reciprocal relationship brought about by their coexistence produces something *other* than such a sum total. We have seen, for example, that the two fictive universes do not entertain what might be called an incremental relationship with one another so that they could be added together to form a whole more complete than either of them, for in the process of adding them together, irreconcilable elements remain. Paradoxically, not only the process of subtraction but also that of addition leaves a recalcitrant remainder.

If we could manage to define the exact nature of this "otherness," then we would have the key to the status not just of the second version but of the bilingual work as such. The only further illumination of the problem I can offer here concerns a more language-system-sensitive aspect of the work than its fictive universe(s).

That the sum total of *Company/Compagnie* is other than or different from the mere addition of the two becomes even clearer once one considers the way each text works itself out on the level of the signifiers. Here the incompatibility of the two texts is virtually complete. As Juliane House puts it in his article "Of the Limits of Translatability": "Obviously, the physical nature of any signifier in language A cannot be duplicated in a signifier in language B; therefore, the relation of signifier to signified in language A, which is no longer arbitrary in literature, can never be rendered in language B." It is virtually impossible for the same pun to exist in two different languages. Thus the English pun "Sole sound in the silence your footfalls" (18) is necessarily lost in the French: "Seul bruit dans le silence celui de tes pas" (18). And once again, the loss is not all in the same direction, for the French pun of "En tenant compte de la teneur en compagnie" (34) is absent from the English: "The test is company" (35). Rhymes suffer the same fate so that "Sunless cloudless brightness" (32) becomes "Clarté sans nuage ni soleil" (32), and "Petite femme maigre et aigre" (27) becomes "A small thin sour woman" (28). Alliteration fares little better: "thus half halving distance between it and homologous hand" (68) is replaced by "réduisant ainsi d'un quart la distance entre lui et la main homologue" (66–67), and "Même ton terne toujours tel qu'imaginé au départ" (46) is substituted for "Same flat tone as initially imagined" (46). It is true that there exists a gradation of incompatibility here in that it is easier to find, if not equivalent, *analogous* rhymes than puns, and easier still to find analogous alliteration between the two languages. It would be most unlikely, however, to find exactly the same *amount* of activity going on in the language of the two texts at the same time in the same passage. This means that the type of analysis I have done elsewhere (*Dimensions*, 127–83) on working out the text on the level of the signifier in the French trilogy could not possibly produce the same result if applied to the English trilogy.

Once again, it is not that something is lost between the first and second versions or even that something is added. Here we have two distinct and indeed autonomous textual systems, each of which has to be studied in its own right. Thus *interdependence* of the two texts, posited earlier, initially has to be placed within parentheses: interdependence now gives way to *independence*. Indeed it is not at all clear that they can ever lose their independence at this level of the text. Any attempt to bring them together will, I suspect, result in a relationship of mere contiguity.

The incompatibility involved is analogous but not identical to that between different language-systems. Indeed, it proceeds directly from the latter. Nonetheless a text-system, as defined by Henri Meschonnic, possesses its own specificity distinct from the given language-system; the very existence of the discipline of text-grammar[3] testifies to the fact. Bakhtine makes this point very well:

> Tout système de signes (c'est-à-dire toute 'langue') . . . peut toujours être, en principe, déchiffré, c'est-à-dire traduit en d'autres systèmes de signes (d'autres langues); par conséquent, il y a une logique générale des système de signes, une langue des langues, potentielle et unifiée. . . . Mais le teste (à la différence de la langue comme système de moyens) ne peut jamais être traduit absolument, puisqu'il n'y a pas de texte des textes, potentiel et unifié. (Todorov, *Bakhtine*, 45)[4]

Whether or not the incompatible is not also incomparable is a moot point. It is clear that the working out of the signifiers has to be language-system sensitive. And to that extent—but to that extent alone—I can be said to have shifted the ground of my argument at this point from maintaining the specificity of Beckett's second versions in comparison with all other translations to highlighting the difference between any translation and its original.

What is more interesting and significant, however, is that it is by no means clear that if one were to have recourse to an analytical tool that was not language-system sensitive, one would be able to effect a comparison between the two text-systems on the level of signifier activity. On the contrary, I am thinking here of the tree-structure analysis undertaken by generative transformational grammar, which would make comparison possible at the level of the Chomskyan deep structures that lay claim to the status of universals and hence possess an obvious pertinence for determining the nature of equivalence between translation and original.

To conclude this preliminary discussion of a most complex problem, the work of the signifiers forms an essential and irreducible part of the remainder that is left over from the process of attempting to fuse *Company* and *Compagnie* into a coherent whole. It confirms the results of the study of the fictive universes which revealed that not only can neither of the universes be substituted for the other without leaving a residue unaccounted for, but neither can they be added together without something being left out. If the exact nature of the interdependence of *Company* and *Compagnie* remains unresolved, the very fact of their interdependence already distinguishes their relationship from that dependence in which any translation finds itself in relation to its original.

Now it may well be that the reception of any translation of a literary work could never be identical to that of its original in the other language due to the inevitable differences of connotation between words in different languages, not to mention the differences distinguishing the two cultures involved and hence their respective reading publics. This would already go some way toward explaining the discrepancy between the impressions one gets in reading the French and English critical writings devoted to Beckett's works (*Problématique*, 98). For readers of the English version are not reading the same *texts* as readers of the French version even if they are reading the same *work*. The existence of two separate texts does not in itself threaten the integrity of the work as an autonomous aesthetic entity inasmuch as any truly and wholly bilingual work must, of necessity, be comprised of two distinct texts. However, when each text conjures up its own fictive universe, as we have seen to be the case with *Company* and *Compagnie*, then the very concept of the literary work is put in question by the existence of the phenomenon that, for the present, can be referred to only as the "bilingual work."

As far as the situation of the Beckettian critic is concerned, even if the writer's second versions were to relate to his first versions in precisely the same way that a translation related to its original, their authorship alone would make them an essential component of the Beckettian canon, and the possibility of ignoring *either* of the two versions would clearly be unacceptable if one sought to give an adequate account of his achievement. Once *Compagnie* is seen to be something other than a translation of *Company* since the world it evokes is not that of its predecessor any more than the way the reader relates to it is the same, then it becomes essential to study each text in its own right. Once that is done, one would inevitably come back to the vexing question of the exact relationship they entertain with each another. And it is this question that is at the core of the status of the bilingual work.

Notes

1. Cf. my articles: "L'Intra-intertextualité interlinguistique de Beckett: La problématique de la traduction de soi," *Texte*, no. 2 (1983); "La Problématique de l'étude de l'oeuvre bilingue de Beckett," *Symposium* 38 (Summer 1984); "The Status of the Second Version of the Beckettian Text: The Evidence of the *Bing/Ping* Manuscripts," to appear in *Journal of Beckett Studies;* "The Status of Self-Translation," *Texte*, no. 4 (1985).

2. Page references in parentheses following quotations refer to *Company* (London: John Calder, 1980). The italics are mine.

3. Cf., for example, the introductory account of this new discipline in Robert de Beaugrande and Wolfgang Dressler, *Introduction to Text Linguistics* (London and New York: Longman, 1981), and for its application to literary texts in particular, see Teun A. Van Dijk, *Some Aspects of Text Grammars* (The Hague and Paris: Mouton, 1972).

4. M. Bakhtine, "Problema teksta v lingvistike, filologii i drugikh gumanitarnykh naukakh. Opyt filosofskogo analiza" ["Le Problème du texte en linguistique, philologie et dans les autres sciences humaines. Essai d'analyse philosophique"], in *Estetika slovesnogo tvorchestva [Esthétique de la création verbale]* (Moscow, 1979), 427, quoted by Tzvetan Todorov, *Mikhaïl Baktine: Le Principe dialogique, suivi de[s] Ecrits du Cercle de Bakhtine* (Paris: Seuil, "Poétique," 1981), 45. Todorov introduces this passage with the observation: "Cette différence entre langue et discours détermine très exactement le paradoxe de la traduction."

MARJORIE PERLOFF

Une Voix pas la mienne: French/English Beckett and the French/English Reader

In conversation with Richard Coe, some twenty years ago, Beckett remarked that he was afraid of English because "you couldn't help writing poetry in it" (Coe, 14). This is not, I think, a facetious remark designed to put off the prying critic. English, for Beckett, is, after all, the language of his childhood, more specifically, the canonical language of English literature as taught to a schoolboy at the Portora Royal School in the Northern Ireland of the early 1920s. Such a schoolboy would of course have been subjected to heavy doses of Shakespeare and Elizabethan poetry, of Milton, and, more immediately, of the great Romantic and Victorian poets. Like it or not, the iambic pentameters of Keat's Odes and the quatrains of Tennyson's "In Memoriam" must have been engraved in some corner of Beckett's mind. Thus, when the "I" of *Enough* says, "I see the flowers at my feet," the English-speaking reader remembers the poet of "Ode to a Nightingale" exclaiming ecstatically:

> I cannot see what flowers are at my feet,
> Nor what soft incense hangs upon the boughs . . .

Beckett's irony is that for the disillusioned speaker of *Enough*, there is no such vision: "I see the flowers at my feet and it's the others I see. Those we trod down with equal step. It is true they are the same."[1] It is an irony lost on the French reader of *Assez*, for whom the sentence "Je vois les fleurs à mes pieds et ce sont les autres que je vois" contains no such buried allusion.

Accordingly, when Beckett tells Niklaus Gessner that "in French it is easier to write without style," when he remarks to Herbert Blau that French "had the right weakening effect,"[2] he is referring, however obliquely, to a certain kind of poetic diction. "Without style" means without, or rather, outside the style of his great English and Irish precursors: Joyce is the most obvious example, but by extension, the "style" Beckett wants to be "without" is also that of Milton or Coleridge, Keats or Swinburne. "The right weakening effect" is one that "weakens" or neutralizes the heavy weight of the Anglo-Irish tradition, which is to say the poetry memorized and recited, as Yeats puts it, "among school children."

In a letter to his German friend Axel Kaun, written in 1937, almost a decade before he became a French writer, Beckett remarks:

> It is indeed becoming more and more difficult, even senseless, for me to write an official English. And more and more my own language appears to me like a veil that must be torn apart in order to get at the things (or the Nothingness) behind it. Grammar and Style. To me they seem to have become as irrelevant as a Victorian bathing suit or the imperturbability of a true gentleman. A mask. Let us hope the time will come, thank God that in certain circles it has already come, when language is most efficiently used where it is being most efficiently misused. . . . Is there any reason why that terrible materiality of the word surface should not be capable of being dissolved?

And he adds, "Perhaps the logographs of Gertrude Stein are . . . what I have in mind. At least the texture of language has become porous."[3]

To dissolve the "terrible materiality of the word surface" so as to create the "literature of the unword," as Beckett calls it (*Disjecta*, 173), became the task of Beckett's great French period, the period of the trilogy, *Godot*, and *Endgame*. Between the writing of *Molloy* in 1947 and *Company* in 1979, all of Beckett's fiction, with the exception of *From an Abandoned Work* (1957), was written first in French, then translated by the author into English. The longing to "write without style," without "poetry," must of course be understood as part of Beckett's larger longing to escape from the oppressive world of his bourgeois, suburban childhood, especially the painful love-hate relationship with his mother. Add to this, as Vivian Mercier points out, the dilemma of the Protestant Anglo-Irish writer who can never be wholly English or wholly Irish, a dilemma Beckett resolved by exiling himself from both and adopting French as his language (*Beckett/Beckett*, 26–27). Further, as Katharine Worth has suggested, Beckett's shift to French may well have been a natural consequence of his work in the French Resistance: forced to play the role of Frenchman in the tense and terrible years of subterfuge and hiding during the war, he reemerged after the war as, so to speak, a French writer (Worth, 6–7).

But of course the Anglo-Irish literary past could not be erased. "What I would do," Beckett wrote Cyril Cusack in 1956, "is give the whole unupsettable applecart for a sup of the Hawk's Well, or the Saints', or a whiff of Juno to go no further."[4] Yeats, Synge, O'Casey: these are not writers usually associated with the spare and austere Beckett. But in Beckett's recent fictions, an interesting phenomenon is at work. Increasingly, in the prose of his old age, the Anglo-Irish schoolroom of the writer's youth is coming in by the back door—

which is to say, the door of translation. When, for example, Beckett translates *Mal vu mal dit* (1981) into English (*Ill Seen Ill Said*), he inserts into the interstices of the text a network of parodic allusions to what we might call the Eng. Lit. canon. Given this particular subtext, the English version demands a rather different reading from the French original. Indeed, if French readings of this and related Beckett texts have been rather different from those in English, surely the critical difference is prompted not only by the different cultural and literary predispositions of Francophone and Anglophone readers, but by the simple practical fact that the two groups are reading *different* texts.

What happens when Beckett's translation is from English to French? *Company* (1980) is less allusive than *Ill Seen Ill Said*, but it resembles the latter in reinstating the poetic rhythms and echoes Beckett had spent so many years purging.[5] Here is a typical passage:

> By the voice a faint light is shed. Dark lightens while it sounds. Deepens when it ebbs. Lightens with flow back to faint full. Is whole again when it ceases. You are on your back in the dark. Had the eyes been open then they would have marked a change. (19)

The ambiguous syntax of the first sentence (Does the voice shed light or is the light shed next to ["by"] it?) gives way to a cadence reminiscent of Dylan Thomas (e.g., "Light sounds where no sun shines"), to the flatness of the declarative "You are on your back in the dark," and then, in the next paragraph, to the archaicizing language of "Whence the shadowy light?" The French translation flattens out these effects:

> La voix émet une lueur. Le noir s'éclaircit le temps qu'elle parle. S'épaissit quand elle reflue. S'éclaircit quand elle revient à son faible maximum. Se rétablit quand elle se tait. Tu es sur le dos dans le noir. Là s'ils avaient été ouverts tes yeux auraient vu un changement. (24)

The passive construction of the first sentence becomes active and unambiguous, the literary echoes don't operate, the lilting "flow back to faint full" becomes the more denotative "revient a son faible maximum," even as the poetic construction "Whence the shadowy light?" becomes simply "D'où le demi-jour"? Indeed, as Brian Fitch has noted, *Compagnie* is a reductive version of the English original: whole sentences are removed, references erased, and literary epithets like "cankerous" are purged.[6]

But of course such reduction functions precisely in the same way as do the additions made when Beckett translates *Mal vu mal dit*. In either case, the Beckett of the recent fiction has reintroduced the long-dormant question of national identity. To put it another way: once the "sans style"—the dissolution of the "terrible materiality of the word surface"—had been achieved, the return to literary origins became a desirable possibility. Provided, of course, that those origins could be sufficiently disguised. Let me begin by examining the double venture of *Mal vu mal dit / Ill Seen Ill Said.*

II

The language of *Ill Seen Ill Said* has, to begin with, a curiously Pre-Raphaelite or Yellow Nineties cast. On the first page we read, "She sits on erect and rigid in the deepening gloom" ("Droite et raide elle reste là dans l'ombre croissante"), and a few pages later, "Watches all night for the least glimmer" ("Guette en vain la nuit la moindre lueur"). "Gloom" and "glimmer": these alliterating nouns appear in poem after poem written by, among others, the young Yeats—"crimson meteors hang in the gloom," "midnight's all a glimmer, and noon a purple glow." The "Shadowy Horses" have eyes that are "glimmering white," and the "Polar Dragon's" "heavy rings" uncoil "from glimmering deep to deep." In *Ill Seen Ill Said*, as in the poetry of the early Yeats or of Dowson or Symons, gloom and glimmer are related to "withered flowers" (15), "slow wavering way" (15), "cold comfort" (26), "Black night fallen" (47), "the westering sun" (48), "olden kisses" (49), "dim the light of day" (51), "Toward unbroken night." Beckett's old woman is seen by her dark window "For long pacing to and fro in the gloom" (47) even as the father in Yeats's "A Prayer for My Daughter" tells us that

> And for an hour I have walked and prayed
> Because of the great gloom that is in my mind.

The voice that "ill sees, ill says" the story of the old woman who sits by the black window, waiting for Venus to rise, is steeped not only in the vocabulary but also in the meters of the Nineties. Indeed, what sound like little rhyming stanzas are introduced at odd junctures: for example,

> Rigid with face and hands
> against the pane she stands
> and marvels long—

which recalls such poems as Arthur Symons's "The Obscure Night of the Soul" ("All things I then forgot . . . All ceased, and I was not") or Wilde's "Requiescat" ("All my life's buried here") in its use of trimeter lines that begin and end with heavy stresses. Such rhythmic figuration is absent from the French text ("Raide debout visage et mains appuyés contre la vitre longuement elle s'émerveille"), which subordinates rhythmic recurrence to syntactic progression, the adjectival modifiers pushing on toward the main verb "s'émerveille," which provides semantic closure.

At the level of word or phrase, then, the tone of *Ill Seen Ill Said* (but not of *Mal vu mal dit*) can be characterized as a kind of parody *fin-de-siècle*, abrupt speech rhythms regularly punctuating the elegant variations on Wildean or Paterian discourse:

> But see she suddenly no longer there. Where suddenly fled. Quick then the chair before she reappears. At length. Every angle. With what one word convey its change? Careful. Less. Ah the sweet one word. Less. It is less. The same but less. Whencesoever the glare. (52)

> Mais voilà soudain qu'elle n'est plus là. Où soudain elle fut laissée. Vite donc la chaise avant qu'elle reparaisse. Longuement. Tous les angles. De quel seul mot en dire le changement? Attention. Moindre. Ah le beau seul mot. Elle est moindre. La même mais moindre. D'où que l'oeil s'y acharne. (66)

Note especially the difference in the final sentence fragment: as in the passage from *Company* cited above, the almost comic archaism of "Whencesoever" has no counterpart in the sober French of "D'où que."

Against this background of late Victorian bric-a-brac, we find intricately jumbled allusions to earlier and later English writers. Here is a partial tabulation:

1. L'herbe la plus mauvaise s'y fait toujours plus rare. (9)
   Ever scanter even the rankest weed. (8)
   —A predominantly trochaic pentameter line whose sound structure alludes parodically to Milton's "Lycidas" (e.g., "As killing as the canker to the rose"), even as its imagery recalls *Hamlet:*

   . . . 'tis an unweeded garden
   That grows to seed. Things rank and gross in nature
   Possess it merely. (II, 1)

   or

   And do not spread the compost on the weeds,
   To make them ranker. (III, 4)

2. Mer invisible quoique proche. Inaudible. (11)
   Invisible nearby sea. Inaudible. (10)
   —Joyce, *Ulysses*, opening of the "Proteus" chapter: "Ineluctable modality of the visible . . . seaspawn and seawrack."

3. Sans pâtre ils divaguent à leur guise. (11)
   Unshepherded they stray as they list. (10)
   —Burlesque of St. Peter's speech in "Lycidas": "Of other care they little

reck'ning make, / Than how to scramble at the shearers' feast. . . . And when they list, their lean and flashy songs / Grate on their Scannel Pipes of wretched straw."

4. Fait baisser le regard dans l'acte d'appréhender. Incrimine l'acquis. Retient de deviner. (19)
   Averts the intent gaze. Incriminates the dearly won. Forbids divining her. (16)
   —These tightly woven three-stress lines recall Satan's first view of Eve in *Paradise Lost*, IV: "When Satan still in gaze, as first he stood . . ."

5. La folle du logis s'en donne à coeur chagrin. (21)
   Imagination at wit's end spreads its sad wings. (17)
   —A burlesque of Hopkins's "God's Grandeur": "Because the Holy Ghost over the bent / World broods with warm breast and with ah! bright wings."

6. Comme si la terre tremblait sans cesse à cet endroit. (21)
   As if here without cease the earth faintly quaked. (18)
   —A collusion of the King James Bible ("world without end") and Yeats's *The Wind Among the Reeds* (e.g., "I Hear the Shadowy Horses").

7. Choses et chimères. (24)
   Things and imaginings. (20)
   —Yeats, "The Tower," III: "I have prepared my peace / With learned Italian things / And the proud stones of Greece, / Poet's imaginings. . . ."

8. Cette vielle si mourante. (24)
   This old so dying woman. (20)
   —The syntactic oddity of the English phrase ("old so dying"), which is not present in its French counterpart, is standard Irish ballad diction and turns up in both Yeats and Joyce.

9. Fermés les yeux ne livrent pas leurs prunelles. L'avenir les dira cernées d'un bleu délavé. (30)
   The lids occult the longed-for eyes. Time will tell them washen blue. (25)
   —Tennyson, *In Memoriam* (e.g., LXVII: "And closing eaves of wearied eyes"; LXXX: "And dropt the dust on tearless eyes"), plus a parody-ballad refrain. The first sentence also recalls Swinburne, "Atalanta in Calydon," IV: "Yet thine heart shall wax heavy with sighs and thine eyelids with tears."

10. L'oeil reviendra sur les lieux de ses trahisons. En congé séculaire de là où gèlent les larmes. (32)
    The eye will return to the scene of its betrayals. On centennial leave from where tears freeze. (27)
    —Perhaps an amalgam of Shakespeare, *Antony and Cleopatra*, IV, 12 ("Betrayed I am. / O this false soul of Egypt! this grave charm, / Whose eye

becked forth my wars and called them home"), Wordsworth, "Tintern Abbey" ("Knowing that Nature never did betray / The heart that loved her"), and Tennyson's "Tears Idle Tears." Note that the second sentence is a perfect Swinburnian anapestic pentameter.

11. Passée panique la suite. (38)
    Panic past pass on. (31)
    —Nursery rhyme like "Pease porridge cold."

12. Sentent-elles seulement la chair sous l'étoffe? La chair sous l'étoffe les sent-elle? Ne vont-ils donc jamais frémir? (40)
    Do they as much as feel the clad flesh? Does the clad flesh feel them? Will they then never quiver? (32)
    —A kind of Swinburnian tongue-twister, playing on such poems as "Atalanta in Calydon" (e.g., "Come with bows bent and with emptying of quivers, / Maiden most perfect, lady of light . . ."). The touch of "clad flesh" is a frequent motif in Swinburne, especially in "The Triumph of Time" and "Laus Veneris."

13. Immortel jour qui agonise encore. (49)
    Death again of deathless day. (40)
    —Poetic Diction, with characteristic Pre-Raphaelite rhythm.

14. Partie sans fin gagnée perdue. Inaperçue. (49)
    Day without end won and lost. Unseen. (40)
    —King James Bible.

15. La chaise squelettique s'y dresse plus blafarde que nature. (51)
    Stark the skeleton chair death-paler than life. (41)
    —Keats, "La Belle Dame sans Merci": "Pale warriors, death-pale were they all."

16. Ombre d'un ancien sourire souri (62)
    Ghost of an ancient smile (49)
    —Play on Pound's "The Return": "host of an ancient people."

17. Refermé l'oeil las à cet effet ou rouvert ou laissé en l'état quel qu'il fût. (67)
    Closed again to that end the vile jelly or opened again or left as it was however that was. (52)
    —Shakespeare, *King Lear:* Cornwall blinding the old Gloucester: "Out vile jelly. Where is thy lustre now?" The allusion gives the sentence in question a sardonic edge that is not found in the French.

18. Jusqu'au moment pour l'heure lointain où les manteaux vont manquer aux fenêtres et au clou le tire-bouton. (71)

Far ahead to the instant when the coats will have gone from their rods
and the button-hook from its nail. (56)

—Ecclesiastes in the King James Bible. A note of bathos is introduced
by the placement in the key nominal slot of the word "button-hook," this trivial object functioning as a central motif in the old woman's meditation.

19. Puis noir parfait avant-glas tout bas adorable son top départ de l'arrivée.
    (75)

    Then in that perfect dark foreknell darling sound pip for end begun. (59)

    —Keats, "Ode to a Nightingale." Beckett's sentence is an elaborate
spoof on the opening of the last stanza: "Forlorn! the very word is like a bell /
To toll me back from thee to my sole self!" The "perfect dark" alludes to the
"embalmed darkness" of stanza 5; "darling" is a play on "Darkling I listen" in
stanza 6.

20. Plus miette de charogne nulle part. (76)

    Not another crumb of carrion left. (59)

    —The allusion is to Gerard Manley Hopkins's "Carrion Comfort":

    Not, I'll not, carrion comfort, Despair, not feast on thee;
    Not untwist—slack they may be—these last strands of man
    In me or, most weary, cry *I can no more*. I can;
    Can something, hope, wish day come, not choose not to be.

Here, in the final paragraph of *Ill Seen Ill Said*, the allusions to Keats and
Hopkins are intricately bound up in the meaning of Beckett's text. In the
coda, the speaking voice alludes first to Beckett's own earlier work: "For the
last time at last for to end yet again what the wrong word?"—and then takes
its final stance in the face of "the last wisps of day when the curtain closes."
Like Keats's "Adieu! Adieu!" the words "Farewell to farewell" bring the
Beckettian speaker back to the realization that "the fancy cannot cheat so
well as she was wont to do" and to the acceptance of the fact that one must
"Lick chops and basta" that, in Hopkins's words, "I can / Can something,
hope, wish day come, not choose not to be."

Ironically, the Hopkins allusion is a perfectly literal translation from the
French. Indeed, the concluding words of *Mal vu mal dit* are rendered in their
precise English equivalent, even if the syntax is slightly altered:

Goulûment seconde par seconde. Ciel terre et tout le bataclan. Plus miette de
charogne nulle part. Lechées babines baste. Non. Encore une seconde. Rien
qu'une. Le temps d'aspirer ce vide. Connaître le bonheur.

Moment by glutton moment. Sky earth the whole kit and boodle. Not another
crumb of carrion left. Lick chops and basta. No. One moment more. One last.
Grace to breathe that void. Know happiness.

The English version "says" exactly what the French does, but the Keatsian and Hopkinsian references give the passage a parodic edge, an edge underscored by such archaisms as "Moment by glutton moment" (where a literal translation would be "Gluttonously, moment by moment").[7] Such phrasing qualifies the romantic idealism of Beckett's conclusion, an idealism that one reviewer has called "a thumping C major chord," "too glib [in its] way of phrasing a refusal to mourn" (Taubman, 16). But neither the French text, with its comic inflections like "Lechées babines baste," and certainly not the English, with its sardonic allusions to Keats and Hopkins, is "glib" in this sense. In reading Beckett, contextualization is always necessary.

III

What, then, do we make of the elaborate web of poetic references that informs the text of *Ill Seen Ill Said?* For one thing, their frequency seems to be Beckett's way of saying that we must be cautious in reading the French and English versions of a given text as if they were quite simply identical. And here we may observe a curious phenomenon. Whereas Beckett's early critics—Ruby Cohn, Martin Esslin, John Fletcher, Hugh Kenner, Ludovic Janvier—were very much aware of Beckett's bilingualism, perhaps because Beckett's turn to French in *Molloy* was such a novelty, recent discussions, even those that deal closely with stylistics, seem to assume that the Beckett text is a stable and unitary entity.[8]

Thus David Read's discussion of the theme of "consciousness of being [as] tertium quid of the interplay between experience and abstinence" in *Company* and *Ill Seen Ill Said* makes no allusion whatever to the textual problem (111–26). Or again, when the difference between the French and English versions is noted, the tendency is to assume that the text in one's own language is the "real" one. Judith Dearlove, for example, in her otherwise exemplary stylistic study, *Accommodating the Chaos: Samuel Beckett's Nonrelational Art* (1982), writes of *Ping* (in French, *Bing*): "Indeed, Beckett's revisions show a movement toward briefer, more ephemeral sounds from paf to hop to bing. In the English text Beckett alters even the voiced b of bing to the voiceless and hence even slighter p of ping (113). Here the French is regarded not as an alternate but as an earlier, hence less finished, version, the title word being made appropriately slight in the text's "final," which is to say its perfected, stage.

Needless to say, the French reader of the French text will see it the other way around: Jude Stefan, reviewing *Mal vu mal dit* for *Nouvelle Revue Française,* reads Beckett's fiction as an existentialist document, as a "cri reduit de la poésie en fin de siècle," the cry of a voice that is powerful but "vigilante jusqu'au soupir final" (344:126). But when the "soupir final" includes the phrases "Sky earth the whole kit and boodle" and "Lick chops and basta," its comic and robust edge suggests that this sigh may not be so final after all.

It is interesting in this connection to compare the early French reviews of Beckett's work to their English counterparts. "[Beckett's] language," said Maurice Nadeau in one of the first reviews of *Molloy*, "dissolves into nothingness (annihilates itself) as soon as it is established, erases instantly its faintest traces." And further, "Beckett settles us in the world of the Nothing where some nothings which are men move about for nothing. The absurdity of the world and the meaninglessness of our condition are conveyed in an absurd and deliberately insignificant fashion" (Graver and Federman, 53). These motifs—the absurdity of the human condition and the consequent dissolution of language, its refusal to signify—are echoed in the Beckett commentaries of Georges Bataille and Maurice Blanchot. Bataille writes:

> Language is what determines this regulated world, whose significations provide the foundation for our cultures, our activities and our relations, but it does so in so far as it is reduced to a means of these cultures, activities and relations; freed from these servitudes, it is nothing more than a deserted castle whose gaping cracks let in the wind and rain: it is no longer the signifying word, but the defenseless expression death wears as a disguise.

And he suggests that the epigraph for *Molloy* could be "Lasciate ogni speranza voi qu'entrate" (Graver and Federman, 57, 59; cf. 64–67). Similarly, Blanchot observes:

> "The Unnamable" is precisely an experiment conducted, an experience lived under the threat of the impersonal, the approach of a neutral voice that is raised of its own accord, that penetrates the man who hears it, that is without intimacy, that excludes all intimacy, that cannot be made to stop, that is the incessant, the *interminable*. . . . The man who writes is already no longer Samuel Beckett but the necessity which has surrendered him to whatever is outside himself, which has made him a nameless being, The Unnamable, a being without being . . . the empty site in which an empty voice is raised without effect, masked for better or worse by a porous and agonizing *I*. (Graver and Federman, 119)

Compare to these representations of Beckett, Donald Davie's assertion, made with reference to the radio play *All That Fall*, written in English for the BBC, that "Beckett is a comic writer. He has yet to write a book that is not a funny book." Having illustrated this thesis by citing snatches of dialogue between Mr. and Mrs. Rooney, Davie comments on the parodic function of Beckett's syntax: "Though language may betray the speaker in a Joycean pun ('Nip some young doom in the bud'), more often for Beckett it does so by syntactical over-elegance." And, as for the "bleak pessimism about the human person and human destiny" of which Beckett stands accused, Davie argues:

[Beckett's pessimism] could equally well be explained as an attempt, like Words-worth's in his progress from articulate men through peasants and children to idi-ots and lunatics, to strip from the human being all attributes save precisely that of being—a common ground on which (who knows?) Beckett might stand, as Wordsworth did, to utter a hurrah for the human race. (Graver and Federman, 154–55)

Is Davie talking about the same writer as are Bataille and Blanchot? Is he merely being insensitive? Here is the opening of Hugh Kenner's *Samuel Beck-ett* (revised edition):

Mr. Beckett's patient concern with bicycles, amputees, battered hats, and the let-ter M; his connoisseurship of the immobilized hero; his preoccupation with footling questions which there isn't sufficient evidence to resolve; his humor of the short sentence; his Houdini-like virtuosity (by preference chained hand and foot, deprived of story, dialogue, locale): these constitute a unique comic reper-toire like a European clown's. The antecedents of his plays are not in literature but—to take a rare American example—in Emmett Kelly's solemn determination to sweep a circle of light into a dustpan. . . . The milieu of his novels bears a moral resemblance to that of the circus . . . (13)

From the vestibule of hell (Bataille) to the circus: the difference in empha-sis between Bataille and Blanchot on the one hand, Davie and Kenner on the other, cannot of course be accounted for simply by the differences between the French and English texts. Nor have all French critics lined up in the former camp and British or American ones in the latter.[9] To understand the difference, one would have to study the contrasting cultural formations of postwar Paris and postwar Britain/America, beginning with the profound malaise of the Occupation, a malaise surely inconceivable for British and espe-cially for American critics, for whom war is always, so to speak, somewhere else.

Beckett, whose day-to-day life during the years of Occupation and Resis-tance was one of constant threat, subterfuge, hiding, and reinvention, was very much the poet of silence and dissolution defined by Blanchot and Na-deau, even as he retained the urge toward comedy, clowning, wordplay, and buffoonery that had already manifested themselves in his first two novels, *Murphy* and *Watt*. His work thus bears out Kenner's reading as well as Bataille's, Davie's as well as Nadeau's. For our purposes, in any case, the im-portant thing is that these two sides of Beckett are reflected in his French/English texts as early as *Molloy*. To give just one example, here is Molloy rumi-nating on his inability to remember names, even the name of the town in which he was born and where his mother lives:

Oui, même à cette époque, où tout s'estompait déjà, ondes et particules, la condition de l'objet était d'être sans nom, et inversement. (40–41)

Yes, even then, when already all was fading, waves and particles, there could be
no things but nameless things, no names but thingless names. (31)

The English translation begins by following the French closely, but with the
articulation of the main clause, the two diverge. A literal translation of the
French would give us, "The condition of the object was to be without a name,
and vice-versa," or "The state of the thing was to be" or, more colloquially,
"It was the condition of the thing to be." But Beckett colloquializes—"there
could be no things but nameless things"—even as he then embellishes: the
terse "et inversement" gives way to wordplay, "no things but nameless things,
no names but thingless names."

Try to think of a thingless name, a name that does not refer to anything,
and you will see that Beckett's Molloy is having a bit of fun. Slight as the difference here and throughout the text may be, the English has a playful edge not
present in the French. Again, the English phrasing often takes on a familiar
Anglo-Irish verse rhythm, as when "la petite nuit où des taches claires
naissent, flamboient, s'éteignent, tantôt vides, tantôt peuplées, comme d'or-
dures de saints la flamme" (36) becomes "the little night and its little lights,
faint at first, then flaming and extinguished, now ravening, now fed, as fire
by filth and martyrs" (28), or when "Tout cela à travers une poussière
étincelante et bientôt à travers cette bruine aussi" (37) becomes "all that
through a glittering dust and soon through that mist too" (29), a phrase that
could be lineated and scanned so as to fit comfortably into a Nineties ballad:

<blockquote>
áll thât thróugh a glíttering dúst
and sóon thrôugh thât míst tôo . . .
</blockquote>

Which version is the "real" or the "better" one? Obviously both and neither.
The scene of Beckett's writing exists somewhere in between the two, a space
where neither French nor English has autonomy. The slippage of language,
its drive toward self-erasure and retracing, takes place not only within the
text, as Nadeau and Blanchot observed, but intertextually as well. More and
more, in the late work, it is a slippage back into the world of Beckett's youth;
the "porous" linguistic texture brings to the surface images and motifs that
had been carefully suppressed. "Language," as Beckett says in the letter to
Axel Kaun, "is most efficiently used where it is being most efficiently mis-
used." Or as the voice of Ill Seen Ill Said puts it, "The eye must return to the
scene of its betrayals."

Notes

1. *Enough*, in *First Love and Other Shorts*, 56. Cf. *Assez*, in *Têtes-Mortes*, 44. For Beckett bibliography and chronology, I am indebted to *No Symbols Where None Intended: A Catalogue of Books, Manuscripts, and Other Materials Relating to Samuel Beckett in the Collections of the Humanities Research Center*, Selected and Described by Carlton Lake (Austin: Humanities Research Center, The University of Texas, 1984).

2. See Coe, *Samuel Beckett*, 14. Cf. A. Alvarez, *Samuel Beckett*, 40–41; John Fletcher, "Ecrivain bilingue, 212–18; Harry Cockerham, "Bilingual Playwright," 139–59. For an interesting analysis from the linguist's point of view, see Ekundayo Simpson, *Samuel Beckett: Traducteur de lui-même*.

3. German letter to Axel Kaun, 7 September 1937, reprinted in *Disjecta*, 52–53. An English translation of this letter by Martin Esslin is provided in the Notes, 170–73; it is this translation that I cite here.

4. Cited in Mercier, *Beckett/Beckett*, 23. The references are, respectively, to Yeats's *At the Hawk's Well*, Synge's *The Well of Saints*, and O'Casey's *Juno and the Paycock*.

5. The case of Beckett's plays is somewhat different. From the radio play *All That Fall* (1957) and *Krapp's Last Tape* (1958) to the present, Beckett has composed many of his plays first in English, and their language and rhythms frequently allude to English literature, to proverbs, and the King James Bible. The most allusive of the plays is *Happy Days* (1962). In his bilingual edition of *Happy Days / Oh les beaux jours* (London and Boston: Faber and Faber, 1978), James Knowlson catalogues the literary references and finds that Winnie's speeches are tissues of quotations from Shakespeare, Milton, Gray, Browning, etc. In some cases, the French version matches the English in that Beckett substitutes, say, Ronsard for Shakespeare or Verlaine for a British ballad, and so on.

Winnie's allusions are, however, rather different from those of *Ill Seen Ill Said*. The dramatic character is always trying to remember a particular "poetic" quotation and announces that she will quote a passage, thus displaying her conventionality, her constant need to resort to authorized ways of saying things. As such, Winnie's citations are more obviously comic than the complex allusions made by the narrators themselves in Beckett's fictions.

6. See Brian T. Fitch's essay on *Company/Compagnie*, in this volume.

7. Raymond Federman has pointed out to me that some of the French phrases cited above similarly allude to the French romantic and symbolist tradition. Thus "Choses et chimères" (Example 7) may allude to Mallarmé's lines, "Quelle soie aux baumes de temps / Ou la chimère s'éxtenue," and the "charogne" of Example 20 points back to Baudelaire's great poem by that name. But such allusions constitute at best a minor chord in the French text and their parodic implications remain undeveloped.

8. For early discussions, see Ruby Cohn, "Samuel Beckett Self-Translator"; Martin Esslin, *The Theatre of the Absurd* 8–9; Ludovic Janvier, *Pour Samuel Beckett* 224–30; Hugh Kenner, "Beckett Translating Beckett: Comment c'est," 194–210; and John Fletcher, "Ecrivain bilingue."

Most British and American essays on Beckett's fictions written over the past decade simply accept the English text at face value, without considering its relationship to the French original. See, for example, John Pilling's otherwise very helpful *Samuel Beckett*, 25–66; and his "Ends and Odds in Prose," in James Knowlson and John Pilling, *Frescoes of the Skull*, 132–94. For a short but notable exception, see George Craig, "The Voice of Childhood and Great Age." Comparing *Mal vu mal dit* to *Ill Seen Ill Said*, Craig talks of the "verbal no-man's land where neither French nor English holds sway."

9. For example, Jacques Lemarchand, reviewing *En Attendant Godot* for *Figaro Littéraire*, 17 January 1953, 10, calls the play a "resolutely comic" work and comments on its "circus" quality: see *Cahier de l'Herne*, 90–91. Again, Jean Anouilh calls *Godot* "the music-hall sketch of Pascal's 'Pensées' as played by the Fratcllini clowns." See *Cahier de l'Herne*, 92; the translation is Ruby Cohn's. Examples of the converse (English and American interpretations that take Beckett as the voice of *angst*, of existential despair, of the failure of language to signify, and so on) are too numerous to list.

DINA SHERZER

Words About Words:
Beckett and Language

Il compito della letteratura è di tenere il linguaggio in esercizio.
—Umberto Eco

The task of literature is to keep exercising language.

It is a commonplace that Beckett distrusts language, that he thinks that language is inadequate, and that in his works he demonstrates the bankruptcy and the nullity of language. Michael Robinson writes: "Beckett's novels are founded upon a profound despair of language, for words cannot be trusted." He adds: "The theater allows Beckett to provide visual evidence of the untrustworthiness of language." Martin Esslin holds that "language in Beckett's plays serves to express the breakdown and the disintegration of language." And Olga Bernal says that "Watt illumine ce processus de désintégration du langage qui se poursuivra jusqu'à *Comment c'est*."[1]

Beckett's skepticism about language has not been invented by these or other critics. It is the result of many statements which Beckett has put in the mouths of his characters. In *All That Fall*, Mrs. Rooney explains that she uses the simplest words and yet she finds her way of speaking very bizarre; in *Molloy*, the narrator talks about icy words and icy meanings; the trilogy contains an impressive array of metaphors such as ants, babble, drops of silence, dust, and scraps which are used to discredit words; Winnie in *Oh les beaux jours* feels that: "on dit tout. Tout ce qu'on peut. Et pas un mot de vrai nulle part"; and in the poem *Cascando*, we read about "the churn of stale words."[2] According to several critics, this skepticism about language might have been kindled or reinforced by the ideas of the German philosopher Fritz Mauthner, himself a skeptic about language, who repeatedly discussed the vanity of words and the impossibility of knowledge through language.[3]

At the same time, Beckett has also made several statements which imply a positive attitude toward language on his part. Commenting on Joyce's writing in 1929, he writes that it is not "about something, it is that something itself," therefore warning that one needs to pay attention not only to the content of

Joyce's works but also to how this content is expressed. Asked about the meaning of *Waiting for Godot*, he responded that it is a question of fundamental sounds and nothing else. His commentary on a passage from Saint Augustine is particularly eloquent: "There is a wonderful sentence in Augustine. I wish I could remember the Latin. It is even finer in Latin than in English. 'Do not despair: one of the thieves was saved. Do not presume: one of the thieves was damned.' I am interested in the shape of ideas even if I do not believe in them. . . . That sentence has a wonderful shape. It is shape that matters."[4]

What does this all mean? How can we interpret and make sense of Beckett's attitude toward language? Is Beckett trapped in a double bind which leads him both to discredit and to value the very tool he uses? In order to answer such questions it is necessary to examine what Beckett does with language. Martin Esslin defines the traits of Beckett's *literary personality* which emerge from his works, whether dramatic or novelistic and whether in English or in French.[5] Similarly we can define Beckett's *linguistic personality* because again, whether he writes in English or in French, or whether he writes plays, novels, or short stories, there are basic features cutting across languages and genres which give Beckett's language its special and particular qualities.

Going back to the statements quoted earlier, it should be noted that when he makes favorable comments about language, Beckett does not discuss words and their incapacity of meaning. Rather, he points to the materiality of language, to his interest in sounds, and to the possibilities of syntax. These are clues to the understanding of Beckett's use of language. The fact that Beckett decided to write in French after *Murphy* in order to write more easily without style, and that recently he has tended to write in English again after many years of writing in French, is another important clue. Such moves show that by not using English, his mother tongue, the language of his cultural and intellectual upbringing, or later going back to English, leaving French, which has become a part of his daily life and creative activities, Beckett wants to escape automatic, ready-made expressions, common cultural or intellectual phrases which all native and competent speakers utter or write unconsciously and mechanically. In other words, Beckett, like Mauthner, also bilingual, feels that the use of language is a rule-following activity. By turning to French and later to English he avoids using language in ways that are predicated by customs and by conventions.[6] Another significant document which is also a clue to Beckett's attitude toward language is the 1932 Verticalist Manifesto, signed by Beckett, which advocates a revolutionary attitude toward word and syntax.[7]

It appears thus that Beckett is interested in the form of language, that he refuses conventions, and that he is striving to find new modes of expression. How does he reflect these ideas in his works? Everyone would agree that the texture of Beckett's literary discourse is characterized by an extreme diversity.

This diversity is due to the nature of the narrative and dramatic situations that Beckett invents. In his novels he establishes an explicit interactional, dialogic structure whereby self-conscious narrators address themselves to narratees, giving them orders, asking them questions, discussing how they are writing, commenting on their topics, speculating on what they have written or will write, and expressing their disgust or their satisfaction in exclamations or interjections, thus interrupting the reporting of events or the description of a particular scene. In his plays Beckett has characters engage in a wide range of verbal activities such as greeting each other, giving orders, asking and answering questions, making up stories, playacting, cursing, telling past events, or describing psychological states. In all of Beckett's works several of these verbal moves, which linguists call *speech acts*, take place successively, with the result that the text is bristling with linguistic activity and heterogeneity, for each speech act entails a specific syntactic, semantic, discursive, and interactional organization.

Paraphrasing Clov, we can say that no one wrote so crooked as Beckett. His language is neither completely conventional nor normal, neither completely incongruous nor nonsensical; it is askew. These properties are caused by the presence of an impressive array of devices which disrupt the logical progression and the syntactical and semantic organization of discourse. Typically a play or a novel by Beckett displays such features as contradictions, accumulations, permutations, non sequiturs, ellipses, exclamations, and interjections which introduce disorder, illogic, and clumsiness into the syntax and the narrative structure. In addition, one encounters many disjunctions between the style and the topic, incongruous juxtapositions of words and stylistic registers, which result in unbalance, clownishness, coarseness, and sophistication in the lexical domain.

Beckett is particularly fond of using existing clichés, proverbs, or sayings, which he transforms. He also invents his own proverbs or maximlike utterances. His modifications are such that the mold or structure of the proverb is recognizable while the content is parodied or deformed, or the context is inappropriate. He thus creates comical intertextual effects.

Repetition is another characteristic of Beckett's discourse and it is created by a variety of devices. It can involve the recurrence of the same words on a page, or of the same sound within an utterance or a group of sentences, or the recurrence of a sentence or a group of sentences within a single text. In addition, there are repetitions with variations which are created when an item is repeated with slight alterations. Repetition has several effects. It is a structuring device in *Waiting for Godot* and in *How It Is*; it introduces a clownish mood in passages where one or several items are repeated mechanically as if skidding was taking place, as in *The Unnamable*; and it creates lulling, incantatory effects in the prose of *How It Is* or in the recent dramaticules *Not I*, *Footfalls*, and *Rockaby*.

What do such linguistic and discursive practices amount to? Beckett's sense of language and his linguistic personality translate a series of philosophical and linguistic attitudes. Or to put it another way, Beckett emerges as a metalinguist who through his linguistic behaviors implicitly comments on the nature of language and language use. By using many speech acts, Beckett shows an acute awareness of and a sensitivity to the heterogeneity and to the multiple possibilities inherent in language. He puts into play what Wittgenstein in his *Philosophical Investigations* calls language-games:

> But how many kinds of sentences are there? Say assertion, question, and command?—There are countless kinds. . . . And this multiplicity is not something fixed, given once for all; but new types of language, new language-games, as we may say, come into existence, and others become obsolete and get forgotten. . . . Review the multiplicity of language-games in the following examples, and in others:
>> Giving orders, and obeying them
>> Describing the appearance of an object, or giving its measurements . . .
>> Reporting an event
>> Speculating about an event . . .
>> Making up a story; and reading it
>> Play-acting . . .
>> Making a joke; telling it . . .
>> Translating from one language into another
>> Asking, thanking, cursing, greeting, praying.[8]

By not observing the conventions of order, causality, and logic, Beckett succeeds in undermining normative uses of language. He plays with and flouts the basic maxims of ideal communication, which the philosopher of language Paul Grice formulates as follows:

> Do not say what you believe to be false
> Be relevant
> Avoid obscurity of expression
> Avoid ambiguity
> Be brief
> Be orderly[9]

By tampering with the components of one of the most conventional of discourse units, the proverb, Beckett undermines its conventionality.

By using repetition Beckett brings about a shift in the properties of novelistic and dramatic discourse. Instead of focusing primarily on the content of the message (the referential function, in Jakobson's terms), he plays up one aspect of language, the phonic, which tends to be emphasized in poetry.

All writers exploit and manipulate language to a certain extent. But Beckett goes considerably further in constantly defamiliarizing language. By combining linguistic entities in different ways he shows that language provides a set of potentials which can be exploited to a very great degree and in a variety of ways. He thus adopts an attitude which corresponds to the views of linguists such as Edward Sapir and Roman Jakobson, who see language as a set of resources, as a powerful tool ready to be manipulated and played with. For them it is in poetry in particular and literature in general that the possibilities of language are pushed to their full force.[10]

Interestingly, Beckett turns the so-called inadequacies of language into elements which become the very ingredients of his creativity and innovation. He takes advantage and plays up the variability of the relationship of language to reality, the fuzziness of the boundaries between what is grammatical and what is not, between what is acceptable semantically and what is not, and between what makes verbal interactions felicitous or incongruous. These logical, syntactic, and interactional problems, which have to do with limits and stretchings of norms and conventions, are precisely issues that are at the cutting edge of contemporary linguistics and the philosophy of language.[11] These stretchings of limits and norms which characterize Beckett's experiments with language are also present in his other semiotic manipulations. Thus in *Not I* there is only a lit mouth and a silent listener on the stage, and only the closeup on the mouth, lips, and tongue on the television screen. A mute character is prompted to actions by objects in *Act without words*, or, in *Quad*, four figures are attracted tirelessly toward a center where nothing happens.

Like the philosophers he might have read (Nietzsche, Mauthner, and Wittgenstein of the *Tractatus*), Beckett probably subscribes to the idea that there is a lack of an exact, tight-fitting relationship between language and reality. He would also probably agree with Derrida, who argues that language is a system of differences, that it is already a copy, a representation, a metaphor, or an analogy and that it does not express but only transcribes. More generally he probably shares the uneasiness of the twentieth-century writers who doubt the efficiency of their medium, insofar as the medium's purpose is to express the truth of lived experience.[12] However, this deconstruction of language does not have a crippling effect on writers or on philosophers. It points to what language is and is not.[13] Beckett, like Joyce, Cummings, or Céline, manipulates language in such ways that readers or spectators are always made aware of its materiality and malleability. These writers do not undermine language. Rather they celebrate it, all the while flouting the belle-lettres style, norms, and propriety which they obviously want to repudiate.

Beckett's language is a perfect medium for his enterprise. It is in keeping with the absurdity, the flux, the indeterminism, with the elusiveness of the I, of reality, of the intellect, of memory, and with the skepticism about science and knowledge, which are the recurring themes of his works. It is also a medium which enables him to create tension, a mode which is basic to all his works. Solitary, desperate, sick individuals who might deplore the lack of value of words and even attack words with animosity, the characters of his plays and the narrators of his novels sustain themselves by talking, writing, addressing, or answering other characters, or merely monologuing or listening to an inner voice which empties a flow of words on empty stages. Language keeps them going.

The baroque mannerisms of the early novels, the clownish metaphysical banterings of the early plays, the fluid and incantatory texture of recent works in drama and in prose, all display the vitality and dynamism of Beckett's language. Indeed, in all his different creations Beckett shows confidence, not Apollonian confidence but a Dionysiac one animated by a sense of carnival and provocation. His is an aesthetic of play which allows him "de créer du jeu avec du jeu," that is, to create imbalance with free play.[14]

Notes

1. Michael Robinson, *The Long Sonata of the Dead*, 229–30; Martin Esslin, *The Theatre of the Absurd*, 63; Olga Bernal, *Langage et fiction dans le roman de Beckett*, 21.

2. *All That Falls*, in *Krapp's Last Tape and Other Dramatic Pieces*, 35; *Molloy* (in *Three Novels*), 31; *Oh les beaux jours*, 70; *Cascando*, in *Collected Poems in English and French*, 30.

3. See the article by Linda Ben-Zvi, "Samuel Beckett, Fritz Mauthner, and the Limits of Language," 183–200, which provides an excellent presentation and references to studies on Mauthner's influence on Beckett.

4. Beckett's essay "Dante . . . Bruno . Vico . . Joyce," in *transition*, no. 16–17, reprinted in *Samuel Beckett: I can't go on, I'll go on*, ed. Richard W. Seaver, 105–26, contains the remarks about Joyce. In letters to Alan Schneider reprinted in the *Village Voice*, 19 March 1958, Beckett talks about sounds. The comment about Augustine is reported by Schneider in "Waiting for Beckett."

5. Martin Esslin, *Mediations*, 94.

6. I use here Mauthner's terminology as it is presented in Gershon Weiler, *Mauthner's Critique of Language*, 115, 273, 336.

7. "Poetry is Vertical," quoted by Sighle Kennedy in *Murphy's Bed*, 304.

8. Ludwig Wittgenstein, *Philosophical Investigations*, 11[e].

9. Paul Grice, "Logic and Conversation."

10. Edward Sapir, *Language*, 221–32; Roman Jakobson, "Poetry of Grammar and Grammar of Poetry," 597–609.

11. Chomskyan linguistics, while focusing on normative language within sentence grammar, has at the same time generated in its wake a concern with the subtleties of the interplay of the grammatical and the ungrammatical, as well as other topics for which Beckett's writings are so relevant.

12. For a discussion on this topic, see Richard Sheppard, "The Crisis of Language," 323–36.

13. Derrida's linguistic performance in *Glas* is a concrete example of the philosopher's optimism toward language. This work is a potlatch of words yielding many possible meanings through uncanny semantic and phonic play.

14. I have analyzed specific instances of Beckett's linguistic manipulations in "Saying Is Inventing: Gnomic Expressions in *Molloy*"; "Dialogic Incongruities in the Theater of the Absurd"; "Didi, Gogo, Pozzo, Lucky: Linguistes déconstructeurs"; "Endgame, or what talk can do"; and in my book *Structure de la trilogie de Beckett*. I have consulted with Joel Sherzer on questions concerning linguistics.

PART 2

Conceptual Transmutations

RUBIN RABINOVITZ

Beckett, Dante, and the Metaphorical Representation of Intangible Reality

Many writers have been perplexed by the distinctions between mental and physical reality. As one wit put it, "What is mind? No matter. What is matter? Never mind."[1] A similar sense of paradox characterizes Samuel Beckett's approach to this issue. On occasion he discusses ideas and matter in a conventional way, referring to well-known philosophical and psychological concepts.[2] But often, especially in his later works, Beckett creates elaborate extended metaphors that suggest the enigmatic nature of the interaction of ideal and material reality.

Beckett's approach owes something to Dante's allegorical method in *The Divine Comedy*. Faced with the task of describing an intangible spiritual realm, Dante used metaphorical settings (such as a dark wood or a frozen lake) based on aspects of material reality. In developing his extended metaphors Dante systematically incorporated details of the physical landscape: the things of this world became the raw materials for metaphors depicting the other. But if Dante's metaphorical settings referred to a spiritual plane of existence, Beckett's refer to existence on a mental level.

As a number of critics have noted, Dante's *Divine Comedy* was an important influence on Beckett's writing generally.[3] An early work, the unpublished novel *Dream of Fair to Middling Women*, describes the hero's sojourn in a "Limbo" that (like his name, Belacqua) recalls *The Divine Comedy*.[4] The settings in later works such as *How It Is* (127), *The Lost Ones* (7), and *Fizzles* (37–39) similarly resemble those in the Inferno. There are many other instances where Beckett's locales are reminiscent of Dante's.

This is not to say that Molloy's gloomy forest, for example, is the equivalent of Dante's dark wood. But both of them are places where a protagonist figuratively loses his way; thus they share a common metaphorical idea. In the same way, many settings in *Molloy* are reminiscent of locales in the *Inferno*, such as those involving ruins (*Inferno*, 23:137; *Molloy*, 52), roads (*Inferno*, 1:18; *Molloy*, 10), rain (*Inferno*, 6:7–8; *Molloy*, 37), or bogs (*Inferno*, 11:70;

Molloy, 14). This list could be extended by including other details of the landscape, such as hollows, ditches, deserts, cities, caves, towers, and plains.

There are many writers, allegorists in particular, who use material objects to depict metaphysical ideas. But Beckett, like Dante, moves beyond the simple allegory of one-to-one correspondences where, say, a loss of wealth is represented by the departure of a figure labeled "worldly goods." Beckett and Dante both develop extended metaphors that refer to transcendental aspects of reality on a number of levels. It takes great skill to invent a figurative language that can rival literal language in its ability to express such complex ideas. This is one of the reasons why Beckett admires Dante's allegorical writing.[5]

In *The Divine Comedy* the literal level (the level that deals with the afterlife) is the one that is most memorable. But Dante also meant for his work to be understood on other levels; hence descriptions of episodes in hell or heaven also refer to abstract concepts.[6] In addition, *The Divine Comedy* can be understood as a portrayal not only of the afterlife but of an inner life, a representation of how Dante's mind was shaped by the world he lived in.

A similar point can be made about Beckett's writing. Even when Beckett describes mental events, there are reminders of the world outside. At times he depicts events in the material world that are in the process of being transformed into mental experiences.[7] He makes it clear how interdependent the two levels of reality are, and how difficult it is to effect a separation between them.[8] It is not only their different attributes but the way the two worlds are conjoined that interests Beckett; and his metaphorical settings reflect the mysterious nature of their interaction.

Another important feature of the settings in *The Divine Comedy* is that they do not always conform to the reality of the material world. From time to time Dante abandons verisimilitude, noting as he does the differences between certain material and spiritual processes. He makes this kind of distinction when he compares the boiling tar in the Fifth Bolgia with that in the Venetian Arsenal: "so, not by fire but by divine art, a thick tar was boiling below there" (Inferno, 21:6). In a similar way he explains why angels flying before the white rose did not obscure its radiance: "Nor did such plenitude of flight coming between the height and the flower obstruct the sight or the splendour; for the divine light penetrates the universe according to the fitness of its parts so that nothing can hinder it" (*Paradiso*, 33:19).

Like Dante's, Beckett's settings go beyond representations of the physical world. Molloy speaks of the "inner space one never sees, the brain and heart and other caverns where thought and feeling dance their sabbath" (*Molloy*, 11). In *Cascando* it becomes clear that features of the landscape are in fact mental entities: "what's in his head . . . a hole . . . a shelter . . . a hollow . . . in the dunes . . . a cave" (11).

Descriptions of objects and actions within a head refer to a related type of metaphorical setting. Such settings usually indicate that the action is taking place in the protagonist's mind, as in these examples:

"All grows dim. . . . It's in the head." (*Molloy*, 8–9)

"Sometimes it seems to me I am in a head." (*Malone Dies*, 47)

"I'm in a head, what an illumination." (*The Unnamable*, 119)

In these works Beckett's descriptions of the inside of a head allude to the idea of action on a mental plane.[9]

References to the interior of a skull serve a similar function. The narrator of "The Calmative" says he will not give too many details of the setting, "for we are needless to say in a skull" (38). The Unnamable speaks of "the inside of my distant skull where once I wandered" (*The Unnamable*, 20). Here and in related passages the descriptions of mental activity are tempered by the connotations of boneheadedness and death conveyed by the idea of a skull.[10]

Beckett often describes the interior of the skull as a confined area, an "ivory dungeon" in *Texts For Nothing* (82), and a "foul little den all dirty white and vaulted, as though hollowed out of ivory" in *Malone Dies* (63). The image of the mind as a prison is linked to the problem of trying to discover one's own identity in *That Time:* "not knowing who you were from Adam no notion who it was saying what you were saying whose skull you were clapped up in" (32).

In some instances references to skulls indicate how the reality of the outer world is blended with inner reality, as in the poem "The Vulture." The locus of the bird's flight, one suddenly realizes, is the mind of the speaker:

> dragging his hunger through the sky
> of my skull shell of sky and earth
> (*Poems in English*, 9)

Such an internalized view of the outer world is given in the poem "Enueg I" (*Poems in English*, 12). Images such as these, drawn from the material world, take on a new significance when they are subjected to the reality of the mind.

At times the skulls are suffused with an inner light that, as some critics have noted, represents thought.[11] In "Fizzle 8" a skull "makes to glimmer again"; in *Enough* there are "gleams" in the narrator's skull; in other works descriptions of dim light convey the same idea.[12] Such examples might suggest that light can simply be equated with mental activity. In fact, Beckett's approach is more complicated: subdued light represents activities that originate in the mind, and bright light is associated with images from the outside world. Since many of Beckett's protagonists dislike the outer world, the bright light is usually unpleasant.

When Belacqua, the hero of *Dream of Fair to Middling Women*, withdraws into his inner world, he is happy to escape from the "prurient heat and glare of living" (55). Molloy reveals that he has destroyed an entity within himself that yearns for heat and light (39). In Beckett's plays, when the main action takes place in the outside world, the stage directions usually call for bright light, as in these examples:

> *Krapp's Last Tape:* "strong white light." (10)
> *Happy Days:* "blazing light."
> *Act Without Words I:* "dazzling light." (*Krapp*, 125)
> *Act Without Words II:* "back of stage . . . violently lit." (*Krapp*, 137)

In those plays where the action occurs on a mental plane, the lighting is dimmer:

> *Play:* "stage in almost complete darkness." (*Cascando*, 45)
> *Come and Go:* "*Lighting* / Soft." (*Cascando*, 70)
> *Not I:* MOUTH and AUDITOR are both "faintly lit." (*Ends and Odds*, 14)
> *Footfalls:* "*Lighting: dim.*" (*Ends*, 42)
> *Ghost Trio:* V says the light is "faint." (*Ends*, 55)
> *Rockaby:* "Light / Subdued." (21)
> *A Piece of Monologue:* "*Faint diffuse light.*" (*Rockaby*, 69)
> *Endgame:* "*grey light.*" (1)

In *Endgame* the sense of inner reality is enhanced by the positioning of the windows, which makes the set resemble the inside of a skull.

In Beckett's fiction the settings that represent the mental world are again characterized by subdued light, such as the "leaden light" in *Malone Dies* (114), the "dim light" in *Ill Seen Ill Said* (21), and the "light infinitely faint" in *Company* (51). Belacqua's experience of "the abdication of the daily mind" is one of "hush and gloom ousting the workaday glare" (*Dream*, 170). Molloy jokes about his proclivity for subdued light: "I don't like the gloom to lighten, there's something shady about it" (112).[13]

In *Murphy*, the light imagery defines the different zones of mental reality. Murphy thinks of his mind as being divided into areas of light, half-light, and darkness. The first zone contains reflections of the physical world; this is where images of material objects interact with mental reality. The second zone is devoted to contemplation. The third, the one most removed from materiality, is "nothing but forms becoming and crumbling into the fragments of a new becoming" (*Murphy*, 112).

The most remote portions of the self are usually associated with darkness, as in a description in *Dream of Fair to Middling Women* of "the inner man, its hunger, darkness and silence" (35). Moran speculates about the "true denizen of my dark places" (*Molloy*, 156), and the Unnamable speaks of his life "here, in the dark" (167).[14] Krapp considers the artistic advantages of accepting "the dark" [he has] "always struggled to keep under" (21).[15] A more personal version of this idea emerges in Beckett's comment that "the daylight world is a realm of blindness for the artist" (Harvey, "Samuel Beckett on Life," 548).

The retreat from daylight therefore represents more than a loss of illumination: the darkness has qualities that Beckett associates with intuition and creativity. A voice in *Company* exclaims, "What visions in the dark of light!" (59). Both Belacqua and Malone speak of "a dark light"; and both Molloy and the Unnamable allude to a process—clearly a kind of inner vision—they call "seeing darkly" (*Dream*, 38; *Malone Dies*, 65; *Molloy*, 58; *The Unnamable*, 11).[16]

Beckett at times links images involving eyes with descriptions of this inner vision. *The Lost Ones* and *Ill Seen Ill Said* refer to an eye of flesh, which is distinguished from a figurative eye that observes inner reality (17, 31). As the Unnamable says, "How all becomes clear and simple when one opens an eye on the within" (77).[17]

The process of inner vision begins as one withdraws from the light of the world and retreats into the depths of the mind. For Murphy, this is expressed as a need to retreat from "the big world" into "the little world" (178). The material world in *How It Is* is a region "above in the light" (8, 35, 123); the inner world is "here" (12, 13, 96), in "the dark the silence the solitude" (8). For the Unnamable, ordinary life is "the wild dream, up above, under the skies" (*The Unnamable*, 83). In "Fizzle 3," an outer aspect of the self is described by a voice from the inner world: "it was he who wailed, he who saw the light, I didn't wail, I didn't see the light" (*Fizzles*, 25).

At times the images of darkness and silence are linked. A character in *Play* says, "Silence and darkness were all that I craved. Well, I get a certain amount of both. They being one" (59). In *Malone Dies* there is a description of "silence . . . in the heart of the dark" (27). There are many other passages where silence and darkness are used in parallel constructions like these.[18]

If the darkness is sometimes alleviated by a glimmer, the silence is occasionally interrupted by a voice. This passage from *Company* is an example: "Slowly he entered dark and silence and lay there for so long that with what judgement remained he judged them to be final. Till one day the voice. One day! Till in the end the voice saying, You are on your back in the dark" (17). In some passages synesthesia is used to equate images of light and sound, as in a description of silence broken by the "sound of light and dark" in *All Strange Away* (52), or in an exhortation to "listen to the light" in *Embers* (*Krapp*, 96).[19]

These sounds, as some critics have pointed out, are very much like the glimmers: they represent images of mental activity.[20] Often they encourage comparisons with the prevailing silence and darkness of the inner world. This idea emerges in a description of inner entities in *The Unnamable:* "when they go silent, it will be dark, not a sound, not a glimmer." (108).

Though light is at times contrasted with darkness, the darkness is capable of generating its own type of illumination. The voices, similarly, are an aspect of silence—a paradoxical concept that is often conveyed paradoxically. As the narrator of "Texts for Nothing 13" says:

> It's not true, yes, it's true, it's true and it's not true, there is silence and there is not silence, there is no one and there is someone, nothing prevents anything. And were the voice to cease quite at last, the old ceasing voice, it would not be true, as it is not true that it speaks, it can't speak, it can't cease. (139–40)

Malone expresses a related idea when he describes an overwhelming silence and then mentions "the voice of that silence" (*Malone Dies*, 27). References to such voices are common in Beckett's works, and they frequently occur in descriptions of entities that represent volitional forces.[21]

The images described so far—those involving heads, skulls, eyes, darkness, light, voices, silence—are part of the basic vocabulary of Beckett's figurative language. Since sensory experiences bridge the gap between the physical and mental worlds, Beckett uses them as sources for metaphors dealing with the interactions of the two worlds. Many of Beckett's images finally operate on a number of levels. They can be seen as descriptions of physical events, of mental activities, or of both: memories of events in the outer world that are reshaped by their exposure to inner reality.

Dante's metaphorical settings incorporate aspects of the landscape such as woods, lakes, or roads, and Beckett's often resemble them. Like Dante, Beckett distinguishes between the light and darkness of the material world and the figurative illumination of an immaterial realm. But in describing the inner self, Beckett, if he borrows Dante's method, also introduces new images based on the physical self (such as the head, skull, and eyes) and on the senses (such as vision and hearing). He uses these to describe remote and subtle aspects of inner reality. This is a reason why Beckett's debt to Dante should not be overemphasized. Dante the allegorist reinvented allegory; Beckett similarly transformed what he borrowed. Each author developed a new type of figurative language, and each used this language to depict a reality that had beforehand seemed inexpressible.

Notes

1. The comment appeared anonymously in *Punch*, vol. 29 (1855), 19; some authorities attribute it to Thomas Hewitt Key (1799–1875).

2. Philosophical aspects of this question are discussed in my book *The Development of Samuel Beckett's Fiction*; the psychological issues are the subject of a forthcoming essay in *Journal of Beckett Studies*.

3. The following studies contain valuable discussions of Dante's influence on Beckett: Ruby Cohn, *Back to Beckett*; John Fletcher, *Samuel Beckett's Art*; Raymond Federman, *Journey to Chaos: Samuel Beckett's Early Fiction*; Lawrence Harvey, *Samuel Beckett: Poet and Critic*; John Pilling, *Samuel Beckett*; Michael Robinson, "From Purgatory to the Inferno: Beckett and Dante Revisited," 60–83; and Walter Strauss, "Dante's Belacqua and Beckett's Tramps," 250–61.

4. *Dream of Fair to Middling Women* (unpublished novel), Dartmouth Library typescript, 38–39, 40, 107, 110 passim.

5. Beckett praises Dante because he avoids the literalness of conventional allegory ("the pictorial transmission of a notion") and makes his allegorical writing so significant that it finally is "electrified into anagogy"; *Proust*, 60. Beckett also discusses Dante in "Dante . . . Bruno . Vico . . Joyce," in Samuel Beckett et al., *Our Exagmination Round his Factification for Incamination of Work in Progress*, and in many of his other works.

6. Dante explains in his eleventh letter to Can Grande that *The Divine Comedy* can be read on three levels beyond the literal: the allegorical, the moral, and the anagogical.

7. In "Dante . . . Bruno . Vico . . Joyce," Beckett gives the Italian version of a scholastic axiom, "Nothing is in the intellect that first was not in the senses" (10). He refers to its Latin version in *Malone Dies*, 43.

8. The difficulty of escaping from the outer world into the mind is a central issue in *Murphy*; see, for example, 179.

9. Similar passages occur in *Molloy*, 37, 68, 188; *Malone Dies*, 50; and *The Unnamable*, 148, 174.

10. The following are references to additional examples of passages where skulls are used to suggest mental activity: *Watt*, 232; "First Love," 12; "Fizzle 8," in *Fizzles*, 56; "Texts for Nothing 3," in *Stories and Texts for Nothing*, 86.

11. A number of critics have provided illuminating discussions of this type of imagery, including Philip H. Solomon, *The Life After Birth: Imagery in Samuel Beckett's Trilogy*, 94ff.; James Knowlson, " 'Krapp's Last Tape': The Evolution of a Play, 1958–1975," 54–56, 59–64; Vivian Mercier, *Beckett/Beckett*, 7–8 passim; and Eugene Webb, *Samuel Beckett: A Study of the Novels* 113–14 passim.

12. *Fizzles*, 55. See also the reference to the "gleams" in "Enough," 54; *Molloy*, 72; *Malone Dies*, 9; *The Unnamable*, 117, 129, 174; and *How It Is*, 22.

13. Other images of gloom: *Dream* . . . , 40, 173 passim; *Malone Dies*, 49; *How It Is*, 96.

14. For other references to darkness, see *Dream* . . . , 39; *Molloy*, 147; *Malone Dies*, 45; *The Unnamable*, 69; *How It Is*, 8; *All Strange Away*, in *Rockaby and Other Short Pieces*, 39, 41; *Company*, 7, 63 passim; "Fizzle 2," in *Fizzles*, 19; *Endgame*, 75; *Cascando*, 14; *Words and Music*, in *Cascando*, 23; and *Play*, 46.

15. Krapp listens to a tape made years before, where he describes this idea; then he angrily switches off the machine. This corresponds to a trend in Beckett's writing generally. His younger heroes enthusiastically withdraw from the daylight world and look forward to exploring the dark inner regions. His older heroes, who may still prefer darkness to light, have experienced the difficulties of inner exploration and are somewhat cynical about its rewards.

16. "Seeing darkly" is of course an allusion to I Corinthians 13:12, "For now we see through a glass, darkly, but then face to face . . ."

17. Other references to eyes and inner vision: *Dream* . . . , 39; *More Pricks Than Kicks*, 161; *Molloy*, 11; *Malone Dies*, 19, 48–49; *Company*, 22; *Ill Seen Ill Said*, 25; *Rockaby*, 9, 19 passim; and *Film*, 11.

18. For other references to silence and darkness, see *Malone Dies*, 9, 31; *The Unnamable*, 109; "Texts for Nothing 13," in *Stories and Texts for Nothing*, 140; and *Company*, 17.

19. See also *Company*, 19.

20. Good discussions of Beckett's use of the voice image can be found in Raymond Federman, "The Impossibility of Saying the Same Old Thing in the Same Old Way: Samuel Beckett's *Com-*

ment c'est," 21ff.; John Fletcher, *The Novels of Samuel Beckett*, 65 passim; Martin Esslin, "Introduction," in Martin Esslin, ed., *Samuel Beckett: A Collection of Critical Essays*, 10–12; Jean Onimus, *Beckett*, 65–71; Hannah C. Copeland, *Art and the Artist in the Works of Samuel Beckett*, 119–27.

21. For other voice images, see *Murphy*, 167–68, 186; *Watt*, 91; *Mercier and Camier*, 59; *Molloy*, 118–19; *The Unnamable*, 172, 173; "The Expelled," in *Stories and Texts for Nothing*, 13, 90, 134, 137; *Company*, 7ff.; *Embers*, 116; and *Eh Joe*, in *Cascando and Other Short Dramatic Pieces*, 38.

MARTIN ESSLIN

A Poetry of Moving Images

I

In looking at Beckett's oeuvre as a whole, I think we can discern two distinct types of approach, two essentially different starting points for his exploration of Being.

The first of these is the strand of internal monologue: the voices that resound in the "sky of my skull shell of sky and earth" telling stories; voices that—"cogito ergo sum"—*are* the Self as it observes itself, trying to obtain knowledge of itself as the observing part of the Self listening to itself as it manifests itself as consciousness, a stream of words, a story, and then notes them down; while, at the same time, it is aware that the very act of listening raises the problem of who it is that is listening—that observing part of the Self that observes or the observed part of the Self; when and how can the two merge? can the observer catch up with the observed? can the two parts of the Self be reunited? The quest is endless, as the listener in turn becomes narrator, observed by a new listener who becomes a new narrator—and so on ad infinitum, through an endless rollcall of named narrators of themselves toward the last, the Unnamable, which must also prove ultimately elusive.

This strand of internal monologue, whether in a single, monophone, voice as in the narratives of the trilogy and *Texts for Nothing*, or split into the dialogic voices of the radio plays like *Words and Music, Cascando*, and *Radio I and II*, has a linear quality—it is a pursuit, an endless quest: the voice murmurs and drones on, from one word to the next, one sentence to the next, one narrator to the next and the next after that . . .

With *Texts for Nothing* Beckett had reached the end of that road. That quest could not continue indefinitely. Now another approach for tackling the problem of Being, of expressing the inexpressible, of how to

mete want with a span?
the sum assess
of the world's woes?
nothingness
in words enclose?

came to the fore: an attempt to compress the individual's experience of Being, his existential experience, into a single visual metaphor, a powerful multi-layered image. This is the second of Beckett's basic modes and methods: the construction and evocation of metaphoric, essentially visual images of the human condition.

How It Is marks a transition: it is still in the form of an internal monologue, but the panting voice no longer pursues an endless quest to catch up with its true Self; as it progresses, it paints a picture, an image of a state of affairs, an unending, static condition.

These images become ever more compressed in later prose works like *Imagination Dead Imagine, Ping, Lessness, The Lost Ones, Ill Seen Ill Said*, or that curious hybrid between "narrative" and "drama," *A Piece of Monologue.*

II

In Beckett's poetry (quite naturally, for such is the nature of poetry), the image *had* always *been* the dominant element. And it might be argued that from his very earliest *dramatic* experiments Beckett was already striving for a poetry of concretized images.

This is already clearly observable in *Eleutheria*, which, while still retaining some of the characteristics of a traditional, realistic play, puts its main emphasis on the powerful image of the split stage gradually turning from the family's room to the solitary cell of Victor's withdrawal. *Waiting for Godot* no longer tells a story: what action there is merely serves to complete the complex image of immobility. The quest, the hastening to catch salvation, unity with the absolute, is still present in the characters of Pozzo and Lucky. But that quest has now become part of the structure of the play's main image. The very progression of what at first sight seems something like a conventional plot ultimately reveals itself as no more than the act of completing the static image.

As Beckett's dramatic oeuvre develops, this imagistic quality becomes stronger and stronger: behind each play there stands an overwhelmingly *visual* idea: the circular chamber of *Endgame*, the old man listening to his own voice in *Krapp*, Winnie sinking into the earth, the urns of *Play*, the pattern of permutations in *Come and Go*, the Mouth of *Not I*, the floating head of *That Time*, the pacing figure of *Footfalls*, the picture of misery in *Catastrophe*, the identical old men in *Ohio Impromptu*, the rocking chair in *Rockaby*.

We might look at that dichotomy between the quest (linear and endless) and the image (compressed and multidimensional) as a manifestation of what Schopenhauer saw as the dual nature of reality—Die Welt als Wille und Vorstellung—the world as Will and as Phenomenal Appearance. (It is perhaps also of some significance that 'Vorstellung' in German also denotes a theatrical performance or 'representation'). Ultimate reality, the ever-inaccessible 'Ding-an-sich' is, according to Schopenhauer, experienced from the inside of human consciousness as an endless surging stream, a pulsing, pushing impetus toward some illusory goal of fulfillment—the "will"; and from the outside as 'appearance', visual, phenomenal reality. For Schopenhauer, music was the perfect expression of the first and drama the perfect expression of the second aspect of reality. Beckett's internal monologue is, in some respects, another kind of music—linear, questing, rhythmic. And in some of Beckett's works music quite clearly is shown as having a function parallel to that of the verbal internal monologue—think of *Words and Music*, *Cascando*, or *Radio I*. There the verbal stream of consciousness is paralleled by the emotional stream of consciousness: music.

III

An "imagistic" drama like Beckett's which rejects the narrative dimension of plot and intrigue and concentrates on creating poetic metaphors with a strong emphasis on the nonverbal, purely visual aspects of the imagery must, by its very nature, be basically "lyrical" as distinct from "dramatic" or "epic" in the traditional senses of these terms. In this respect Beckett stands in a line of development which goes back to the symbolists and Neo-Romantics. (Hofmannsthal's "lyrical dramas" and the plays of Yeats clearly fall into a similar category.)

But Beckett, always fascinated by the visual aspect of the world, more at home in the company of painters than that of writers, has always been striving to go to the very limits of this tendency: this already manifested itself fairly early in his career as a playwright with his *Acts Without Words*. There already he strove to reduce the image to the visual element alone, without the intervention of words.

But in these mime plays there remained the difficulty of conveying the exact image to the performers. They still had to rely on words in the form of descriptive stage directions that outlined the action. (In a play with spoken dialogue, the dialogue carries a great deal of the visual within itself—the rhythm and timing of the language, the "gestural" character of the language, dictates a very considerable amount of at least the unfolding in time of the visuals of a play; but of course even there, attaining the exact visual image that corresponds to the author's own vision is impossible, hence Beckett's increasing involvement in directing his own plays, unofficially and officially. In *ballet* it is the music which guarantees adherence to the time dimension of the development of a basic visual pattern.) But how could the pure, the almost wordless visual moving image be fixed once and for all—be given a truly permanent form?

IV

It is in this light that we must see Beckett's fascination with the mechanically recorded visual media—film and television. The silent cinema obviously had an enormous impact on Beckett (witness his attempts to study film with Eisenstein). The iconography of the silent cinema plays an important part in his concept, for example, of the two main characters in *Waiting for Godot*, whose general phenotype is that of pairs of silent film comedians like Laurel and Hardy or Pat et Patachon. Hence, when opportunities offered themselves to Beckett of experimentation with film and television, he was eager to embrace media that are not only visual but also allow the artist to fix his vision in permanent form, once and for all.

Film (1965) was an early effort: it still carries the inheritance of traditional cinema with a plot—however minimal. Nor did the cinema with its high production cost and hierarchical structure of technicians allow Beckett complete control of the visual image.

Through his successes with his early radio plays Beckett had won an entree to the BBC—and when the directors of some of his radio work, notably Michael Bakewell and Donald McWhinnie, moved on to BBC television, Beckett had established a foothold in the television medium, which, with its video-recording techniques and less complex technical structure, allowed him to take almost complete control of the production process, even when he was not officially credited as the director. A similar progression from radio to television also occurred in Beckett's relationship with the Süddeutscher Rundfunk in Stuttgart (for whom he had written the radio play *Cascando*). Here too he gained access to television and was invited to direct some of his work himself.

Yet in his earliest play for television the two strands of Beckett's imagination were still in balance: in *Eh Joe* (1966) the image is that of a man sitting on his bed listening to a woman's voice that clearly resounds within his consciousness. Here the internal monologue merges with the camera's eye: the more insistent the voice of remorse within his conscience becomes, the closer the camera moves in on Joe's face until, in the final image, we are left with a closeup of his eyes wide open in terror.

In Beckett's next television work, *Ghost Trio*, ten years after *Eh Joe*, the voice is no longer an interior voice. It is still a woman's voice, but it is external to the action, objective, a master of ceremonies. It greets the viewer with: "Good-evening. Mine is a faint voice. Kindly tune accordingly." Having thus warned the public not to turn up the volume nob, the voice gives a faintly ironic, self-parodying description of the by-now-familiar Beckett room—

gray, bare, bereft of color, with the pallet by the window. Each item that is described is shown, as though we were watching a real-estate agent's demonstration of a dwelling and its inventory. This first of the three sections of the script, marked by the Roman numerals I to III, ends, after we have been shown the external elements from which the image we are being offered will be built up, with the introduction of the protagonist: "Sole sign of life a seated figure," an old man bent over an object at first difficult to identify.

In section II the voice announces and introduces the actions of this figure (referred to in the script as F): "He will now think he hears her," as he goes to the door to listen if someone is coming; to the window, the mirror, the pallet, and the door again.

In the third section, the voice, having fulfilled its function of introducing the image, vanishes altogether. We have reached the stage of complete wordlessness and we realize that the first two sections merely served to set the scene, to prepare us for the unfolding of the wordless action, the image itself. The old man thinks he can hear someone coming; his expectation is disappointed. When he opens the window to look out, there is only the rain outside. He goes to the mirror and for the first time we see his face and get a closeup of his haggard features. But then footsteps are heard outside in the corridor, there are knocks on the door, the door opens: outside there stands a small boy dressed in an oilskin against the pouring rain:

> Boy shakes head faintly. Face still, raised. 5". Boy shakes head again. Face still, raised. 5". Boy turns and goes. Sound of receding steps.

The door closes, the old man remains seated. We have gradually realized that the music we have been hearing—passages from the Largo of Beethoven's fifth piano trio, the "Ghost Trio"—emanates from the object over which he has been bent: a cassette player. *Ghost Trio* ends with the old man raising his head and a second closeup of his ravaged face. The camera takes another last general view and then the image fades.

Ghost Trio, originally entitled *Tryst*, displays some intriguing parallels to *Waiting for Godot:* the little boy who shakes his head to indicate that the expected person, with whom the tryst, or rendezvous, of the original title was to be, would not be coming, except that in this case the tryst seems to have been with a woman, that "lost one" who haunts so many of Beckett's works.

What is striking in *Ghost Trio* as well as its companion piece, *... but the clouds ... ,* is the technique of first demonstrating and verbally introducing the ingredients from which the image is built up, after which the image is, wordlessly, left to speak for itself. This is almost reminiscent of the Elizabethan technique of preceding a play with a mimed enactment of its "argument," except that here the order is reversed—the argument is verbal, the play itself a mime.

In ... *but the clouds* ... the voice which instructs the viewer is in the first person singular. It is the voice of an old man who is shown in his daily round of arriving home in the evening after having roamed the roads all day, shedding his greatcoat, donning his nightshirt, and then settling down to try and evoke the image of a long-lost love. Then emerging again from his sanctum in the morning, changing his nightshirt for his greatcoat and hat, and leaving to roam the backroads once more, and so on and on ... The image on the screen is that of a circle of light surrounded by darkness, into which the man enters from the left (East), exits to the right (West) to change his clothes, and retires in the center, back (North). When he is seen trying to remember the beloved face, the old man sits in Belacqua's fetal position, his head between his knees. The voice demonstrates the moves, talks the viewer through them as it were, like an air-controller talking a pilot through a maneuver. This is not an internal monologue, it is a *mode d'emploi* for viewing a visual experience.

We are shown four possible variants of what could happen in response to the man's begging for the woman's image to appear: she might appear and be gone almost instantly; she might appear and linger a moment; she might appear and her lips might be moving soundlessly; or indeed she might not appear at all—the most frequent case.

After all the moves have been named and demonstrated the final image develops in silence, except that, when, at the climax the woman's face appears superimposed on the screen and we see her lips move, we hear the old man's voice repeating the lines the lips are obviously forming, lines from Yeats's poem *The Tower:*

> ... but the clouds of the sky
> When the horizon fades:
> Or a bird's sleeping cry
> Among the deepening shades.

The reference here clearly is to the preceding lines of the poem—they are not quoted; Beckett clearly presupposes that they are known to his ideal viewer—the lines which speak of

> ... the death of friends, or death
> Of every brilliant eye
> That made a catch in the breath ...

that now seem "but the clouds of the sky."

Beckett directed both these short television pieces twice—for the BBC and for the Süddeutscher Rundfunk. There are differences between the two versions: the German ones are later and perhaps incorporate some of Beckett's own second thoughts about the first versions. Perhaps they are closer to the definitive images he was striving for. (In *... but the clouds...* there is a textual difference: a much longer passage from Yeats's poem is quoted at the end, unfortunately in a translation so imperfect that it is hardly discernible whether what we hear is poetry or prose.)

What is striking about these two works—one hesitates to call them plays, although *Ghost Trio* is subtitled "A Television Play" and *... but the clouds...* "A play for television"—is precisely that they have ceased to exist as works of literature. The script has become little more than a mere technical notation of camera positions (diagrams) and indications of timing. The lines of text that remain are a relatively insignificant ingredient. And they merely serve to instruct the viewer, to teach him how to look at and contemplate the actual, wordless visual experience. In *Ghost Trio* music also plays a vital part; it alone depicts the internal aspect of the protagonist's experience—the ebb and flow of his stream of *emotional* consciousness. Yet even this comes, strictly speaking, from the outside: F, the figure, is listening to a recording which he switches on and off, winds backward and forward—and if his emotion matches the music, that is merely because he internalizes this external sound. In *... but the clouds...*, quite analogously, the only hint at a verbal inner monologue is a quotation from a remembered preexisting literary text, lines from the poem by Yeats.

V

In Beckett's two latest television pieces the verbal element has completely disappeared. Both of these were written by him for Süddeutscher Rundfunk and also directed by him. In *Quadrat I + II* (1981—the production started on Beckett's seventy-fifth birthday, 13 April 1981; the original typescript in English is titled *Quad*), the script is basically a diagram and a string of what looks like a series of mathematical formulas.

The camera, stationary throughout, looks from above at an oblique angle at a square outlined on the ground. There are four figures, dressed in long cloaks and cowls, so that it is impossible to tell whether they are male or female. The colors of these costumes are white, blue, red, and yellow. Each figure has a fixed route described by the sequence of the corners of the square through which it must pass—A, B, C, and D. As this often involves a diagonal crossing of the square. To get, for example, from A to C or from B to D, the moving figures should have to pass through the central point E. But that center point E seems to contain a deadly danger: when the figures approach it, they hesitate in a moment of panic and then must circle around it, always in a clockwise direction.

The structure of the four figures' movement is like that of a canon or fugue. First one figure pursues its prescribed and eternally fixed path alone, then a second one joins it on its second circuit just after the first figure has reached the second point on its path, then, when both have completed theirs and started the third circuit of the first, the second of the second, a third figure enters, then a fourth, then the numbers are reduced to three, two, one. Then the process starts again. When all four figures are moving at the same time, the congestion around the central point becomes acute as they move around it in their clockwise circle.

The entire fuguelike movement is shown twice. Each figure's moves are accompanied by its own percussion instrument—Javanese gong, African woodblock, African talking drum, and a wastebasket—so that the addition and subtraction of each figure alters the rhythmical accompaniment to the action.

In the original typescript, merely titled *Quad*, these two movements comprised the entire work. In performance, however, a second part, *Quadrat II*, was added. The producer at Stuttgart, Reinhart Mueller-Freienfels, told me the story of the genesis of *Quadrat II*. The recording, the first television piece by Beckett to use color, had been completed, and in the evening Mueller-Freienfels played the tape back to Beckett on his video machine at home. Beckett liked the finished performance, and Mueller-Freienfels mentioned that it had also looked very good on the additional black-and-white monitor (which has to be present in any television studio so that the director can judge whether the colors are compatible for those viewers who do not have color sets). Beckett was intrigued by this observation and suggested that they go back the next day to make a recording in black and white of only one complete circuit, but much slower and this time without the percussion accompaniment, the only sound being the shuffling of the four figures' feet. When this had been recorded and Beckett viewed it, he said: "Good—this is a hundred thousand years later!" And so with the addition of the black-and-white section *Quad* became *Quadrat I + II*.

The impact of this wordless piece is tremendous. It is both wildly funny and deeply frightening. Are these figures in a Dantesque hell, doomed to repeat their prescribed circuit to all eternity? Or is the image that of all human destiny, where, seen from an objective vantage point outside ourselves, each of us has his preordained path on his journey through life and is thus destined to collide with all those whose preordained path he is preordained to cross at preordained moments. And does the center that must be avoided signify the impossibility of genuine contact between the endlessly journeying figures? These are some of the questions the image raises, without, of course, answering them or even opening the way toward a valid answer. (There is a parallel here with *How It Is* and its complex image of endless traumatic encounters—but now it has been reduced to a single visual metaphor).

What is clear in any case is that this, as so many other works by Beckett, is another attempt to compress the concept of Eternity, eternal recurrence, as an endless permutation of a limited number of existing elements, into as concise an image as possible. The motif of the preordained paths and the inevitable fruitless encounters is already present in *How It Is;* Eternity as an endless recurrence of preexisting elements in *Play* as well as in *Lessness*—to name but a few examples. Beckett's second piece produced at Stuttgart, in 1982, also dispenses with the spoken word altogether. *Nacht und Traeume* is the title of a late Schubert song, based on a short poem of eight lines by the Austrian poet Heinrich Josef von Collin (1771–1811):

> Heil'ge Nacht, du sinkest nieder
> Nieder wallen auch die Traeume
> Wie Dein Dunkel durch die Raeume
> Durch der Menschen stille, stille Brust.
> Die belauschen sie mit Lust
> Rufen, wenn der Tag erwacht:
> Kehre wieder, heil'ge Nacht
> Holde Traeume, kehret wieder.

(This at least is the text of Schubert's song. In Collin's collected poems the text is slightly different. I presume Schubert himself changed the words, which are even triter in the original version.)

Beckett's televisual image is that of an old man sitting in "a dark, empty room lit only by evening light from a window set high in back wall." He is the archetypal Beckettian character, old and gray, bent over a table. The last seven bars of the song are heard, without words, melody alone, "softly sung, male voice." These are the bars corresponding to the last two lines of the text:

> Kehre wieder, heil'ge Nacht
> Holde Traeume, kehret wieder.
>
> Come again, o holy night
> Lovely dreams, o come again.

As the light fades on the image of the dreamer, the last three bars are heard again, this time with the words "Holde Traeume, kehret wieder" (Lovely dreams, o come again) clearly audible.

The old man reappears and now we can see his dream: In the upper-right-hand quarter of the screen there appears the "dreamt self" of the dreamer in the identical position. A hand, marked in the script as a left hand, (L), then gently touches the dreamt self's head from above; it withdraws. A right hand appears with a "cup of water" and conveys it gently to the dreamt self's lips; he drinks from it; the hand disappears. After a pause the right hand reappears with a cloth and gently wipes the dreamt self's brow. The dreamt self raises its head to gaze up at an invisible face. The dreamt self "raises his right hand and holds it raised palm upwards." The right hand of the unseen person appears again and rests on the dreamt self's hand; the dreamt self raises its left hand and rests it on the joined hands. And then an unseen person's left hand reappears and rests gently on the "dreamt self's" head.

The song is heard again, and now the image that had been in the right-hand corner, rather like a thought balloon in a cartoon, moves into the center and occupies the entire screen; the entire sequence of actions is repeated in closeup and more slowly; after which the camera moves back to its initial position and first the dream, then the image of the dreamer, fades. The structure of this piece closely corresponds to that of *Ghost Trio* and . . . *but the clouds* . . . , except that here Beckett has succeeded in eliminating the spoken "argument." He still starts by instructing the viewer, as it were, in what to look for, but now he does it by simply showing the elements of the image first as an insert with the dreamer visible and then moving into the dream in closeup. Again what results is an extremely powerful (if, in this case, for my taste, somewhat too sentimental) image.

VI

Quad I + II and *Nacht und Traeume*, then, are neither ballet nor mime play. They seem to me to represent a wholly new genre: they are visual poems.

This is what I feel Beckett had been striving toward for a very long time: the compression of the maximum of experience into the most telling and graphic metaphor which could then be incarnated, made visible and audible, in the most concise and concrete form of a living, moving image: a poem without words.

As early as 1937, in a letter written in German and now published in Ruby Cohn's collection *Disjecta*, Beckett expressed his dissatisfaction with language and literature:

> It is indeed becoming more and more difficult, even senseless, for me to write an official English. And more and more my own language appears to me like a veil that must be torn apart in order to get at the things (or Nothingness) behind it. . . . As we cannot eliminate language all at once, we should at least leave nothing undone that might contribute to its falling into disrepute. To bore one hole after another in it, until what lurks behind it—be it something or nothing—begins to seep through; I cannot imagine a higher goal for a writer today. Or is literature alone to remain behind in the old lazy ways that have been so long ago abandoned by music and painting? Is there something paralysingly holy in the vicious nature of the word that is not found in the elements of the other arts? Is there any reason why that terrible materiality of the word surface should not be capable of being dissolved, like for example the sound surface, torn by enormous pauses, of Beethoven's seventh Symphony, so that through whole pages we can perceive

nothing but a path of sounds suspended in giddy heights, linking unfathomable abysses of silence?

A piece like *Quad* seems to me to be the culmination of that kind of endeavor. Here the metaphor, the poetic image, has been freed from the word altogether. It is not drama anymore, it is poetry, but not poetry in words. Nor is it strictly speaking cinema: it lacks the epic quality, the storytelling element of cinema. It is most akin to some types of contemporary performance art, where also often two distinct phases are distinguishable: first the ritual of building the image, second, the display of the image. In some sense this is a kind of painting, the creation of an "emblem" to be deciphered by the viewer, except that the image moves and has sound.

Ultimately, this new genre seems to me to abstract *one* element from traditional drama, the concretized metaphor where the story of a play suddenly coagulates in one unforgettable poetic image: Lear, naked, raging against the storm; the Pope being dressed in *The Life of Galileo*; Hedda Gabler burning the manuscript; the red carpet being unrolled for Agamemnon; Oedipus blinded. In the earlier plays of Beckett and in the drama of Ionesco and Genet, the emphasis shifted decisively toward this kind of poetic metaphor, while a narrative, storytelling element still remained to sustain it. Yet, clearly, the "Theatre of the Absurd" increasingly tended toward this kind of imagistic presentation of visual poetic metaphors.

In Beckett's new televisual poetry, as indeed in stage plays like *Not I*, *That Time*, *Footfalls*, *Rockaby*, *Ohio Impromptu*, *Catastrophe*, and *What Where*, the ultimate limit of that tendency has been reached. The metaphoric, poetical image is here isolated and presented in its purest state. And the *television* images have the additional advantage that they are fixed, and fixed by the poet himself, so that they attain a state of permanence denied to texts for live production. Here the poet's own imagination has been directly translated into concrete form and preserved for posterity.

The preoccupation with the visual image clearly has been dominating Beckett's mind ever since he first ventured into film and television. The semi-dramatic *Piece of Monologue*, for instance, clearly tries to fix a visual image with words, almost in the terms of a camera script:

Umbrellas round a grave. Seen from above.

And the same is true of the elaborate visual image of *Ill Seen Ill Said:*

The hands. Seen from above.

It is as though in these late texts the internal monologue, which is that of an author urging himself on to write (or making critical remarks about what he has written), no longer quests for union between the observing and the observed Self but merely strives for the evocation of as exact an image as possible. Perhaps it is the perfect image that might compress all of experience into a single, all-embracing metaphor and bring that final, liberating insight.

Words can only describe, circumscribe that image; they will never be able to carry the image itself. Film or videotape may perhaps show it and preserve it. And they can do so without the heaviness and thraldom of language.

When I first met Beckett twenty-five years ago, he mentioned, half jokingly, that he was trying to become ever more concise, ever more to the point in his writing—so that perhaps at the end he would merely produce a blank page. The visual poetry of incarnated metaphors, like *Quad*, in some ways, it seems to me, is in fact that blank page—a poem without words.

ROSETTE LAMONT

Crossing the Iron Curtain:
Political Parables

In the spring of 1984, when I revisited Poland after a nine-year hiatus, I traveled from Warsaw to the stately, somber, magnificently preserved historic city of Cracow. For many years I had been promising myself to undertake the pilgrimage to Auschwitz.

To effect this visit I had to hire a car and driver since there is at present no other way of reaching the camp site. The only groups taken there by chartered buses are school children shepherded by their teachers. The Auschwitz visit is built into every high-school curriculum throughout Poland. Future generations will not be allowed to forget that the Nazis (one never hears references to "Germans" since East Germans are the official friends and allies of Communist Poland) had a program for the destruction of the Polish nation, with the exception of a small body of agricultural slaves who would serve the Master Race.

Nothing ever prepares one for the discovery of Auschwitz and particularly of its memorial museum. The latter is a two-floor red brick building, one of the remaining blockhouses. Not far from it stands the most infamous of them all, the "hospital" where experiments were carried out on living victims. In yet another, one can visit the underground cell in which Father Kolbe, the priest who was canonized by Pope John Paul II, perished when a camp guard hastened the end of his flickering life with an injection of acid. Father Kolbe, a Polish Catholic priest, had volunteered to take the place of a fellow prisoner, a family man still alive today, who was condemned with nine others of his block to die slowly of thirst and starvation after an inmate of their house staged an unsuccessful escape. The narrow cell in which the ten condemned men were herded together is now a shrine.

The most horrifying and enlightening visit is to the Auschwitz museum. The ground-floor walls are covered with the photographs of those who perished in the camp. One flight up are the "display cases." Large glass cases occupy the length or the width of the rectangular rooms. The displays testify to the carefully orchestrated program of putting to various "practical" uses parts of the human anatomy, together with the personal belongings of the prisoners. One case, for example, contains nothing but strands of blond, dark, gray hair. Tresses and locks fill the case from top to bottom. Next to this case, a smaller one holds a piece of cloth woven from the women's hair. It is a simple burlap of the kind one might use for sacks, or even a rough smock or apron. Untinted, its yellowish color echoes that of the shorn tresses. In the next room, a similar large case holds nothing but glasses. Many are broken and twisted. Steel frames are entangled with elegant horn ones. The glasses lie in a heap upon a sand base. It is as though they had just been torn off the faces of those sent into the showers, the gas chambers. Further still, one encounters a bizarre display of canes, crutches, prostheses. Most are strewn upon the sandy base, while others lean against the back wall, as though their crippled owners had just limped off, out of sight. Perhaps the most Kafka-esque of all these displays is the one that contains only valises and handbags. Again, these are not placed in any kind of order. They have been piled up to look like a junk heap, a piteous remnant of an existence that was once orderly, dignified, until it was cut short by inhuman brutality. Name tags attached to the handles proclaim their owner. One reads "Kafka."

All of these remnants are metonymies of a mute dirge to those who came to die. Yet they are not figures of speech but terrifying realities, fragments that testify to a relentless dismemberment, to planned annihilation. But what I found most amazing and unexpected was the striking analogies between Beckett images, Beckett stagings, and the display cases. They confirmed what I had sensed rather than reflected upon for many years—that Samuel Beckett is one of the great Holocaust writers of our time.

Upon my return to Paris I met with Beckett. He was eager to hear about his Polish friends, particularly his translator and critic, Antoni Libera. After a moment's hesitation I decided to tell him about my reaction to Auschwitz, in particular to the museum displays. I said that nothing reminded me more vividly of some of the images he had created on the stage than those glass cases full of artificial limbs, valises, eye glasses. He listened with deepening sorrow. Then he began to talk about his close friend Alfred Péron, who died as a result of having been sent to a concentration camp. Péron was arrested when a spy who had infiltrated the Resistance group in which he and Beckett worked together denounced them to the police. "We were amateurs," Beckett said with his self-deprecating irony, "and therefore naive, vulnerable. We never identified the traitor in our midst. One day Péron was arrested by the Gestapo. His wife managed to warn us by telegram. The moment we received it, Suzanne and I walked out of our apartment. We took nothing with us. For a day or two we were hiding with friends while papers were being forged for us. With these we made our way into the 'free zone.' "

In 1942 Samuel Beckett and his companion became wanderers. They reached the southern city of Roussillon-de-Vaucluse, where the couple was to spend two difficult years. Beckett worked on a farm. At night he was writing *Watt*, "in order not to go quite mad," as he told me in conversation. He also went on with Resistance activities, joining occasionally with the *maquis*. As Alfred Simon writes in his *Beckett:* "The vagabonds Gogo and Didi owe much to the Sam-Suzanne couple without Beckett ever imposing upon us his personal memories of the Occupation of France" (28–29).

Perhaps it was at that time that Beckett became keenly conscious of the fact that "*unheimlich* is in some way or other a sub-species of *heimlich*" (Freud, "The Uncanny"). As a man without a *heim* (a home), a foreigner in a land which had become estranged from itself, he must have experienced the full meaning of *Unheimlichkeit*. He met others like him, men torn from their surroundings, men who had become aliens in their own country. In his famous essay "Das Unheimliche," Freud describes and discusses Hoffmann's *Nachtstück*, "The Sand Man." There is something prophetic about this fantastic tale. Indeed, our epoch has witnessed the unbridled rampage of Coppelius/Coppola, the lawyer who sanctioned the burning of little children in furnaces, the optician who sells not glasses but living eyes. Although the supernatural plays no role in Beckett, everyday reality is touched with strangeness and the dead are never out of reach. Often their voices rise, sound in the mind of lonely, haunted men like the Joe of *Dis, Joe*, or our double stares at us from the reflection we fail to recognize in the mirror.

Beckett is not a political writer, but history has stamped him with its pain. Most of the time the dramatist blurs specificity, striving for the universal. Thus, in the manuscript of *En attendant Godot*, Gogo was first called Levy throughout Act I. As he started his second act, Beckett decided to be less explicit. The name was changed to Estragon, and Levy crossed out. Beckett must have met many Jews who were also in hiding, or worked in the Resistance. He also knew that, like his friend Péron, they were being sent to concentration camps. For him, Gogo must be one of the faces of innocent agony. Although the name Levy disappeared from the published text, "agony" remains at the core of the modest herb, *estragon* (tarragon in English). Allied to wormwood, tarragon is aromatic and bitter. The earthy Gogo may be the salt of the earth, but he is also the victim of life's bitter absurdities. Beaten at night by some unknown, unidentified assailants, he comes to accept pain as one of the constant presences, or components, of existence. This apprehension surfaces once again in Beckett's most recent plays, *Catastrophe* and *What Where*.

Catastrophe was originally written in French for a single performance at the summer 1982 Avignon Festival day in honor of the then-jailed Czech dramatist Vaclav Havel. Its English-version premiere took place on Wednesday, 15 June 1983, at the Harold Clurman Theater in New York. Written for the Graz summer festival, *What Where* received its world premiere on the same day.

The two *dramaticules*, as Beckett calls his short pieces, were accompanied by *Ohio Impromptu*, which Beckett wrote for the Ohio State University three-day symposium (7–9 May 1981), "Samuel Beckett: Humanistic Perspectives."

Catastrophe does not deal directly with Havel's situation, although the published text is dedicated to the Czech writer. The play takes place in a theater where a Female Assistant is costuming the Protagonist (P) for the Director's approval. Offstage, a character called Luke (L) is in charge of lighting. P is seen standing quite still upon a black pedestal. His bowed head is covered by a wide-brimmed hat that hides most of his face. His fragile form is enveloped by a grayish dressing gown covering his ash-gray prison pajamas. P stands motionless, his hands deep in the dressing gown's pockets. The Director walks in dressed in a Russian-looking fur-lined coat and a fur hat. Puffing on a cigar, he settles in a comfortable armchair while the Assistant, wearing a coverall that suggests both the uniform of a stagehand and that of a nurse in a psychiatric ward, waltzes attendance on the big boss. He directs the young woman to remove P's hat and his robe, to roll up the trousers of the mute man's pajamas. A "moulting" cranium will be exposed, then pitifully thin legs, and finally hands turned to claws by "fibrous degeneration," a crippling malady known in France by the name of its discoverer, Dupuytren. For those who are aware that Beckett himself suffers from this illness the reference acquires particular poignancy.

D is businesslike but impatient. He has a pressing engagement. He refers to his "caucus." The Director may not be a theater man after all, but a member of the Politburo, or a KGB investigator. The word "caucus" flashes a signal inviting us to follow another path.

As D steps off the stage into the ambient darkness, his voice seems to come from a great distance. Luke is ordered to cast a spot on the bare head of P, but that head must be kept lowered. When P seems properly humbled, D shouts approval. A storm of applause is heard. Is it the invisible audience, or the crowd composing a Presidium? We are shown the individual's demise and humiliation.

All of a sudden, when all seemed set forever, something utterly unexpected takes place. As the applause dies down, P raises his head very slowly and looks out. By this one gesture, the actor is able to convey man's irreducible spirit, the triumph of the individual will and conscience over a tyrannical regime that could crush it only with his life. People who saw Havel shortly after his release say that he was deeply moved by the text of the play, as well as by the fact that a Havel evening had been organized at Avignon by AIDA (Association Internationale de Défense des Artistes).

A question remains: If the play ends on a silently triumphant note, why call it *Catastrophe*? Perhaps because like all of Beckett's dramatic pieces it is more metaphysical than political. The word "catastrophe" suggests the Gnostic notion that this world is a bungled job. A catastrophe was unleashed by the demiurge before the fall of man in the Garden of Eden. The Fall in fact is not man's fall but a cosmic fall. For the Gnostics there was no order or beauty in the world, no consolation for the absence of God. Man is separated from the divine by a hierarchical system, chains of emanations. At the bottom of the abyss in which we are plunged there is only a flickering, ever receding light. If Kafka was, as some claim, a modern Gnostic, so is Samuel Beckett.

There is also a joke in *Catastrophe*; it has to do with the impossibility of artistic creation. What can you do with this paltry creature, Man? You can work on him, *ad infinitum, ad nauseum*, and he will still resist definition. You can place him on a pedestal, strip him bare, spotlight his puny form, and what do you have in the end: "the thing itself." As King Lear says, looking at the naked Edgar, a madman in disguise: "Unaccommodated man is no more but such a poor, bare, fork'd animal as thou art" (III, iv, 106).

The Israeli painter Avigdor Arikha, whom I met for the first time at the opening of the new Samuel Beckett theater in New York, told me the following: "For Beckett politics is not an abstraction. His interest in them comes from personal pain, from his apprehension of human suffering." Although pain is present in Beckett's entire *oeuvre*, it seems to me that in *What Where* it is palpably present. Again the play is both metaphysical and political, or perhaps one ought to say that its metaphysical, even Gnostic, structure is presented in terms of a modern political image: the interrogation chamber.

The dramatic personae of *What Where* are four men, identically dressed, their heads covered by identical wigs of matted gray hair. The fifth presence on the stage is an object: a suspended megaphone. This ominous object explains the statement: "We're the last five." Bam, Bem, Bim, Bom—the four characters—are irretrievably tied to one another by the complicity of senseless torture, the punishment they must inflict upon each other in order to find out *what* happened and *where*. Again and again Bam inquires whether the tortured man wept, screamed, begged for mercy. However, although he has, nothing has been revealed. As in *King Lear*, but in a different sense, "nothing will come of nothing."

The sadomasochistic inquisitors of *What Where*, their bell-like names tolling a death knell, are latter-day reincarnations of subsidiary characters in Beckett's early novel *Murphy*. Bim and Bom are twins, the chief members of a sadistic clan of male nurses in charge of the Magdalen Mental Mercyseat, the hospital where Murphy holds his first and last employment.

The head male nurse is Mr. Thomas ("Bim") Clinch, "a huge red, bald, whiskered man of overweening ability and authority in his own department" (156), who, for Uranian love of his assistant, the former Dublin pot poet Austin Ticklepenny, hires Murphy in order to release his beloved "from the torments of the wards" (156). "Bom" is the "younger twin and dead spit of Bim" (165). Murphy is delivered into his care on the first floor of Skinner's House, "between the psychotic and psychiatric points of view" (165). In addition to

Bim and Bom there are "no fewer than seven male relations, linear and collateral, serving under [Bim], of whom the greatest [is] Bom and . . . the least an aged uncle [Bum]" (166).

Beckett's 1938 novel is strangely prophetic of the Soviet Union's system of *psikhushkas*, the psychiatric prison wards used as "reeducation" centers to bring dissident intellectuals back in line by means of the chemical straightjacket. This is how the Soviet dissident mathematician Leonid Plyusch, who was imprisoned in a series of such hospitals before he was allowed to leave Russia through the offices of Amnesty International, describes "treatment" at the Dnipropetrovsk hospital:

> I could see the effects of the potent sedative haloperidol on my fellow inmates and wondered why drugs were administered in quarantine. . . . One inmate was writhing in convulsions, head twisted to the side and eyes bulging. Another patient was gasping for breath, and his tongue was lolling. A third was screaming for the nurse and begging for a corrective to alleviate the physical effects of haloperidol. The drug was given in such large doses in order to reveal the malingerers and to break any resistance. . . . That very first day a criminal who had been simulating amnesia gave up and went to see Kamenetskaya (the psychiatrist) to confess. (*History's Carnival*, 305)

At the M.M.M. the patients sleep in convulsed attitudes, like the tormented creatures of the "Pergamene Barlach" or Puget's "caryatids of Strength and Weakness," glimpsed by Murphy in Toulon on "a wild waning winter afternoon" (239). As he walks through the wards or peers into the cells, they seem to him to be recoiling from nature's solicitations. Beckett's "Kamenetskaya" is Bom, a sadist who "encouraged what is vulgarly called sadism in his assistants" (238). Those who resisted were reported as "uncooperative, not cooperating in the routine of the wards, or, in extreme cases, 'restive.' They were liable to get hell at night" (238).

Bom instructs Murphy in the ways in which he must give care. Since this is "a mercyseat," he must not be rough, although of course "restraint and coercion [are] sometimes unavoidable" (158). When it becomes difficult to handle a patient singlehandedly without hurting him, he may "call the other nurses to his assistance" (159). No wonder that Murphy, "the surd" (77), develops kindred feeling toward the psychotics who are as "cut off" from reality as he is. He can see no value in restoring people to all the emotions they seem to have cast off. In fact, the most comforting space for this other Belacqua is the microcosm of "the pads" with their cushioned ceiling, walls, door, floor, and their temperature, which allows only for "total nudity" (181). It is with the imperturbably insane that Murphy can enjoy "vicarious autology" (189). His own circumscribed existence in his Cartesian, stove-heated garret is much like that of the uncertified at the M.M.M. This may account for the instant dislike Bim takes to Murphy. As to Bom, another Pilate, he rubs his hands clean, releasing him "to his folly" (170).

Although the highly developed system of psychiatric wards used as effective prisons for recalcitrant dissidents, such as Sakharov, had not yet been put into place in 1938, the names used by Beckett in *Murphy* leave us no doubt as to his subtextual reference. In her chapter "Murphy the Morph," Ruby Cohn writes: "The sadistic attendants, Bim and Bom, are apparently named for the Russian clowns who were allowed to tell the cruel truth about the Soviet system as a joke" (*Comic Gamut*, 62). Their reappearance in Beckett's most recent play, the one he wrote after *Catastrophe*, points clearly to the dramatist's intention to "translate" the political in a subtle but eloquent way. Nor is this a new concern on Beckett's part. Coming full circle, *What Where* connects with the "sanatorium" (160), where Murphy plays his Christ-like role until the end, until his end.

The young Beckett, writing his first full-length novel in English after having moved permanently to Paris, and the great classical writer of today are both metaphysical poets, yet never for a moment do they forget their responsibility toward those who must suffer in mind and flesh the cruelty of persecution.

What Where is not a play that can be apprehended by the mind alone; it must be grasped intuitively. On its most profound level it deals with the impossibility of knowing. It raises the questions that haunted Origen, Valentinius, Plotinus, the Manicheans, and the Albigensians. The men we see entering and exiting in the semidarkness are suffering cosmic alienation. They are the victims of a failure in the realm of the spirit.

Beckett's stage directions are, as always, highly precise. A dimly lit rectangle (three meters by two meters) is the cell-like space in which the characters confront one another. The megaphone over which Bam's recorded voice will be heard hangs downstage, on the left. The voice begins to speak. It is, in fact, the voice that seems to put on the light, as though it were that of the invisible Creator. The season, we are told, is spring. Life is about to begin. But what manner of living?

We see Bam standing on the left side of the rectangle of light, head high. Bom stands on the side parallel to the back wall, head low. The recorded voice speaks its disapproval of this start. The light goes off. The Creator or Demiurge says he is about to start all over again. This time, as the light goes up slightly, we see that Bam is standing alone. He proclaims this fact and then announces Bom's entrance, reentry.

The next scene is silent, a shadow play. All four characters enter briefly in groups of two, the second always following the first one out. Each time there is a reversal of roles: the character who has made a proud entrance, head held high, will eventually return meekly, head low. The erstwhile leader becomes the follower, the victim, until Bam's final entrance, head low. Clearly there are no victors, no permanent leaders. Even Bam, who seemed to initiate the cycle, is only a cog in the cosmic machine. All will be ground down, yet, somehow, the infernal wheels will continue grinding, working, moving. It is a perfect image of the Gnostic universe with its chains of emanations, its spirits become demons, its plunging motion that takes us deeper and deeper into the abyss.

The vocabulary Beckett uses, however, has nothing mystical about it. It is almost gangster language. Bam tells each tormentor who has failed to secure a confession that he must now "be given the works." In the English version the word is ambiguous. The "works" could refer to the writings of a party ideologue. In French the menace is less ambiguous: "On va te travailler jusqu'à ce que tu avoues." The French text refers explicitly to torture, although a philosophical level is hinted at by the reiterated question: "Are you free?" Two of the characters interrogated by Bam answer in the affirmative. Their freedom, however, is limited to being available to inflict or bear torture.

Nor are we made to feel that the situation we are viewing is new. It has gone on for some time, perhaps for an eternity. Is it a game, like Gogo and Didi's word games, their dream of hanging themselves from one of the weak branches of the only tree? Here, however, there is little humor, no relief. Bam, the Inquisitor, is grim, relentlessly cruel. The others are cooperative prisoners, willing to torture, submissive enough to endure torture in turn. They cannot break the chain since there is nothing to confess; they are in the dark, ignorant of *what* and *where*. The torture ends only when the tortured man faints, when nothing can bring him back to consciousness. In the almost total darkness that bathes the stage all we can make out are vague forms, the wigs that seem to have been made from the shorn hair on display at the Auschwitz museum. The cycle of suffering will never cease.

What is miraculous about this short play is the way in which intense tragic feeling is contained within a cool, seemingly detached form. The familiar, haunting twentieth-century image of the prison cell, the psychiatric ward, the slave labor camp, is evoked over and over again by the narrator/writer whose voice we hear over the megaphone, but who is also the cruel Demiurge, the force that set it all in motion by saying: "Let there be light!"

What Where is a seamless amalgam of the metaphysical and the political. It dramatizes Beckett's own art of endless questioning, his self-inflicted torment, his rapturous pain in probing the bottomless void. The Creator is not pleased with his creation; the writer feels he ought not to go on, yet he goes on. The only change we are made aware of is that of the seasons. By the end of *What Where* it is winter. A year has passed and the cycle will begin anew.

Like Aeschylus in his *Prometheus Bound*, Beckett shows that we are all victims of cruel divinities who have tied us to the rock of endless suffering. It is the fate of humanity to suffer, to endure, to wait for the end, their personal end but not the end of suffering. Beckett's message is the same as that of the great classical writers and, like them, Beckett is not a pessimist. A pessimist does not lift pen to paper. The last words of his latest work, *Worstward Ho*, are: "Said Nohow on."

RICHARD KELLER SIMON

Beckett, Comedy, and the Critics: A Study of Two Contexts

From the beginnings of Beckett scholarship in the late 1950s, and for more than a decade afterward, critics regularly explained his work as a form of philosophically and theologically complex comedy, one that affirmed the values of humor, laughter, and mockery against suffering and despair. Murphy and Molloy, Vladimir and Estragon, Hamm and Clov, all of Beckett's central characters were described as clowns, clochards, and music hall comedians who demonstrated the clown's special ability to survive under the worst of circumstances. Among the earliest critics to take this position were Maurice Nadeau in France (1951) and Gunther Anders in Germany (1954). In England and the United States, all of the first major critics developed a comic interpretation, establishing the context in which Beckett would be read and understood by others: Hugh Kenner in essays published in 1958 and 1959, then in *Samuel Beckett: A Critical Study* in 1961 and *Flaubert, Joyce, and Beckett: The Stoic Comedians* in 1962; Ruby Cohn, in essays published between 1959 and 1961, then in *Samuel Beckett: The Comic Gamut* in 1962; and Martin Esslin, in essays on the modern theater in 1959 and 1960, then in *The Theatre of the Absurd* in 1961. Kenner called Beckett's techniques "a unique comic repertoire, like a European clown's" (*Samuel Beckett*, 13). Cohn wrote, "As he moves from a baroque to a colloquial style, Beckett retains his comic vision. An analysis of his humor therefore traces an attitude that is pervasive in his work, at its complex core, and an understanding of that humor may elucidate the core" (*Comic Gamut*, 7). Esslin wrote, "the Theatre of the Absurd transcends the categories of comedy and tragedy and combines laughter with horror" (301). Others followed: Frederick Hoffman in *Samuel Beckett: The Language of Self* in 1962, Josephine Jacobsen and William Mueller in *The Testament of Samuel Beckett* in 1964, Nathan Scott in *Samuel Beckett* in 1965, John Fletcher in *Samuel Beckett's Art* in 1967, Michael Robinson in *The Long Sonata of the Dead* in 1969. And numerous journal articles during this period similarly develop the comic approach to Beckett. His work was compared to the circus (Kenner, Robinson), the music hall (Esslin), film slapstick (Hoffman), commedia dell'arte (Kern, Robinson), humour noir (Esslin), Sterne, Cervantes, and Swift (Fletcher); it was identified as "metaphysical farce" (Lamont, Cohn), "ontological farce" (Anders), "wilfully aborted comedy" (Mercier), "comitragedy" (Cohn), "tragicomedy" (Hoffman), "epistemological comedy" (Hoffman), and "the new *Book of Job* in buffo" (Kott). Beckett himself was labeled "comedian of the impasse" (Kenner).

But just as these critics were establishing the essential comic nature of Beckett's texts, Beckett stopped writing such comic texts. Apparently while affirming the values of laughter, the strengths of the clown, and the abilities of the comic attitude to withstand suffering, decay, and despair, Beckett came to the conclusion that the laughter, clowning, and the comic would not do. It did not happen one day, the way Pozzo goes blind and Lucky goes mute, but quite slowly: each successive work contains fewer and fewer pratfalls, fewer jokes, fewer echoes of the musichall. Beckett was careful in making up his mind. And after *Happy Days* there are virtually no provocations to laugh and little that can be called comic in the increasingly stark literature. "The tears of the world are a constant quantity," Pozzo explains in *Godot*. "For each one who begins to weep somewhere else another stops. The same is true of the laugh" (22). The same, it turned out, was true of Beckett and his critics: as more and more critics began to laugh, encouraging the mass of readers to laugh with them, Beckett gradually stopped.

Because the literature Beckett has written since *Happy Days* is not comic, Beckett critics have turned away from the problems of comedy; what was once a dominant theme in the criticism has almost completely disappeared. Thus the first readings of Beckett stand as the major treatments of comedy, but however brilliantly they explain some of the comic qualities of these texts—and nothing in this essay is meant to denigrate their fine perceptions of Beckett—they are wrong about others. Although there are obvious comic elements in his work, they are *not* affirmations of the comic spirit. Humor is *not* at the complex core of Beckett's worldview, and in fact it no longer appears to be in his work at all, even in the margins. The later criticism of Beckett, which has concentrated on the noncomic texts written after *Happy Days*, has never reevaluated the problem of comedy in the earlier texts, those which established Beckett's reputation. But if the first critics were at least partially mistaken about the nature of the comic in Beckett's works—something we can see now in retrospect—then the problem of comedy remains. In what sense are the works before *Happy Days* comic? How did those critics read the texts as endorsements of the comic, of clowning and laughter, and what can we now understand about their meanings from Beckett's rejection of laughter, humor, and the figure of the clown?

There are two critical contexts against which the problem of comedy can be understood in Beckett. One is the first decade of Beckett scholarship in England and the United States, between 1958 and 1969, when there was widespread interest within literary criticism in comedy as a defense against pain and suffering, when critics would therefore have been predisposed to see such themes in a writer's work (there are major reevaluations of many authors in this period which make similar claims for them; and it was at this time that university classes were developed on "black humor"). The other is the period from 1928 to the end of World War II in Europe, England, and the United States, when Beckett was composing his "comic" literature. What literary, psychological, and theological critics were writing about laughter and comedy in this period provides the context in which Beckett's project in the comic can best be understood, and they were by no means convinced that laughter and humor were effective or even healthy responses to pain and suffering. A debate can be reconstructed between and among the major critics of the comic in this period—Sigmund Freud, Theodor Reik, Ernst Kris, Anton Obrdlik, and Helmuth Plessnėr, between Max Eastman, Anthony Ludovici, Wyndham Lewis, Kenneth Burke, and Reinhold Niebuhr. In the simplest terms, most of the European critics argued that humor and laughter were effective coping mechanisms against suffering, while most of the Anglo-Americans felt that such comic responses had limited effectiveness and could be more dangerous than the conditions they were designed to offset.

The issue had special relevance for the Jews of Central Europe and for the Jewish critics of humor in this period, especially those within the psychoanalytic movement, for it was by such defensive joking that Jews had learned to cope with the conditions of their own powerlessness and oppression. World War II demonstrated the validity of both positions—that of the Europeans and that of the Anglo-Americans. Humor did not prevent the destruction of Central European Jewry, but it apparently allowed some of the survivors to endure concentration camps and Nazi occupation. There were survivors who so testified, among them Victor Frankl and George Mikes.

It was in such a context, this extended and carefully considered argument over the comic from the late 1920s to the aftermath of World War II, that Beckett wrote his major works. Whether or not he was aware of the debate it is not possible to say, but what can be asserted is that his plays and novels in this period contain very similar considerations of the meanings of laughter and the functions of humor. And in the texts written after World War II Beckett finally concludes that, although laughter and humor are certainly understandable human responses, they are not adequate as coping mechanisms. Within the larger debate on comedy, humor, and laughter, Beckett sides with critics like Ludovici, Burke, and Niebuhr. In their understandable hurry to explain the obscurities of Beckett's texts, the first critics took the presence of comic elements as an indication that the texts were "comic," but these texts can more accurately be described as inquiries into the nature of the comic, of humor, and laughter. What laughter signifies and what not (Watt Knott), what comedy and the comic sense can deal with effectively and what not—these are among the issues Beckett deals with in this period. These are of course the issues Beckett forced onto his critics, but they took them up without very much recognition that he was similarly preoccupied. Beckett's work does provoke audiences to laugh, but it is also full of laughter, occasions when characters laugh, and full of descriptions of laughter, occasions when characters discuss the problems of the comic or the laughable. To see this as comedy is a first step in understanding Beckett's project as a writer; to see this as metacomedy is the next. He is a major theorist of the comic, and his works are significant and sustained evaluations of laughter and the comic.

Arsene's classification of laughter in *Watt*, into bitter, hollow, and mirthless, respectively, the responses to that which is not good, not true, and not happy, has been appropriated frequently by critics as a way of understanding Beckett. Beckett, sounding like a critic of comedy, entices his critics to sound like him sounding like a critic of comedy. But Arsene's classification can also be read as a parody of comic theory. There are similar classifications of the modes of laughter in much nineteenth- and twentieth-century theory, and in 1941, one year before Beckett began *Watt*, Helmuth Plessner wrote in *Laughing and Crying*, "The curve of laughter stretches from the mediate occasions of boundless joy and titillation to the boundary situations of embarrassment and despair. The top of the curve . . . indicates laughter in its full development" (113). Beckett's classification rather neatly inverts Plessner's. Arsene too finds the top of a curve, but it is "the laugh of laughs," the mirthless. Besides, Arsene is only one of many comic theorists in Beckett. While her primary point concerns the mirthless laugh, in *Endgame*, Nell's primary point concerns laughless mirth. The two are not the same: Nell rather neatly inverts Arsene (37). At the complex core of the works written up to *Happy Days* is a struggle with the problems of humor.

II

In *Godot* the worst insult Vladimir and Estragon have in their extensive repertoire of abuse is "critic," worse than moron or vermin, more devastating than curate or cretin. When Vladimir hears it, he wilts. Beckett of course was a critic very early in his career, and it should not be surprising that he would write texts with critics in mind. In *Godot*, Vladimir and Estragon constantly comment on and evaluate their own performances, explain their possible meanings, play the game of reviewer and critic in front of audiences of reviewers and critics. And in a curiously comic way *Godot* plays a game with its critics by anticipating their obvious responses and confounding them. The two most common critical interpretations of the play are as religious parable and as clown show, and yet both are little more than elaborations of statements contained within the play. An extensive discussion of the Bible occurs early in Act I, but before the critic or reviewer can find a moment to think about this during the intermission, Vladimir and Estragon compare themselves to Christ as the act ends. If the critic wishes to sound either intelligent or original, he must find something else to say about the play. In Act II there is the long piece of comic business, the hat trick, which would suggest the play is a clown show, but in Act I, before such explicit borrowings from comedy, Vladimir and Estragon have already compared their performance to the music hall and *twice* to the circus. The play undercuts the critic by making its themes so explicitly obvious: Will he simply repeat what the characters tell him (and everybody else) the play means?

No one should belabor the obvious, at least without examining the evidence carefully. Yet it was into this particular trap that Beckett's first critics fell, looking for ways of explaining the obscurities of the play. Esslin used the lines to support his argument that the play was comic: "And the parallel to the music hall and the circus is even explicitly stated" (*Theatre of Absurd*, 14); Kenner wrote, "Thus a non-play comments on itself" (*Samuel Beckett*, 135); Jacobsen and Mueller wrote that it "reminds us of the milieu in which, we must never forget, all takes place" (14); Fletcher wrote, "Beckett's characters never forget that they are present at their own spectacle" (66). The lines about the music hall and circus were taken at face value: the characters were taken as reliable guides by critics who did not consider that Vladimir and Estragon are not always the best of authorities, or, for that matter, that what a character says is not what the author says. About the relationship between Beckett and his critics, Esslin argued in 1965, "Inevitably there exists an organic connection between his refusal to explain his meaning . . . and the critics' massive urge to supply an explanation. Indeed, it might be argued that in that correlation between the author's and the critics' attitude lies one of the keys to the whole phenomenon of Samuel Beckett, his *oeuvre*, and its impact" (*Samuel Beckett*, 1). But here Esslin seems mistaken. At the beginning at least, the organic connection was rather between the meanings Beckett tossed out to the critics, much as Pozzo tossed out bones, and the ways in which the critics grasped hungrily at them, digesting often without a second thought. Beckett very obviously invites us to see *Godot* as religious parable and a circus performance—it is part of his complex playing. No critic is necessary to provide us with these meanings. But it was on evidence like Vladimir's and Estragon's blather about the music hall and the circus that critics built the case for Beckett as comedian.

There were in fact two kinds of evidence cited by the first critics: the obvious kinds of comic business in the texts, the borrowings from circus and musichall, and the unmistakable fact that audiences laughed at productions of the plays. The explicit comic references in the texts include the hat trick in *Godot*, the flea-powder-in-the-pants routine in *Endgame*, the long, drawn-out slip on the banana peel in *Krapp's Last Tape*, and numerous statements about clowns and clowning throughout the literature. There was also Beckett's own subtitle to the English version of *Godot*—a tragicomedy. Critics gathered this evidence together and concluded, reasonably enough, that Beckett wrote tragicomedy. But there were problems with the evidence, as some of them acknowledged. The French version of *Godot* is not subtitled a tragicomedy, and as for the English version, Cohn admitted, "one cannot be sure what Beckett means by the word" (225).

A number of early critics, acknowledging the strange qualities of audience laughter, argued for a strange quality of comedy. Vivian Mercier, reviewing *Endgame* in 1959, wrote: "The night I saw it . . . the audience laughed many times, but the laughs were all of one kind, a kind that Mr. Beckett himself describes in *Watt* . . . the mirthless laugh" (*Griffin*, 14). Mercier suggested the play was both "purposefully aborted tragedy" and "wilfully aborted comedy." Cohn wrote in 1962, "So ambiguous are Beckett's comic heroes that we scarcely know why we laugh, and whether we laugh *at* or *with*" (8). "Instead of laughing in a civilized or detached way at comic figures . . . we come in Beckett's work, to doubt ourselves through our laughter" (295).

The weaknesses of these kinds of evidence should now be obvious. The presence of comic elements does not by itself make a play or novel comic. Neither *Hamlet* nor *Lear* is comic, even though their comic elements function much as they do in Shakespearean tragedy—as a kind of relief, momentary interruptions in the tedium and despair. In retrospect, what we can now see is that they were simply the most recognizable elements, and that the first critics seized upon them as a way of explicating Beckett's difficult texts. What was most obvious about them became what was most essential. But by no generally held definition can these texts be called comic—they do not celebrate the golden mean, integrate the individual into society, or show the victory of young lovers over blocking characters. Neither are they about rebirth, marriage, festivity, saturnalia, or fertility of any sort. In fact, by most of these definitions, Beckett's texts are clearly anticomic, precise inversions of the comic literature, about death, sterility, disintegration of the individual. Comedy has sometimes been defined as an inversion of the normal and the everyday, as the world turned upside down; Beckett's literature is an inversion of that inversion, a perversion of the comic. And therefore the comic elements in plays like *Godot* and *Endgame* may not be incidental comic relief after all, but among the primary objects of the author's attack. By only one very general definition can the texts be called comic—that they provoke audience laughter and therefore are perceived as "funny," but such laughter is a notoriously unreliable guide to the generic meanings of a text. Forced somewhat awkwardly into problems of audience response, the first Anglo-American critics converted this kind of subjective response into the objective characteristics of the texts; by a critical sleight of hand, laughter became comedy. But Beckett was writing something more complex: drama and fiction that was about comedy, humor, and laughter. But then Beckett's first critics were faced with a very difficult set of texts to explicate, and if they sometimes misinterpreted evidence, they much more frequently proved themselves to be brilliant interpreters. It is not what they got right that needs repetition of course, but what they did not that needs revision.

<h1 style="text-align:center">III</h1>

Beckett's evaluation of and ultimate rejection of the comic can be more easily understood when it is placed in the context of the larger critical debate over comedy, humor, and laughter. Between the late 1920s and the early 1960s, when Beckett was creating the work on which his reputation depends, the relationship between humor and suffering was of interest to many critics of comedy and laughter. It is this aspect of comic inquiry which should be understood as background to Beckett's "comic" literature.

As early as 1905 Freud had introduced the concept of humor as a defense against suffering and pain (in *Jokes and Their Relation to the Unconscious*), a concept which depended on his understanding of Jewish jokes as the way a powerless people had made the best of their powerlessness. "By making our enemy small, inferior, despicable or comic, we achieve in a roundabout way the enjoyment of overcoming him," Freud wrote (103). By the mid-1920s, however, humor as a defense against suffering began receiving increased attention from a wide variety of critics. In 1921, for example, Max Eastman cautioned in *The Sense of Humor* that "there are pains and disappointments too great, even when they are imaginary, for any interior machinery of light-heartedness to turn them into comic enjoyment" (93). Dismissing Freud's analyses of the comic, Eastman argued that the comic depended instead on "playful" pain. Throughout the decade, moreover, as the condition of Jews worsened in Central Europe, Freud's analysis of Jewish humor became a subject of intense scrutiny within the psychoanalytic movement. In 1928 Freud returned to the subject, writing in "Humour" that "its fending off of the possibility of suffering places it among the great series of methods which the human mind has constructed in order to escape the compulsion to suffer" (163). But in relating humor to the id/ego/superego model of consciousness, he qualified the praise, explaining that, "in bringing about the humorous attitude, the super-ego is actually repudiating reality and serving an illusion" (166). In humor, then, the protective superego suddenly changes from a "severe master," allowing the individual to perceive the dangers of the world as a mere plaything. Freud downplayed the obvious negative aspects of this process: it is not, after all, the place of the superego to repudiate reality and serve an illusion, however charming or entertaining the illusion may be. But Freud's understanding of the psychodynamic mechanisms of humor clearly indicated potential difficulties, and at this time other critics began making explicit warnings about humor. In 1932 Nietzsche's English translator, Anthony Ludovici, wrote in *The Secret of Laughter:* "It is high time to think of other remedies than the exaltation of humour" (117). Dismissing Freud's work on the comic, he argued that "there seems to be a danger that laughter is becoming no more than one of the many anodynes with which modern men are rocking themselves into a state of drowsy insensibility. There is a very distinct danger that it is helping to make tolerable a condition which should be intolerable and utterly beneath the dignity of adults" (115). In order to escape the debilitating sense of inferiority characteristic of modern life, Ludovici wrote, men and women had turned to the comfort of laughter, humor, and the comic—and thereby increased their own helplessness. Laughter was a sign of cowardice, he argued; humor promoted weakness.

Offering an alternative explanation for the relationship between humor and suffering, Wyndham Lewis wrote in "Studies in the Art of Laughter" in 1934 that suffering was an appropriate object of laughter. Although society prevents men and women from laughing at the shell-shocked, the dying, and the deformed, such are "often very funny" (47). "Who has not on occasion (with shame) suppressed an involuntary laugh at the injured, the shell-shocked, and the deformed? But that is like laughing at the contortions of a dying man, and it would be too brutal a society that made a habit of laughing at its shell-shocked persons—especially as it would be to the society of laughers to which ultimately the responsibility for those disfigurements would have to be brought home" (47). It is not difficult to see Beckett's work as a correction of Lewis's position—the deformed and the dying are precisely what audiences *are* invited to laugh at.

But the greater debate concerned humor as defense, not offense. In 1937 Kenneth Burke wrote in *Attitudes Toward History* that humor "tends to gauge the situation falsely." The "customary method of self-protection" for humorists, he wrote, "is the attitude of 'happy stupidity' whereby the gravity of life simply fails to register; its importance is lost to them" (43). What Burke suggested instead was a comic frame of acceptance, one that saw clearly and perceived comedy but still retained the ability to act. "It is neither wholly euphemistic, nor wholly debunking—hence it provides the *charitable* attitude towards people that is required . . . but at the same time maintains our shrewdness" (166). And while Burke makes no reference to Freud in this context, other commentators did take up Freud's argument explicitly, modifying, defending, sometimes simply repeating. Taking an opposite position to Burke (again without any explicit reference to him), Ernst Kris wrote in "Ego Development and the Comic" (1938) that, while the comic "cannot bring permanent relief," humor could—by banishing man's fear of loss of love. "The precious gift of humor makes men wise; they are sublime and safe, remote from all conflict" (216). Nevertheless Kris did modify Freud. "The comic alone cannot overcome emotion for it presupposes a certain control over anxiety before it can become effective" (212). This is an important change. In "The Psychology of Caricature" (1934), Kris wrote, "things which simply arouse anxiety or unpleasure cannot be adapted to comic expression . . . until they have been reduced in intensity and undergone some degree of working over" (185). For Kris, then, humor was clearly not as potent as Freud had argued it was. Other psychoanalytic commentators made other revisions to Freud's model of humor at this time, sometimes considering its meaning for the Jews specifically, sometimes considering its general psychodynamic mechanisms. Reik called Jewish humor masochistic (1926), and Bergler argued that all humor was a dynamic of hostility and aggression between ego and superego; the attack was not on external realities but on internal ideals (1937). It was thus not nearly as healthy a process as Freud had suggested.

In 1941 the phenomenologist Helmuth Plessner made a refinement of the relationship between laughter and despair, similar to Kris's, explaining in *Laughing and Crying* that when a despairing person laughs, "he has not yet given himself up for lost, for he is still actualizing a distance from his situation. . . . But in despair itself, which has found no outlet either in self-surrender or gallows humor, laughter and crying are equally out of place" (110). "Only those boundary situations excite laughter which, without becoming threatening, are nevertheless unanswerable"—otherwise we must either learn how to cope successfully, or flee. But in gallows humor or self-surrender, "we have conquered our despair" (111). In 1942 the sociologist Antonin Obrdlik reported on gallows humor in Czechoslovakia both before and after the Nazi occupation, arguing that it "bolsters the resistance of the victims and at the same time, it undermines the morale of the oppressors. As long as the Nazis know that their victims ridicule them, they cannot be sure of the final victory" (713). He concluded that "humor in general, and gallows humor more specifically, is a social phenomenon the importance of which, under certain circumstances, may be tremendous. . . . Its positive effect is manifested above all in the strengthening of the morale and the spirit of resistance of people who struggle for their individual and national survival" (716). In the same year William Dana Orcutt wrote in *Escape to Laughter* that "humor possesses a peculiar and saving quality that it so often asserts itself in crises where no other form of relief can possibly avail" (42). And in 1944 Gunnar Myrdal in *An American Dilemma* included a similar assessment of humor for American blacks and their survival under hostile circumstances: "Much of the humor that the Negro displays before the white man in the South is akin to that manufactured satisfaction with their miserable lot which the conquered people of Europe are now forced to display before their German conquerors" (960).

This position was seriously challenged in 1945 by Reinhold Niebuhr, who wrote in "Humor and Faith" that "to meet the disappointments and frustrations of life, the irrationalities and contingencies with laughter, is a high form of wisdom. . . . One thinks for instance of the profound wisdom which underlies the capacity of laughter in the Negro people." But, Niebuhr qualified, "there is indeed a limit to laughter. . . . We can not laugh at death. We do try of course." But we must fail. Citing the particular humor that occurs during war, he warned, "If we persist in laughter when dealing with the final problem of human existence, when we turn life into a comedy we also reduce it to meaninglessness" (145–46). But after the war, Jews who lived through it testified that there was humor in the concentration camps, that by laughing at death, some of them at least were able to endure it. Niebuhr, the Gentile, had not understood. "The attempt to develop a sense of humor and to see things in a humorous light is some kind of trick learned while mastering the art of living," Victor Frankl wrote. "Yet it is possible to practice the art of living even in a concentration camp, although suffering is omnipresent" (*Man's Search for Meaning*, 69). George Mikes reported on a friend who had survived Auschwitz by seeing the experience as comic and who, after the war, had written a comic novel about it: "Like everybody else, he had somehow come to terms with this frightful experience, to survive not only Auschwitz but also its aftermath" (29).

Freud's cautionary analysis in 1928 and the postwar testimonies of Frankl, Mikes, and others frame the period in which Beckett was writing the drama and fiction most often identified as comic. It is not that Beckett's texts are to be reduced to the comic theory of the period, but that they are to be seen as comparable considerations of the problems of the comic within fiction and drama, as complex fictional and dramatic enactments of theory. What Freud and Burke, Kris and Frankl, evaluated in straightforward essays, Beckett made into his plays and novels. It is another way in which his work has important connections to the intellectual history of his time and place.

JESSICA PRINZ

The Fine Art of Inexpression:
Beckett and Duchamp

Duchamp's *Objet-Dard* (1951) is an art of eroticism that contrasts sharply
with Beckett's art of impotence and despair, yet some striking similarities
exist in their work.[1] Both produce an art in which ambiguities and enigmas
prevail, where nonsense, nonsequiturs, and short-circuits to meaning subvert
stable interpretation and call attention to epistemological limits. Humor is an
essential component of their work and it is often employed to heighten an
ironic negativity concerning life and art. The machine and man-as-machine
is a central feature of their art as well; Duchamp and Beckett generate images
of mechanical systems—human, logical, and linguistic—that function but do
not "work." Most important, both use language to subvert it, to call words
into question as a means of communication and as a vehicle for truth.

Watt is the novel that most closely parallels Duchamp's styles and strategies, and many of its images and techniques resemble dadaist jokes. The "Ad-
denda," for example, includes the description of the second painting in
Erskine's room. The heightened realism, combined with absurd imagery,
gives the impression of not just one but two tasteless artists: the naked piano
player complete with dirty torso and the naive realist who paints his portrait
(250–51). The passage, the painting, and *Watt* as a whole parody the notion
of "significant detail" by conveying with excruciating exactitude exaggerated
details that are not realistic but absurd. Indeed, Sam (the narrator) does unconsciously what a dadaist artist does consciously: he mixes the tasteful with
the tasteless, supplants the sublime with the scatological, confuses art and reality, and creates a dirty pun.

Beckett, however, calls attention to his own artistic ploys by linking the
words "art" and "con" throughout the novel. The portrait of the piano player
is painted by one "Art Con O'Connery," whose name puns on Descartes'
conarium (Cohn, 1964, 34), female sexual organs, and perhaps the dadaist
con game of art. The novel also presents the twin dwarfs, Art and Con, who
are impossible to distinguish:

the resemblance was so marked in every way that even those (and they were many) who knew and loved them most would call Art Con when they meant Art, and Con Art when they meant Con, at least as often, if not more often than, they called Art Art when they meant Art, and Con Con when they meant Con. There were not wanting those to insinuate that he [Sam] was the father of his cousins Art and Con. (106–7)

Indeed Beckett's dirty joke with the word "con" is very much like Duchamp's continual pun on "cul," as in the "oculist witnesses" (au cul) of *The Large Glass* or, more important, in *LHOOQ* (*elle a chaud au cul*), famed for its blasphemous treatment of the *Mona Lisa* ("she's got a hot rump"). Both Beckett and Duchamp satirize the pretensions of high art by their use of low and bawdy puns, and in both cases the object of the satire is realistic art.[2]

Just as important as the irreverence directed at art is the ironic treatment of man presented by these artists. Both employ the most common dadaist device and portray the human being as a machine in a despairing comedy of inefficiency. Watt's way of walking, for example, includes mechanical, robot motions that are ridiculously inept (30). Like his walk, his systematic analysis of experience also fails to produce any effective result. When the machinery of his mind breaks down, he gets stuck, like a machine, in reverse. The novel as a whole sustains the tension between Watt as a kind of apparatus and Watt as an all-too-human character with a passionate need to please and a poignant desire to know.

The Bride Stripped Bare by Her Bachelors, Even similarly confuses human and mechanical attributes. *The Green Box*, which contains Duchamp's notes, drawings, and diagrams for *The Large Glass*, describes the bride, who "blossoms into stripping" and is activated by an "automobiline, love gasoline."[3] Confusing the natural, the mechanical, and the human, she is a "motor" of "timid power," yet she retains some human characteristics: her feelings for relatives and girlfriends, her desires and her imagination.

In many ways *The Large Glass* is "a total object complete with missing parts," for the erotic union it promises is conspicuously missing. This is not just because Duchamp left it unfinished (in 1923), but because he planned all along to frustrate not only the bachelors' but the spectators' desires. One note in *The Green Box* describes the electrical connection between the bride and the bachelors, and Duchamp's intention to "short-circuit [it] if necessary." The grand erotic apparatus is unplugged, as it were, constructed meticulously and precisely in order to fail, to create an irresolvable ambiguity concerning whether or not the characters reach their "happy goal."

Duchamp's couple has actually been a "pseudocouple" all along; terminology of autoeroticism is included from the outset. The structure of the work that keeps male and female apart, caged in glass, suggests an inevitable and bitter isolation. Beckett, too, is fond of creating "pseudocouples" (*The Unnamable* 297), one example of which is Watt and Mrs. Gorman.[4] Beckett short-circuits

MARCEL DUCHAMP, *The Large Glass.* Courtesy Philadelphia Museum of Art, Bequest of Katherine S. Dreier.

this affair as he does most human relations, but in this case the failure of human intercourse resembles a slapstick joke. The way in which Watt and Mrs. Gorman shift positions on each other's lap presents a machinelike image of repeated and circular motions—first Mrs. Gorman on Watt, then Watt on Mrs. Gorman. When all the changes of position and all of the kisses are finally added up, there is a "total for the day of one kiss only . . . for during the interversions they could not kiss, they were so busy interverting" (141).

Watt's system of interverting succeeds only in tiring him, and his mode of walking exhausts him entirely. Beckett's human mechanisms, like Duchamp's, are always in the process of malfunctioning. In the same way that the entire mechanism of *The Large Glass* is carefully constructed so it can fail, so Beckett employs automated and mechanical processes to undercut any real sense of control. Thus the parallel with dada is more appropriate for Beckett's work than any other machine-oriented art movement of the century. In contrast to the futurists, who create an aesthetic of the machine for its sensations, or the constructivists, who herald the machine as the potential source for a new technological society, and even the cubists (Léger, for example), who use machine images for visual effect, the dadaist machine is always broken and self-destructing; it is employed ironically to criticize both the machine and human life.

Underlying the humorous portrayal of man is a pervasive cynicism regarding human life. At the very core of this Bergsonian humor, we find the source for tragedy as well: "All that is serious in life," says Bergson, "comes from our freedom. What, then, is requisite to transform all this into a comedy? Merely to fancy that our seeming freedom conceals the strings of a dancing jack" (79).[5]

The "Bachelor Apparatus," in the lower portion of *The Large Glass*, contains the "chariot mechanism" which oscillates back and forth and sings the "litany" of the whole "celibate machine." By referring back to the materials and construction of *The Large Glass* as a whole, the refrain enacts the self-obsession and self-reflexiveness which it describes:

> Slow life
> Vicious circle
> onanism
> Horizontal
> Round Trip
> For the Buffer
> Junk of Life
> Cheap Construction
> Tins, Cords
> Iron wire
> Eccentric Wooden Pulleys
> Monotonous fly wheel
> Beer Professor

The autoerotic imagery simultaneously devalues life and art; as in *Krapp's Last Tape*, artistic creation is presented as self-reflexive, masturbatory activity.[6] Indeed the Bachelor Machine is a kind of "masculine hell" (Lebel, 72) in which life is presented as a series of confined and repeated motions. While this machinery is comic, it also entails a pessimistic vision of man, a nihilism the tragic consequences of which Beckett explores in later works, like *The Lost Ones:* "Slow life/Vicious circle."

For both Beckett and Duchamp, the mechanical is associated with loss of human freedom, with intellectual and aesthetic automatism, and with habit,[7] so it must be resisted, undermined, and broken. Thus they satirize not only the machine but also all mechanized forms of order, including the ones that they themselves construct.

Watt, for example, is composed entirely of systematic forms of logic that do not work. It is a novel filled with mathematical calculations and permutations in which everything adds up to *pi* (Kenner, 105). Watt himself is an "untiring logic machine" (Hoefer, 167), whose logic is faulty and misapplied. His extended analysis of Knott's eating arrangement not only includes errors of logic but calls into question the very premise of his search for original causes. The source of Knott's eating arrangement is just one of the numerous questions of causation that, like the repeated question marks scattered throughout the text, the novel raises but does not answer.

Like Beckett, Duchamp uses rational techniques to produce irrational effects. Just as the ordered systems of Beckett's characters, like Molloy's stone sucking (69), give way to randomness and chance, so the careful articulation of mechanisms within *The Large Glass* gives way to nonlogic and irrationality. Like the elaborate system for coordinating random glances of the academic committee in *Watt*, which is designed to help the committee accomplish nothing in a more efficient way, the "boxing match" component of the Bachelor Machine operates to no purpose. It is an intricate network of interlocking motions and causal reactions: a marble releases and activates various "rams" in a "clockwork" mechanism that is designed to but does not strip the bride. Like other elaborate contrivances described in *The Green Box*, it parodies mechanistic precision and the notion of causation.

Anytime a complicated system operates too smoothly, it is undermined by contradiction or self-conscious references to its fictionality (as in *How It Is*, 144). When Mercier and Camier fail to meet at the opening of the novel, Beckett calls attention to the controlled miscalculations as an elaborate contrivance: "What a stink of artifice" (9). A comparable technique appears in *The Green Box*, where Duchamp describes the intricate process in which the "gas" of many bachelors is transformed into "spangles," a "vapour of inertia," "splashes," and then a few distilled and refined "drops." The lengthy pseudoscientific description concludes with, "What a drip!" The remark not only puns on the word "drop" and the ejaculation it represents, but also and more importantly it ridicules Duchamp's own intricate causal system and be-labored description.

Both Beckett and Duchamp toy with the terminology of logic as well. The subtitle for *The Large Glass* later becomes the title for Duchamp's last work, *Etant Données (Given)*. But what sounds like the beginning of a syllogism gives way only to non sequitur and nonlogic. Beckett, too, toys mercilessly with the holy language of logic: the "qua qua" (caca) of *How It Is*, or Watt's question, "But a fortiori were several dogs the same thing as the dog?" (96). In the work of Duchamp and Beckett, reason and logic are constructed and used only to be dismantled and destroyed. In their work we find pockets of logic, loci of order, and mechanisms of control, but the ordered systems are emptied of purpose and surrounded by a prevailing nonsense and absurdity.

The works, moreover, produce a particular kind of nonsense, one that is in-extricably tied to our logical forms and our notions of truth. Both Beckett and Duchamp are fascinated by the paradox of tautology, in which statements can be both true and meaningless at the same time.[8] Beckett's interest, for ex-ample, in the "law of the excluded middle," is expressed in his oft-quoted praise for St. Augustine's statement:

> "Do not despair; one of the thieves was saved. Do not presume; one of the thieves was damned." That sentence has a wonderful shape. It is the shape that matters. (Hobsen, 153)

Watt is in fact structured by a grand tautology: each life is just one term in an endless cycle of lives without value, *and* each life is charmingly idiosyncratic, filled with poignant emotion, absolutely unique and inherently valuable. Both of these statements are true in the novel (as they are, perhaps, in life as well), and every character is viewed through this paradigmatic tautology—from Arsene and his fictional creation Mary, to Watt, Erskine, Arthur, to the great Knott himself.[9] While Beckett continually uses contradiction to under-mine logic, the excluded middle is an even more effective and paradoxical de-vice for criticizing rationality, for it empties logic from the inside while allow-ing the structure of truth to remain. It is, like *Watt* as a whole, a structure of "great formal brilliance and indeterminable import" (74).

Duchamp's interest in the excluded middle is expressed in a number of ways. He constructs a door between two frames so it can be both "open" and "closed" at the same time. For the center section of *The Large Glass*, close to where the imagined union takes place, he designs a "Wilson-Lincoln" ef-fect—one image containing the profiles of two different men. *The Green Box* includes another visual tautology: a step or fan formation can be seen both protruding from and receding from the picture plane. *The Large Glass* as a whole functions in much the same way: it is simultaneously a figure for union and disunion, love and isolation, completion and fragmentation, chance and control. Thus Duchamp's work, like Beckett's, is constructed so that it can be read in mutually exclusive and contradictory ways.

Both Beckett and Duchamp create art that forces us to confront the limits of intellection, that traps us in a hermeneutic game. Duchamp once nailed a hatrack on the floor, designed, like his work in general, to "trip" people up. He titled it *Trébuchet,* a chess move that sacrifices a pawn to "trip" the opponent. His work, and much of Beckett's, is comprised of just such moves in the realm of art. Both produce essentially nonsensical and absurd art designed to short-circuit the intellect even as it engages the mind. In an article entitled "Chess with the Audience: Samuel Beckett's *Endgame,*" James Acheson describes the play as being "deliberately designed to resist even the most ingenious of explications. . . . In no matter what direction we move as audience we are in check" (33). Duchamp and Beckett multiply meanings and possibilities for interpretation in ways that suggest the instability of truth and reality. In the same way that *Watt* is about the different ways of knowing "nought," so Duchamp's work is about man's urge for understanding and its inevitable failure. In effect, *The Large Glass* is a grand joke on the discovery and disclosure of truth; no totalizing idea or stable truth is disclosed (dis-clothed) or "stripped bare" in this kind of art.

The use of tautological structures is a favorite device of authors determined to sketch out epistemological limits.[10] In the case of Beckett and Duchamp, the tautologies within and shaping the works can also be related to a particular view of language, namely, that language is itself a closed and tautological system. Linda Ben-Zvi and Jennie Skerl have convincingly argued for the influence of Fritz Mauthner upon Beckett: "Mauthner pointed out that all true propositions are tautologies; they are not true because of empirical truth but because of our prevailing mode of speaking. . . . The result of this critique of language is that external reality is unknowable" (Skerl, 477). Though it is unlikely that Duchamp read Mauthner, he did read language philosophy, and his radical skepticism regarding language closely resembles Beckett's. "Language is just no damn good," he once said. "I use it because I have to, but I don't put any trust in it. Once I became interested in that group of philosophers in England, the ones who argue that all language tends to become tautological and therefore meaningless" (Tomkins, 31–32). Indeed both Beckett and Duchamp take as a central subject the inability of language to describe or explain reality. In the same way that Beckett's writings and writers continually express the failure and impotence of language, so Duchamp's incessant language games and linguistic devices all use language in order to subvert it, to parody it as a means of communication and as a vehicle for truth.

The writings of Duchamp and Beckett are extremely different, yet they do overlap in a few interesting ways. Both turn language into mechanisms of sorts, in order to short-circuit meaningful connections and any successful communication. For example, Watt's inverted language is a mechanical and logical reversal that paradoxically combines coherent method with dissociated speech. The exhaustion of logical possibilities throughout the novel turns discourse into a repetitive and compulsive but inefficient system. Throughout Beckett's work, language is produced automatically by machines and machinelike speakers, who are strangely dissociated from the words that they utter (*Waiting for Godot, Not I, Radio II*).[11] Words flow mechanically and uncontrollably from some characters once, like Krapp's tape machine, they are switched on. Communication is satirized throughout, but nowhere so bitterly as in *How It Is*, where to learn a language is to become a victim—"mechanically at least where words involved" (64).

Duchamp also constructs mechanisms of language: in *Anemic Cinema*, a machine spins words and phrases into dizzying spirals. In *The Green Box* he designs a series of strange and original dictionaries, one, for example, using extreme closeup images to create a new "language" of film.[12] David Antin observes that in his proposed dictionaries Duchamp "approaches [a] malevolent, mechanical analysis of language" (104). Like Watt's systematic inversions, Duchamp's new linguistic systems are based on a series of logical relations; the result, however, is an infinite regress of new conventions and complete verbal confusion. The new "languages" function only to satirize communication and to underscore the conventional nature of ordinary discourse.

In addition, both Beckett and Duchamp subvert definition in a variety of ways. Duchamp's titles neither define nor describe his strange ready-mades, but they do situate his objects in a linguistic field in a way that suggests the disjunctiveness of words and things. *Fresh Window*, as Antin observes, creates semantic contradictions between which the object oscillates without resolution. The object is neither a "fresh widow" (though its black windows imply death), nor what we would normally call a "french window" (104). In general, the ready-mades exist in an odd space purposely designed to render ordinary language inoperative. By sustaining the tension between their status as art objects and their status as objects of life, they cannot really be defined as one or the other.

Thus Duchamp's *Fountain* is a nonsensical object: it both is and is not a "fountain," both is and is not a "real" urinal, both is and is not "art." Not to suggest any possible influence but merely to examine an interesting parallel, consider Knott's "pseudo-pot" (83), which like Duchamp's, both is and is not a pot:

> It resembled a pot, it was almost a pot, but it was not a pot of which one could say, Pot, pot, and be comforted. It was in vain that it answered, with unexceptional adequacy, all the purposes, and performed all the offices of a pot, it was not a pot. (81)

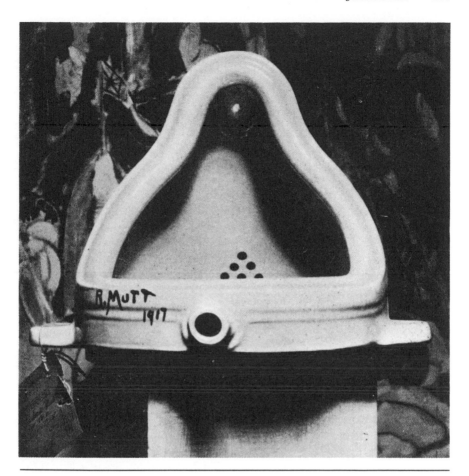

MARCEL DUCHAMP, *Fountain.* Courtesy Philadelphia Museum of Art, Library #18356, Arensberg Archives.

Aside from the obvious humor and the intrusion of pots, slops (*Krapp* and *Fizzles)* into the realm of art, in both cases words are disengaged from things. Simple everyday, familiar objects are employed to mark the limits of language, which fails not only to define metaphysical truth but fails also to define commonplace reality.

Nor, for these artists, is language effective in defining a coherent identity. Duchamp's masquerade as "Rrose Sélavy" divides the self and (by means of a pun, "érose c'est la vie") linguistic meaning as well. Consider this passage from Duchamp's interview with Pierre Cabanne:

C: But what do you believe in?

D: Nothing, of course! The word belief is another error . . .

C: Nevertheless, you believe in yourself?

D: No. Not even that. I don't believe in the word being. . . . It's an essential concept, which doesn't exist at all in reality and which I don't believe in, though people in general have a cast iron belief in it. No one ever thinks of not believing in "I am."[13] (89–90)

Certainly, Beckett thinks of "not believing in 'I am,' " and he continually associates the problematic consciousness of his characters with the problem of language. The Unnamable attempts but fails to find words appropriate to the self (324–26). "And then," says Molloy, "sometimes there arose within me, confusedly, a kind of consciousness, which I express by saying, I said, etc. . . . or . . . by means of other figures quite as deceitful" (88).

The confusion of genres and the confusion of the boundaries of "art" and "life" are part of this assault on language. Quite often the works cannot be labeled or defined in any clearer way than the objects within them.[14] The art not only describes but also produces semantic slippage. Words no longer "fit," and we witness a world in which objects, experiences, and works of art all become "unnamable."[15]

Thus the human being, logic, and language are all presented as mechanisms that are inefficient and broken down. Perhaps for Beckett, as for the dadaists before him, the irrationality within art is a response to war, its extremes of rationalism and absurd destruction. Beckett, however, more fully explores the risk involved in dismantling conceptual systems (like language) and dissociating mechanisms of control (like logic). To the extent that his absurd unleashes a cruelty, suffering, and violence of its own, his art is very different from Duchamp's. Nevertheless, both take their point of departure from a failure of language and produce a paradoxical art that uses words to mark their limits.[16]

Linguistic pessimism and modern nihilism combine to shape an anti-art aesthetic, an art of nonrelation (Dearlove) or "inexpression" in which art, too, is presented in a state of collapse and disintegration. Beckett and Duchamp both create work that gives the superficial impression of artlessness; both use chance procedures (Duchamp's *Three Standard Stoppages*, Beckett's *Lessness*), to counter the image of artist as master of his materials.[17] In both cases, the artistic oeuvre is purposely fragmented and suggests breakdown. This is the art and the "literature of exhaustion," where, in the words of John Barth, "to cease to create altogether would be fairly meaningful" (31). Indeed Duchamp's abandonment of art for chess in 1934 was a logical and "fairly meaningful" step in his progressive devaluation of art. Since he persistently (if quietly) continued to produce work, neither Duchamp nor Beckett "cease[d] to create altogether." On the contrary, both play out their endgame moves within the realm of art. They create an art of inexpression that suggests "there is nothing to express" (no adequate materials, certainly not language), "nothing from which to express" (no stable identity or ego), "no power to express" (artistic control gives way to chance), "no desire to express" (art is completely devalued), and "still the obligation to express" (Duchamp worked secretly for years on *Etants Données*, while Beckett continues to produce forceful, if increasingly fragmentary, texts).

The production of "inexpressive art" is a fundamentally irrational and paradoxical gesture. In fact, the ironic stance of Beckett throughout "Three Dialogues" (with Georges Duthuit) closely resembles Duchamp's most famous self-portrait, *With My Tongue In My Cheek:*

> Duthuit: Are you suggesting that the painting of [Bram] van Velde is inexpressive?
> Beckett: (*A fortnight later*) Yes.
> Duthuit: You realize the absurdity of what you advance?
> Beckett: I hope I do.
>
> (19–20)

The satiric tone, ironic pedantry, the contradictions in Beckett's essay recall Duchamp's continuous ironies concerning art. In both cases, the art is doubly ironic. The devaluation of art leads to more art, and the rejection of mastery leads to masterpieces. In the case of Beckett especially, the aesthetic of inexpression is posited only to be contradicted in work that expresses human emotion in powerful and original ways.

Notes

1. On the profound importance of the visual arts for Beckett, see McMillan. See Mercier (1977, 90) and Bair (465–67) for discussions of Beckett and Duchamp that stress the artists' interest in chess and the use of endgame imagery in their art.

2. Beckett is not a "con" artist to the same degree as Duchamp, yet other critics have also noted such tendencies in his art. See Brater (1975) and Kristeva.

3. See *The Bride Stripped Bare by Her Bachelors, Even,* ed. Richard Hamilton, trans. George Heard Hamilton. All quotations are from this edition.

4. A different Beckettian pseudocouple (*First Love*) is compared by Julia Kristeva to the "clockwork autoeroticism" of *The Large Glass* (248).

5. On Beckett's humor and Bergson, see Ruby Cohn, *The Comic Gamut.*

6. For the comparison of *Krapp's Last Tape* to *The Large Glass,* I am indebted to a discussion at the Samuel Beckett Conference, University of Texas at Austin, March 1984.

7. The term "estheticized automatism" is from "Three Dialogues, by Samuel Beckett and Georges Duthuit," (21). For Beckett's discussion of habit, see *Proust,* 9–12.

8. A person who says "either it is raining or it is not" has said something true but meaningless. The statement offers no information about the weather and tells us nothing at all.

9. Other kinds of tautology are employed by Beckett as well. All lengthy calculations and extended analyses serve to accomplish nothing; at the end, "x is still x" (Kenner, 151). See, for example, Arsene's speech on "beginning again" (*Watt*, 47).

10. For a more recent example of the excluded middle used as a structuring device, see Pynchon's *The Crying of Lot 49*.

11. See, for example, *Not I:* "or the machine . . . more likely the machine . . . so disconnected . . . never got the message" (17).

12. Duchamp generates his "dictionaries" in an effort to find a suitable language for the bride's "commands, authorizations" through which contact (not physical but verbal) is made with the bachelor machine.

13. Establishing yet another parallel with Beckett, Duchamp's systematic skepticism arose from what he called his "Cartesian mind": "I refused to accept anything, doubted everything," he once said (Tomkins, 17).

14. On the confusion of genres in Beckett's work, see Perloff and Abbott (1984). See also the essays in this volume by Abbot, Dearlove, and Zeifman. On Duchamp, see Buffet. Duchamp says he was looking for a way of working "without being a painter, without being a writer, without taking one of those labels" (Schwarz, 7).

15. Linguistic skepticism thus inspires the de-definitional strategies and intergeneric tactics that make Beckett and Duchamp such important precursors for (and early practitioners of) interdisciplinary art. At a symposium entitled "Intermedia Art: The Era of Interdisciplinary Collaboration" (UCLA, 12 May 1985), composer Philip Glass described Beckett's work as a *major* source of inspiration and influence for contemporary interdisciplinary artists.

16. See Sheppard, who says, "Perhaps the people who first investigated and answered these problems to any extent were the Dadaists. . . . They ventured the daring conclusion that the experiences of nothingness and linguistic aridity can be dealt with not by retreat . . . but by accepting them" (333).

17. On the chance compositional procedures of *Lessness*, see Cohn, *Back to Beckett*, 265.

PART 3

Genre Transformations

DAVID HAYMAN

Beckett: Impoverishing the Means—Empowering the Matter

In the fall of 1972, I asked Samuel Beckett what he was doing at the time, meaning what was he writing. His response was predictable: "Nothing." But then, as often happens, he volunteered the information that he was about to go to London to witness (and doubtless oversee) the rehearsal of a new play which would feature the speaking mouth, a neglected part of the actor's anatomy. The play was of course *Not I*, and Beckett went on to describe his strategy: to mask the actor behind a curtain in which a hole would be cut to reveal only her spotlit mouth in ceaseless activity. Though he did not say so, the voice was an extension of the character Winnie in *Happy Days*, Winnie reduced to the absolute minimum. What he did say was that she would not say anything of interest, that the point of the play was to be the device. He exaggerated, as he often does in the service of his typically wry wit, but the emphasis is not without importance. For him that play, like so many of his other works, was premised on what may well have been its stimulus or *amocce*, a device which certainly permitted him to give flesh to his verbal impulses.

From the beginning, though not quite so transparently, Beckett seems to have aimed at achieving expressive wealth through the progressive impoverishment of his means.[1] If we limit ourselves as I propose to do to questions of form and ignore philosophical and temperamental considerations, three procedures characterize each of his works.

First, the chosen medium is stripped of one or more of its givens. It is as though Beckett had decided, like Walter Abish in *Alphabetical Africa*, to impose and reveal arbitrary restrictions on the letters he could use in his narrative discourse. Thus, prefiguring the New Novel but extending tendencies already visible in other modernist texts and traceable to Sterne, he insisted on the lack of credible individuality in characters located in the "real" space of Murphy's Dublin and London, explicitly creating a universe of comic puppets bereft of adequate motivation. More emphatically than Eliot or even Pound, his early verse revised poetic diction, discarded meter, roughened texture, and made his most serious points through a screen of outrageous wit and arcane illusion.

Second, by dropping hints, dangling hooks, referring to the missing or spurned paraphernalia, the normative discourse of the subverted convention, he made certain that his audience would experience that discourse as a subtext. Thus, all the givens of the novelistic tradition are vibrantly present in the increasingly static and minimalized development of the trilogy. Character, situation, plot, and setting are simultaneously and repeatedly imposed and denied. Satisfaction is offered to and withheld from the tantalized reader, who would be disappointed were Beckett actually to draw upon narrative resources, to turn his disempowered fictions into conventional novels. The Unnamable cannot, must go on! Full stop. As Judith E. Dearlove puts it, though Beckett's works "never proffer completed conventional structures, his pieces depend on the reader's perception of the disparity between the recognizable fragments he is given and the tradition they deliberately do not fulfill" (*Accommodating the Chaos*, 39–40). But we should go on to say that evidence of the struggle with convention, the mode of subversion as statement, is a central source of reader enjoyment against the grain of a uniformly dreary and uncompromisingly honest vision.

Finally, the very tension established so carefully between the actual and the potential text, between his vehicle and the powers so palpably and firmly spurned, is made to contribute mightily to the significance of the dual text we experience. It matters that Didi and Gogo are clowns in *slow motion* within a modern morality play on a denuded stage. It is important that *Endgame* appears to be taking place within a skull with its eye sockets turned toward the unseen stage of a terminal existence. And what about the Unnamable, which is being forced to project itself into a sequence of active bodies, generating in the process narrative situations more or less adequate to the absence of specifics? In each case Beckett has removed some strategic pillars, leaving others, though never the same ones, in place to support a tottering edifice. Reaching for the sublimated presence in our efforts to accommodate the real absence, we experience powerful tensions that turn such deliberate diminution to increasingly poignant and desparately comic, if not metaphysical, ends. Perhaps Beckett's procedures can be likened and contrasted to those of Matisse, who produced his drawings by a process of elimination, cutting back to the expressive minimal line. In Beckett's case the line itself is attacked, though haunting vestiges of the trappings of discarded conventions remain.

In a career spanning more than fifty years, Beckett has tried his hand at poetry, short fiction, novel, play, pantomime, TV drama, radio script, film. In each case, while remaining rigorously true to his muse, he has reworked and even revolutionized the form, frequently eliciting critical astonishment. As one might expect, the development, anchored as it is in the tenets and even

the conventions of post-Flaubertian modernism, and displaying the character
of a rigorously disciplined creative intelligence, has been gradual. Yet even
the early verse and prose were predictive. The poems, so admirably studied
by Lawrence Harvey, push beyond Eliot in their disjunct concision, in their
oblique allusions, in the simplicity of their discourse larded with arcane language, and in their gestural precision, as in this passage from "Sanies I":

> all the livelong way this day of sweet showers
> > from Portrane on the seashore
> Donabate sad swans of Turvey Swords
> pounding along in three ratios like a sonata
> like a Ritter with pommelled scrotum atra cura
> > on the step
> Botticelli from the fork down pestling the
> > transmission
> tires bleeding voiding zeep the highway
> all heaven in the sphincter
> *the* sphincter
>
> > > (*Poems in English*, 30)

Not only are the by-now familiar themes already evident, but the sexual and
scatological wit are put to clearly antipoetic uses; the language and the
rhythm are clipped, the reference to Irish towns (an instance of privileged information carried to an almost absurd extreme), the insertion of German and
Latin, the opposition established between sound and meaning, the curious
juxtaposition of tires that bleed, void, and zeep, and the driver's presumably
hemorrhoidal sphincter or the car's faulty exhaust system—all of these and
other effects are thoroughly modern and, even so, even today, surprising.
Here and elsewhere, Beckett displays his adherence to the latest trends, indeed his extension of them in what must be seen as a young man's effort to
outdo as well as *épater*.

If anything, this quality is clearer in the world-weary "Enueg II," where the
language and the local color are more transparent and where prose, laced
with slogans and citations, undercuts the occasional near-poetic image:

> world world world world
> and the face grave
> cloud against the evening
>
> de morituris nihil nisi
>
> and the face crumbling shyly
> too late to darken the sky
> blushing away into the evening
> shuggering away like a gaffe

> veronica mundi
> veronica munda
> give us a wipe for the love of Jesus
>
> sweating like Judas
> tired of dying
> tired of policemen
> feet in marmalade
> perspiring profusely
> heart in marmalade
> smoke more fruit
> the old heart the old heart
> breaking outside of congress
> doch I assure thee
> lying on O'Connell Bridge
> goggling at the tulips of the evening
> the green tulips
> shining round the corner like an anthrax
> shining on Guinness's barges
>
> the overtone the face
> too late to brighten the sky
> doch doch I assure thee
>
> (*Poems in English*, 26–27)

Whatever the serious implications of this poem, its image of a world-weary and disenfranchised identity set against a disheartening urban backdrop, the complex play upon the very nature of poetic discourse, the elaborate distortion of clichés, pushes the reader toward formal pleasures. It is a trait shared with the later work that this poem, with its exposure of what is generally left subliminal, can be enjoyed immediately by the unlettered and gradually by the lettered. Perhaps this is an inevitable outcome of a formal strategy that systematically disempowers the tools it employs, the coy withdrawal of proffered satisfactions, the subtle intertextual games. More likely, it is a mark of the writer's sensitivity and tact.

The early poetry and prose both display weaknesses, such as the occasional lapse into leaden wit or the self-conscious aping of a too-much-admired Joyce. Of this, *More Pricks Than Kicks*, for all the brilliance of its subversions, is a case in point. This jagged sequence of tales, whose inconsequent action features a fantastic and semiautobiographical protagonist, is characterized by ellipses, a disparaging narrative voice, epiphanic revelations, and disturbing behavior. We can trace all such procedures back to Sterne, to Flaubert's *Education sentimentale,* and to Joyce's *Dubliners* and *Portrait* if we wish to see Beckett as elaborating upon the theme of the antihero while systematically stripping and distorting narrative attributes. But we will still be struck by the ability of these disjunct episodes to deliver realistic illusions, to establish contexts, to elicit sympathy, even while milking their circumstances for the readily available absurdity. In short, the misadventures of a patently inadequate Belacqua satisfy us despite, as well as by virtue of, their disruption of the ordinary means of conveying action and their delivery of incomplete and even tentative messages. Even lobsters feel the heat.

Let's skip by the splendors of *Murphy*, with its Sternean narrator given to uttering pseudo-Dickensian judgments, its cast of emblematic but vulnerable clowns, its outlandishly stilted dialogue, its use of specifics to convey philosophical generalizations, and its stripped-down, schematic plot. A more spectacular instance of the sort of productive poverty to which I am alluding is *Watt*, which blends Sterne, Flaubert, Joyce, Dante, and perhaps Kafka to produce a most austerely comic narrative. Here, the rhetorical exuberance, the intricate catalogues of gestures and opinions, the elaborate formal play, seem only to substitute narrative strategy for content while putting traditional point of view through fantastic paces. It can be argued, and doubtless proved, that such moments as the wonderful spoof on an academic meeting, the exposition on the various verbal codes used by Watt to fail to deliver his message, the treatise on the disposition of the food uneaten by Mr. Knott, all lend substance to the novel's message potential. But the pleasure of this text is drawn far more from the zany tactics by which it frustrates development and the elegance of its subterfuges than from its action. At best, the speaker of this narrative is a madman; at worst, he is utterly without authority, a prefiguration of the figment Malone spinning his tale from the fibers of his verbal environment.

Here as elsewhere, Beckett's procedures put in question all aspects of narrative validity. Thus the myth of Watt's encounter with Mr. Knott has the same validity as the myth which he himself is said to have concocted to account for the distribution of that godlike lunatic's leavings. We are in the realm that vibrates between but never quite touches the poles of the probable and the improbable, consequence and inconsequence. The diversions that enable Beckett to join the late Joyce and Sterne, by virtue of their dual dedication to irrelevance and style, become the substance of this tale, a substance through which we occasionally glimpse self-annulling but intriguing meanings and even human joy and distress. Gone is the pretense of and appeal to causality and the lure of verisimilitude, but not gone without a trace. For here, as in all of Beckett's work, we are haunted by the ghost of narratives past, the efficacious echo of a novelistic decorum that has been left to glimmer in the shadows.

Not only is the intertextual burden, the echoes of other books and discourses, everywhere available, but the very reflexes of tale telling are continuously manifest. It is not unimportant that readers of Joyce's last book can discover in the middle of Arsene's interminable address of welcome and farewell to Watt a rewriting of the central event in Joyce's *Finnegans Wake*, the encounter of HCE with the cad in Phoenix Park.[2] But we are more likely to be struck at every turning of this hilarious-in-the-telling tale by its power to conjure up *the hope of* a story, a coherent allegory and perhaps a truly credible act or persona, a hope it will invariably dash and effectively crush underfoot as it makes its erratic progress, much in the manner of the Watt-like specter Watt sees as he peers back down the road from the railway station:

> The feet, following each other in rapid and impetuous succession, were flung, the right foot to the right, the left foot to the left, as much outwards as forwards, with the result that, for every stride of say three feet in compass, the ground gained did not exceed one. This gave to the gait a kind of shackled smartness, most painful to witness. Watt felt them suddenly glow in the dark place, and go out, the words, *The only cure is diet.* (*Watt*, 226)

World War II was a watershed period for Beckett, and *Watt* was the first major work to follow it, but the most startling results are the works in French. Whatever the reasons for Beckett's decision to write in French, the practice resulted in a deceptive loosening of the rhetorical fabric of his narratives and in the elaboration of his later style. Thus, beginning with *Mercier et Camier*, with its obvious echoes and instructive distortions of Flaubert's last fictional work, Beckett's overpowering doubt asserts itself as a shaping force, seemingly restricting his ability to say but actually strengthening and tightening his utterance while doing further violence to narrative conventions.

If *Mercier et Camier* prefigures aspects of *Godot*, the message of *Watt* infects the articulation of the trilogy by means that are in large measure formal, turning what had been a discourse on the improbable into a frontal attack on the impossible. Beckett's language becomes something more than a means of saying, just as it has earlier been more than a means of telling. *Molloy*'s monologue, for example, brings into being a vision that refuses to exist on a referential plane, that refuses to request or impose a suspension of disbelief at the same time that it engrosses the reader in its texture and development.

Beckett's four major French novels are all variations on the monologue becoming increasingly interior and "poetic" without, for all that, turning into interior monologue. Indeed, they are nearer to the convention of the eighteenth-century confessional narrative than to either Jamesean and Proustian modernism, with its emphasis on subtle nuances of character and situation and veiled plot developments, or to Joycean stream-of-consciousness, with its elaborate versions of the world as experience. Like Joyce's *Wake* but more like Kafka, they are generated by a sort of oneiric logic, a seemingly subliminal associative process that closer scrutiny reveals to be a mode of self-generation, of language growing out of its own potential. Unlike Kafka's fictions, however, they resist the tug of metaphor and reject the possibility of a viable and rational universe.[3]

Or perhaps we should see this as a two-tiered development in the novel beginning with *Watt*. On the macrotextual level of the "action," we find events conjoined in a whimsical and seemingly haphazard manner, even though the text pretends to make every effort to rationalize its development. We note, for example, how Watt is introduced through a distanced encounter before he is followed to the house of Mr. Knott. Neither his appearance nor the trip to Knottland has been adequately rationalized, and the same may be said of just about every narrative element in the text as well as about the various narrators and narrative procedures it employs. The only predictable element, once we have left the bench of Mr. Hackett, is the presence of Watt in each passage. Everything else is arbitrary, against the grain both of narrative logic and of the quixotic quest pattern. The whole text can be thought of as oneiric or subliminal in the sense that it echoes the operation of the unconscious, or at least it seems to be drawn from levels of experience we have no way of verifying.

What can be said about *Watt* is in different ways applicable to the two voices of *Molloy*, with their double unreliability, as well as to the double quest theme and structure of that novel with its deceptive analogical component. All of Beckett's fictions are false or partial multiple allegories, just as all of his protagonists and voices are clownish without being farcical. We might add that, because the actions described are precisely those that more conventional novelists would omit, *Molloy* and the other novels call to mind an amazing range of intertexts even without citation of direct allusion. Indeed, not action or even inaction but nonaction is the substance of these nonnovelistic developments, and the most emphatic and convincing clown is the shaping force that articulates the text, the "authoritative" voice "*mise en abîme*."

On the microtextual level, self-generative procedures dominate and Beckett willingly lets the language tell the tale, becoming action in its own right. In passage after passage, the narrative voice seems caught up in its own web of associations. Contexts are derived from the need to elaborate upon words that have found their way into the utterance. Humor is frequently a function of the potential of language to exhibit its inner absurdity, to fail. More important, the microtext provides the clues needed to disclose subtexts that frequently overwhelm the dominant discourse. In the trilogy, for example, as in a rigorous allegory or satire, there is at least one carefully elaborated infranarrative development, which is signaled by a system of accentuated rhyming details. As I have argued elsewhere, *Molloy* establishes this dimension in part by counterpoising the two narratives in such a way that readers may perceive most, if not all, the phenomena in one half as revisions of details from the other.[4] Thus the sucking stones gathered and distributed with such care and then carelessly jettisoned by Molloy in Part I are analogous to the keys Moran accidentally scatters during a violent encounter and then must painfully recover.

The reader is confronted with dozens of similar details, challenged to account for them, though free to ignore them, in the process of assimilating a text that does not lend itself to full recuperation either as narrative or as allegory but continually raises the possibility of doing both. More important, we eventually discover that there are also systems keyed to the trilogy as a whole, systems which can be recuperated by the industrious reader willing to play the games. Those same systems, belied though they are by a seemingly inconsequent surface, inevitably return us to the verbal texture from which we have departed. All of this and more flies in the face of novelistic tradition, establishing, as all truly viable innovations must, a new tradition or rather a cluster of new conventions, partial readings in a post-Beckettian vein.[5] Such tactics, and there are far more than I have indicated, suggest the central defamiliarizing mannerism of the Beckett text, its deliberate impoverishment of the powerful, but perhaps overfamiliar, formal conventions within which he pretends to be working. Beyond that, we may discern the entire body of narrative (and philosophical) writing mouldering under and bearing fruit within these antinovels.

If anything, the plays, the TV and radio scripts, the film, provide even clearer evidence of these disencumbering, dismembering, and reanimating procedures. Beckett's *Film* is all too obviously an exercise in rigorous excision. Who else would choose to photograph an actor famous for his face almost entirely from the rear? Who else would make a mechanical sequence of inconsequent movements the subject of his discourses while insisting on the meticulous recording of an undistinguished context? Who else would make use of sound in a conventionally silent context only for a single "shhh"? In this instance, as in every other, the medium clearly serves to constitute the message in ways that Marshall McLuhan might approve of but could not necessarily predict. Further, as elsewhere, though Beckett's *amocce* was an attempt to counter Berkeley's dictum "esse est percipi," the result is a radically unstable visual message, an open work capable of delighting on many levels the openminded viewer but presented as a conundrum by virtue of what it does not do in a context where absence is presence.

This view of *Film* flies in the face of an interesting argument advanced by S. E. Gontarski, who feels that, since technical difficulties prevented Beckett from completing his project, "to explore the human consequences that follow from" Berkeley's proposition, the work is unsatisfactory. This is true even though, as Gontarski is careful to note, Beckett himself said the proposition is to have "no true value" (*Film*, 130). For Gontarski, whose conclusions could also be drawn from Beckett's remarks concerning *Not I*,[6] such an attitude is central to Beckett's aesthetic: "Beckett's art is often more concerned with formal relationships than with . . . theme" (130). Gontarski seems to beg the question of why in fact, here and elsewhere, Beckett does elaborate themes (generally metaphysical in nature) and why themes, like subject matter, are so frequently designed to underscore the disadvantages of the chosen form.

One would almost say that Beckett has deliberately overturned the classic Flaubertian dictum that matter must equal manner. In *Film* he has certainly applied his Berkeleyan theme in such a way as to subvert the seeing nature of the camera (a fact underscored by his use of still photos). The progress of his conception speaks eloquently for the way he fought (and acquiesced to) the medium to achieve the desired internal dynamic. Interestingly, Gontarski sees this struggle as a sign of failure: "Despite Beckett's technical achievements with *Film*, the work never coalesces. Beckett seems, at almost every stage in the creative process, to have engaged in a battle with his medium" (35). This obvious and correct observation could doubtless be made about almost any of Beckett's works. It is in fact central to my argument that the (always at least partly unsuccessful) struggle with different media was the necessary creative condition from the start. It derives from Beckett's preoccupation with inexpressible and incommunicable states and the nature of absence or nonmeaning in a human context that insists on naming and justifying itself. In terms of the precise project, one could agree that *Film* was a particularly resounding defeat, but I would suggest that defeat snatched from the jaws of victory is frequently Beckett's hallmark. We have long known that inevitable failure, as in the case of Mallarmé's "Livre" and Flaubert's "Book about Nothing," can be as useful a goal or goad as possible success. *Film*, which attempts and fails to convey the shifting identities of the camera I and the viewing I/object/actor, finally succeeds—by using and abusing its medium, de-realizing even the camera's ability to record trivial aspects of our world, tensing our filmic habits against their abuse—in refreshing our perception of filmic potential by making us register both image and trace as part of the narrative procedure.

A final example, this time from Beckett's theater, should bring us back to the point at which we began this discussion. Though hardly his most radical play, *Comédie* or *Play* is a powerful and remarkably successful instance of the use of theatrical space and conventions against the potential for dramatic expression. The title, like that of *Film*, strips this work of specificity while promising the sort of pleasure that accompanies theatrical events. (In French, it has an even stronger double potential.) Three ashen heads protruding from the great urns in which their decaying bodies are confined are obliged or permitted to speak in monotonous voices. Thus the space of the stage is the theater for the absence of human gestures of all sorts, an absence that underscores its presence by virtue of the rigor of its presentation. No audience will miss the anomalous quality.

As if to reinforce that powerful diminution of the actor's capacities, we have the trivial tale the characters tell and the monstrous cliché their French triangular tragedy represents. Beckett's supreme achievement is to have made of such materials a searing comic drama. But his trump card is paradoxically the ability to cast the least visible component of modern theater, its *spotlight*, as star performer, to raise this device to the condition of controller as opposed to reinforcer of the action and, by the same token, to include the viewer in the procedures of production, turning the terror of attention into the endless process of living with pointlessness. Our three impenitent penitents are finally doomed to repeat a transitory tick of the flesh for eternity. The splendors of existence are, on the one hand, reduced by the trivial situation and the persistently inquisitory light, the light of a postmortal and eminently theatrical third degree, to the lowest common denominator of boulevard farce. On the other hand, they rise to the level of Dante.

Beckett is completely attuned to the tendencies of post-Flaubertian and post-Symbolist modernism, with its commitment to the right word in the right place and absolute formal liberty. He is also attuned to the various components of what we loosely call the avant-garde, which is, after all, ancillary to that tendency. But there is, as we must note, another dimension—the crucial one. Unlike many of the brasher proponents of the new, the different, the outrageous, and the unacceptable, and far more in the direct line of Flaubert and other monks of literature, Beckett's form is in each instance the perfect vehicle for his deeply held personal philosophy of the at-once motiveless and necessary nature of the human predicament, the philosophy that has driven him at each stage in his career toward ever fresher and more precise formulations against the grain but in the best spirit of the great traditions that have mapped out that predicament through the ages. Beckett's move back to basics is a full-dress affair.

In this case, artistry lies in knowing what to eliminate as well as what to say. It lies in knowing how not to say and how much power can be entrusted to the insignificant word, gesture, pause. Beckett's understanding of the nature of form underlies his response to silence, inaction, and absence, goes far beyond the limits of the absurd into the realm of absolute significance. His timing goes beyond that of the consummate clown. His self-deprecation, honest as it is, an attitude that invests even the least of his creative (and personal) acts, is the ultimate in self-assertiveness. What he denies to his conventions he bestows upon his forms and his *in*formed reader/viewer/self.

As a corollary to this, we should note how every word, gesture, silence, is precisely calculated, pondered . . . excessive . . . a blot on the absolute. Here, to Flaubert, Beckett joins Mallarmé, for whom the minimal mark is both too much and essential. Though Beckett's achieved elegance is neither the ultimate statement nor the perfect utterance, though his vision appears at times closer to that of the German post-dadaist Joseph Beuys, whose best-known work is a kitchen chair loaded with what appears to be animal fat, there is an adequacy in every wrinkle of the verbal skin, from the obsessive catalogues of *Watt* and *Molloy* to the oppressive silences of *Rockaby* and the babble of *Not I*. A terrible adequacy of delight results, joining aesthetic truth to participatory madness in a species of total intertext through the means art and society have concocted to impose order on the unflattering image of experience.

Notes

1. The position taken here is, on the surface at least, not unusual. Critics of various persuasions have noted Beckett's manipulation of conventions. My approach differs in that it sees the forceful diminution of means as a fundamental strategy pretty much from the start. The tactic derives in good measure from the tradition in which Beckett's muse is anchored: the post-Flaubertian, post-Joycean, and post-Proustian modernism and its parallel manifestations in the other arts. Beckett's manipulations are, however, unusually consistent, as are his thematic concerns, and though he never attacks conventions simply to expose their soft underbelly, his systematic dismantling seems unprecedented and singularly appealing. For a sampling of parallel and divergent readings, see A. Alvarez, *Beckett*, 50–51 and passim; S. E. Gontarski, *The Intent of Undoing in Samuel Beckett's Dramatic Texts*, 2–3 and passim; and Judith E. Dearlove, *Accommodating the Chaos: Samuel Beckett's Nonrelational Art*, 39–40; and Stephen J. Rosen, *Samuel Beckett and the Pessimistic Tradition*, 217. Of these, Alvarez is probably closest to sharing my approach to form. But Gontarski's description of Beckett's "phenomenological reduction" of theatrical discourse is to the point, as is Dearlove's view that Beckett "sought to create a nonrelational art by breaking apart . . . pieces of identity, time, space, and language."

2. See my "A Meeting in the Park and a Meeting on the Bridge: Joyce and Beckett," 372–84.

3. I have developed the concept of self-generation in Beckett in a brief essay, "Joyce—Beckett/Joyce," in *The Seventh of Joyce*, ed. Bernard Benstock (Bloomington: Indiana University Press, 1982), 38–40; see also *Journal of Beckett Studies*, no. 7 (Spring 1982): 102–5. But see also Richard Pearce's discussion in *The Novel of Motion*, 38–55.

4. In all fairness, I should say that only a handful of critics have accepted this early reading. Dearlove (*Accommodating the Chaos*, 73) simply places it in a sequence of conflicting views so as to show (correctly enough) the undecidability of all readings. David Hayman, "Quest for Meaninglessness: The Boundless Poverty of *Molloy*," in *Beckett Now*, 140–45.

5. Among the writers who have reread Beckett through their own texts, we may list Raymond Federman, the later Alain Robbe-Grillet, and Ludovic Janvier.

6. See the beginning of this essay.

H. PORTER ABBOTT

Beckett and Autobiography

> He thinks words fail him, he thinks because words fail him he's on his way to
> my speechlessness, to being speechless with my speechlessness, he would like
> it to be my fault that words fail him, of course words fail him. He tells his story
> every five minutes, saying it is not his, there's cleverness for you.
> —*Text for Nothing 4*

When *Not I* was first staged in 1972, there were those who saw it as autobiography.[1] The play seemed to express vividly the predicament of its shy author, a man by then known everywhere, but known only through his words ("whole body like gone"). The repeated reference to his age ("coming up to seventy") was hard to resist, while the flat denial in the title and the pointed reference to the speaker's gender ("she!") were so insistent as almost to require that we take them as a form of protesting too much.

If *Not I* is indeed a kind of microautobiography, is it an aberration—an eleventh-hour effort, perhaps, to scoop the biographers? Or is autobiography, or something like it, what Beckett has been writing all along? Could autobiography provide a key to the astonishing formal strangeness and diversity of Beckett's output—a strangeness and diversity that become more, not less, astonishing as Beckett comes up to eighty?

I want to make the argument that if Beckett is not engaged in autobiography, he is engaged in something in the near vicinity, something formally repeatable, with identifiable roots. The immediate problem with this argument is that Beckett's work does not look like autobiography. Further, it is all coded as fiction. To treat it as autobiography is to invite the kind of diminution of fictive art that autobiographical criticism so frequently produces. Whatever Beckett may have said in a rash moment, Hamm and Clov are not the author and his wife, and to identify them as such is to make the play a case history, that is, to trivialize it.

There are, however, two basic kinds of autobiographical act, only one of which invites a confident alignment of details in the life of the author with details in the texts he or she creates. This one type of autobiographical act is dominated by the assumption that one can produce a text that expresses or stands for oneself, a "readable" text (in Barthesian terms), one that aspires to a pleasing narrative shape through which the author says "This is my life." Writing it, the author creates for him or herself a finished artistic existence. The author can be either deceived or undeceived in this, but, in effect, the self in its undefinability and unfinishedness is escaped or denied by a literary stand-in. Though it asserts its nonfictional status, such an act draws heavily from fiction. This is a natural consequence of the desire to confer public and conventional status on the autobiographer. This kind of autobiographical act fits Northrop Frye's identification of autobiography as a subdivision of the novel.[2]

The other kind of autobiographical act is animated by an acute distrust of conventional art. It seeks to escape public forms in order to recover, preserve, at the very least pay homage to, a live presence of self. Such acts seem considerably closer to what Beckett does, for they continually discourage any easy alignment between the text and the "facts" of the author's life. Such autobiographical acts are dominated, as Beckett's art has been, by an awareness of the treachery of literary expression, its tendency (because of its public nature) to alienate or dissociate from self. Genre, as Sartre wrote, is a kind of bloodsucking ghoul with whom one wrestles as one writes: "He will hold onto the pen until the end of this exercise and then disappear. But whatever I start on next—pamphlet, lampoon, autobiography—other vampires lie in wait for me, future intermediaries, between my consciousness and my written page" (*Foreward*, 10). An autobiographical act of this second type is never, as is that of the first type, found in its pure form. It is always mixed uneasily with the first type, "neither . . . fiction nor nonfiction," as Louis A. Renza described it, "an endless prelude . . . a purely fragmentary, incomplete literary project" (*Veto*, 5–22). Thus Mary McCarthy in *Memories of a Catholic Girlhood* sets herself down in a series of finished stories, each systematically undermined by afterthoughts that foreground the artful and fictive qualities of those stories. The instability of this kind of autobiographical act has kept it from settling into a recognizable genre and kept the classics of the type strikingly original. A still-gathering wave of theoretical work by critics like Renza, Elizabeth Bruss, Paul de Man, James Olney, Janet Gunn, Michel Beaujour, and Avrom Fleishman has been animated by a concern to accommodate precisely this instability of the second type of autobiography.[3]

There is, then, a loose similarity between works of the second category of autobiography and the works of Beckett. Both are created *against* genre. In Beckett's development since the early 1960s especially, what stands out in work after work is emphatic difference—*Imagination Dead Imagine*, *Ping*, *Lessness*, *The Lost Ones*—each insisting on its departure not only from conventional genres but also from its neighbors in the author's canon. Beckett himself is hard put to classify the things he writes. He calls them "shorts," "fizzles," "dramaticules," "residua," "ends," "odds." Still, for all their similarity to autobiography in this regard, they appear to lack both autobiography's aspiration to nonfictional status and its effort to make the author the subject.[4] Is there, then, some category of fiction, related to the second class of autobiography and characterized by a similarly ostentatious originality?[5] But then what, for that matter, characterizes Beckett's fiction beside this quality of rebellion? What else is repeatable in it? What is the form of its antiformality? How do we recognize Beckett as Beckett?

I can propose three elements by way of an answer. They are not meant to be either exclusive or necessary, but they are elements that belong to Beckett. First, he has reduced narrative and dramatic action to an absolute minimum. Second, he has islanded the narrative or dramatic subject, spotlighting it in its frequently mute eventlessness. Third, he has, in direct proportion to this stripping of action and character, increased the garrulousness of the narrative monologue. There have been striking departures in Beckett's unvoiced pieces, but these three elements are very sturdy recurrences: meager action, stark isolated images, and sheer monological logorrhea. In varying ratios, you find this triangle persistently in Beckett, and with increasing concentration in the later work.

It is now possible to generalize with more force. If one looks at the fictional narrative of Wordsworth, particularly at his blank-verse narratives and lyrical ballads, one finds a similarly consistent formal originality marked by the same triangle of narrative deformations. Take as an example "Simon Lee," twelve stanzas in the short ballad meter that appeared in the first edition of *Lyrical Ballads*. It is a poem (like many of Wordsworth's) with an elaborate wind-up and a dud delivery. Simon Lee, once the fastest and merriest of huntsmen, is now the smallest and frailest of old men, working the soil with his aged wife. This is the windup, in seven and a half stanzas. In the next one and a half stanzas, the narrator admonishes the reader not to expect the wrong thing in this poem, then delivers in the final three stanzas the barest event: the narrator, coming across Simon one day hacking at the root of an old stump, severs the root in one blow and is deeply saddened by the old man's profuse gratitude.

In this, as in all of Wordsworth's ballads, the rich diversity of incident and character one expects in a ballad gives way to a static concentration on a single person. In the process, the person is stripped to what is enduringly and indisputably human. For this reason, Wordsworth prefers for his subjects children and ancient folk. (In "Simon Lee" the effect of reduction is compounded by a concentration on the physical process of reduction: what Simon was, compared to what he is now, literally "dwindled.") When Wordsworth finds his fit subject, he isolates it: a child alone in the countryside, a leech-gatherer on the moor, an old Cumberland beggar "by the highway side," a maid "among th'untrodden ways," Simon working on a stump.

The third quality we observed in Beckett (the foregrounding of the narrative voice) is stressed in "Simon Lee" through a shift of attention from the mimetic subject to the narrator. One finds this shift almost everywhere in Wordsworth: in his modification of the meditative lyric, his use of the double narrator device. His epic project, *The Recluse*, was itself redirected into an extended scrutiny of the narrator (*The Prelude*). Once the poem about Simon is in full swing, the narrator breaks the momentum with a turn to the reader, bringing himself into the foreground as a narrator engaged in his own drama of expression. This wordy self-consciousness of Wordsworth contributes to the frequent contrast in his work—a contrast eerily like that so frequent in the work of Beckett—between the self-absorbed verbosity of the poet and the muteness of his human subject. In this repeated pairing of verbose narrator and mute subject, one can see an emerging anxiety about the poet's profession. On the side of words, the poet is necessarily *not* on the side of truth. In the poem "Resolution and Independence," one finds the impossible solution to the dilemma, a subject who speaks and doesn't speak at the same time. We never hear the leech-gatherer's words, but our authorial agent reports that he heard a voice "like a stream / Scarce heard; nor word from word could I divide." What he heard was a poetic ideal, inexpressible in poetry. In the major reflexive moment of "Simon Lee," the narrator destabilizes the meaning of the term "tale," at once asserting and denying both the presence of a tale in the poem and the viability of "tale" as a description of literary activity:

> My gentle reader, I perceive
> How patiently you've waited,
> And I'm afraid that you expect
> Some tale will be related.
>
> O reader! had you in your mind
> Such stores as silent thought can bring,
> O gentle reader! you would find
> A tale in every thing.
> What more I have to say is short,
> I hope you'll kindly take it;
> It is no tale; but should you think,
> Perhaps a tale you'll make it.

I am going to disappoint you because "you expect / Some tale," yet there is "A tale in every thing"; this "is no tale," yet "perhaps a tale you'll make it." Whatever a tale is, the responsibility for it is placed on the assiduously cultivated, alternately stroked and admonished, gentle, gentle reader. And this is because, the tale-teller seems to say, "tale" may be superficially a technical generic term applying to narrative, but a true tale is something off the page, something the reader both finds and makes and that depends on "stores of silent thought."

If what I have isolated cannot go by the name of autobiography, the poet in whose work I have isolated it is one of the major figures of the first great period of autobiography. Wordsworth's autobiographical narrative is, moreover, strikingly like his fictive narrative—spare in action, studded with isolated figures and objects, loaded with reflexive discourse. Both his fiction and nonfiction are the work of a sensibility that features both the preeminent importance of a nontextual presence of being and the great odds against the textual recovery of that being. If the *Lyrical Ballads* are not autobiographical, they are still dominated by an intense focus on being, a focus that distorts inherited narrative forms in the three-part way I have described. Call it a fiction of being, the narrative has been squeezed in such a way that attention oscillates between the voice (being as self) and the human subject (being as other). The talkative representative of consciousness pores over the mute, inactive subject in whom his own being is implicated. In his dreadful diminution, Simon Lee is an expression of the mystery of being on earth in whom the narrator mourns his own passage on the same planet.

To be fair to Wordsworth, his range of interest included other concerns such as how children think and how people care for each other, how the mind grows and how it "associates ideas in a state of excitement." But throughout his work, he continually recurred to the enigma of being itself and an effort "to see into the life of things." If the main sentimental interest of "The Idiot Boy" is Betty Foy's maternal concern for her son, the idiot himself and the mysterious source of his joy occupy a goodly portion of this long, slow poem. "I have often applied to idiots, in my own mind," wrote Wordsworth, "that sublime expression of Scripture, that *their life is hidden with God*" (*Lyrical Ballads*, xxviii). The bafflement that greeted this poem and the other lyrical ballads is much like the bafflement that greeted the works of Beckett when they came fully on the scene 150 years later. "No tale less deserved the labour that appears to have been bestowed upon this," wrote Robert Southey of "The Idiot Boy" (xxxviii), a comment that anticipates the initial response of many to Beckett's *Godot* and the trilogy. Readers of both authors did not immediately see in the reduced, stubbornly persistent human figure the power of ontological enigma that Wordsworth and Beckett did. All the decrepits of Wordsworth look forward to Beckett. Molloy is a direct descendent of the Old Cumberland Beggar.

We have now sketched the contours of a fictional literary type: the fiction of being, which is perhaps most immediately notable for the way it produces bad stories. It appears as an affliction of narrative, a prolix energy of discourse that swarms over the tale like a virus. Can one find it outside of Wordsworth and Beckett? *Tristram Shandy* springs to mind with its laborious bringing to birth of both itself and its subject, as do *Childe Harold*, *Notes from Underground*, *Lord Jim*, *Heart of Darkness*, *Absalom, Absalom!* Consider in *Heart of Darkness* how Kurtz, the human subject, is reduced (nearly a skeleton), isolated (in the very heart of the Congo), almost mute (to our ears), difficult of attainment, and, once physically attained, spiritually elusive. Marlow, Conrad's authorial agent who finds his own being implicated in that of Kurtz, manufactures discourse in direct proportion to the reduction of character and incident in the story. He talks and talks. Like the narrator of "Simon Lee," he frequently aims this talk back upon the talk itself, underscoring the inadequacy of discourse to its object ("Do you see him? Do you see the story? Do you see anything? It seems to me I am trying to tell you a dream—making a vain attempt" [27]). Again, as in "Simon Lee," what emerges is both a tale and not a tale, literary production in a new shape to which we are warned not to bring our old familiar notions.[6]

Over the course of Beckett's work, the weight of this pressure on the narrative became so great that it eventually squashed the story flat. In *The Unnamable*, only the barest remnant of a tale and a human subject are allowed to emerge, while the discourse runs on in a fictional eternity of words. The sheer brutality of human reduction in this book is an index of the author's ontological frustration. Mahood is stripped of his arms and legs, crammed in a jar, and before long erased completely from the text. The only replacement allowed to appear in the way of a mimetic narrative subject is a bare name, Worm, a fictional hypothesis whose sole function is to express the absence of his development.

One feature of the variety of Beckett's experimentation has been his more than occasional adaptation to theater of what we have described so far as a condition of narrative. When he has done this, he has effected it principally by combining stark, static visual imagery with continuous monologue. There is no monologue in *Catastrophe*, yet even this recent "dramaticule" is every bit as susceptible to the kind of analysis we performed on "Simon Lee." The characters are (D) the Director, (A) his Female Assistant, (P) the Protagonist, and Luke (in charge of lighting, off-stage throughout). They rehearse the catastrophe of what appears to be some larger play. Following successive instructions from D, A strips P of his dressing gown and hat, unclenches his fists, lowers his head, bares his neck, rolls up his pajama legs, focuses the spotlight on him, and makes a note to whiten all exposed flesh. The conclusion is a highly concentrated juxtaposition of the rehearsed catastrophe and a final nuance, what might be called a catastrophe of the rehearsal:

> D: Stop! (*Pause*) Now . . . let 'em have it. (*Fadeout of general light. Pause. Fadeout of light on body. Light on head alone. Long pause.*) Terrific! He'll have them on their feet. I can hear it from here.
>
> *Pause. Storms of applause. P raises his head, fixes the audience. The applause falters, dies.*
>
> *Long pause.*
>
> *Fade-out of light on face.*

Here again is Beckett's familiar unfamiliarity. Frequently in his late works, the distance from repeatable literary kinds is underscored by an echo, a sometimes delectable shock of recognition: the elegy in *Enough*, the utopia in *The Lost Ones*, the nativity story in *Ill Seen Ill Said*. The effect is often that of a magnification of detail—a remnant torn from its generic context. In *Fizzle 1*, for example, the genre of the quest has become simply "the body on its way," from start to finish, without cause or motive, endlessly lurching through stone passageways. In *Catastrophe* it is catastrophe itself—a remnant of Aristotelean form—which is enlarged and made strange. As in Beckett's other mutilations of genre, as in Wordsworth's and Conrad's mutilation of "tale," the expectations of genre are willfully overturned. When P displaces D's catastrophe with his own, the applause falters, dies, and is replaced with silence. D wants to put on a safe, reassuringly conventional play. When A timidly enquires, "What if he were to . . . were to . . . raise his head . . . an instant . . . show his face . . . just an instant?" D scoffs "For God's sake! What next? Raise his head! Where do you think we are? In Patagonia?" suggesting a kind of elemental barbarity in P's final raising of his head: something that transgresses decency, violates our tacit communal agreement to repress awareness of ourselves.

The triangle of deformation is as pronounced here as anywhere. As in Beckett's other late, short works where action is a slow pacing back and forth, a hand turning at the end of its arm, a sigh, a blink, a breath, one finds here the same decomplication of dramatic development. Where in the other works the subject is isolated and reduced to two figures in a rotunda, a man in a chair, a blue-eyed creature in a box, a mouth, one finds here the same concentration on sheer human being. The action of the play is the stripping of P, while P stands alone and mute, islanded at the center of dramatic space, the focus of light and attention. But in a fascinating departure, the garrulous narrator— the third leg of the triangle—is replaced in *Catastrophe* by a theatrical director. At first view, there would appear a much greater distance between the real author and this director than one finds between author and narrator in *Heart of Darkness* or in Wordsworth's poems or in Beckett's monologues. D is upstaged at the very end by a character beyond his control, a character who would appear, moreover, entirely opposed to D's repressive will. Draped in furs (no ratty overcoat this time) and speaking in the inflections of Hollywood, this pompous American type would appear to be the anti-Beckett.[7] But such protesting too much is of a piece with the mouth Beckett put on stage more than a decade before and called *Not I*. The disguise is thin, now as then. In *Catastrophe*, there is no missing the commentary on the presumption of creative endeavor. The artist is a pathetic thug, a kind of Pozzo. Every inch of the play, up to its final moment, is an expression of the authorial will to order. D's human subject is the meekest of human material. Yet even here D fails. As in Wordsworth, the contrast between the verbose authorial surrogate and the mute subject is acute. "Sure he won't utter?" asks A. "Not a squeak," says D.

Paul de Man may have been right: "The distinction between fiction and auto-biography is not an either/or polarity but . . . undecidable" ("De-facement," 921). Still, this term *autobiography*, that first appeared in print a year before "Simon Lee,"[8] has proven stubbornly persistent. Something there is that calls up the name, and what Beckett has been writing all these years may be closer to it than we have so far given credit.

Notes

1. My own version of this reading was made in "A Poetics of Radical Displacement: Samuel Beckett Coming up to Seventy."

2. Northrop Frye, *The Anatomy of Criticism*, 307–8. A strong case can be made that the modes of sincerity originated in fiction; see, for example, Philip Stewart, *Imitation and Illusion in the French Memoir-Novel, 1700–1750: The Art of Make-Believe*.

3. Elizabeth Bruss, *Autobiographical Acts: The Changing Situation of a Literary Genre*; Paul de Man, "Autobiography as De-facement"; James Olney, "Some Versions of Memory/Some Versions of *Bios*: The Ontology of Autobiography," in ed. James Olney, *Autobiography*, 236–67; Janet Varner Gunn, *Autobiography: Towards a Poetics of Experience*; Michel Beaujour, *Miroirs d'encre: Rhétorique de l'autoportrait*; Avrom Fleishman, *Figures of Autobiography: The Language of Self-Writing in Victorian and Modern England*.

4. The stress here is on "aspiration" and "effort" in order to enlarge the field as defined by Philippe Lejeune—"DÉFINITION: Récit rétrospectif en prose qu'une personne réelle fait de sa propre existence, lorsqu'elle met l'accent sur sa vie individuelle, en particulier sur l'histoire de sa personnalité." *Le Pacte autobiographique*, 14.

5. Since the autobiographical novel, as a type, represents the kind of generic conformity one finds in the first class of autobiographical act, one would need to find a type of fiction at the opposite remove from, say, *David Copperfield*, fiction predicated on a rebellion against character and convention.

6. "The yarns of seamen have a direct simplicity, the whole meaning of which lies within the shell of a cracked nut. But Marlow was not typical . . . , and to him the meaning of an episode was not inside like a kernel but outside, enveloping the tale which brought it out only as a glow brings out a haze, in the likeness of one of these misty halos that sometimes are made visible by the spectral illumination of moonshine," *Heart of Darkness*, 5.

7. American to my ear. At the same time I don't want to deny the Eastern European quality of D's furs (one finds them on Kafka's bureaucrats) or the powerful political meaning in this play. But Beckett has quite successfully disengaged his political commentary from any particular historical situation and in the process fused it with the play's commentary on the artist. Shades of Mann's *Hitler, My Brother*.

8. By the linguist William Taylor, reviewing Isaac Disraeli's *Miscellanies* in the *Monthly Review* (1797). See Thomas Cooley, *Educated Lives: The Rise of Modern Autobiography in America*, 26.

FREDERIK N. SMITH

"A land of sanctuary":
Allusions to the Pastoral in Beckett's Fiction

"Beckett seeks to deny the lyrical impulse," claims Judith Dearlove (9), verbal-izing what has become almost a shibboleth in our criticism. This view seems to be based on the assumption that Beckett's relentless rationalism, cold nega-tivism, and vaudevillian situations are incompatible with the lyrical impulse. When sensitive descriptions of lovely, ordered nature occur in his fiction—and they *do*, and not as infrequently as we imagine—we believe they must be offered ironically, must be undercut in some way. Indeed sometimes they are. But not always, and not entirely. True, the lyrical in Beckett is often nearly squeezed off the page, but its minimal presence is an effective counter to the frenetic intellectualizing and dead-end attempts at storytelling which dominate his fiction.

Of course to refer to Beckett as a pastoralist pure and simple would be ri-diculous. He is nothing pure and simple. Nevertheless, not unlike the poets Spenser, Milton, Marvell, Pope, Thomson, Wordsworth, Shelley, Yeats, Frost, and Dylan Thomas, Beckett harks back to the pastoral for his own purposes; like them, he knows he can manipulate the familiar motifs of this tradition—and what one commentator has called its "disciplined nostalgia" (Tayler, 176)—with assurance that his reader will understand what he is doing. Nor is there anything new in a novelist borrowing from the tradition. The pastoral figures significantly in British and American fiction from Sterne's *Tristram Shandy* (as unlikely a novel as Beckett's *How It Is*) through Hardy's *Tess of the D'Urbervilles* and right up to Faulkner's *The Hamlet*, Dickey's *Deliverance*, and Fowles's *The French Lieutenant's Woman*. In each of these novels, moreover, the pastoral exists rather uneasily in its prosaic surroundings. Paradoxically, by importing something from such a highly artificial form, the novel—which fears the poetic like the plague—in effect spotlights the poetic. It is the nature of one genre's borrowing from above or below itself that the fit should not be perfectly comfortable. That's really the point.

Pastoral allusions—and I refer here not to all lyrical descriptions of nature but to allusions to the genre itself—occur throughout Beckett's fiction, although his attitude toward the form has evolved over the years. The allusions in *More Pricks Than Kicks* and in *Murphy* (not unlike other features of these works) have a certain glibness, borrowing from the tradition while at the same time having fun at its expense; the allusions in *Molloy* investigate new possibilities for the pastoral, seem far less contrived, and are tonally far more complex, exploiting simultaneously the sense of rejuvenation as well as tragic loss which accompanies an imaginative flashback to an idyllic past; finally, the far simpler allusions in *How It Is*, *Company*, and *Ill Seen Ill Said* pick up on the elegiac attitude in the tradition, and these works seem almost to be *about* the failure of the writer's ability to call up allusions to the pastoral. What is perhaps most surprising is that Beckett seldom mocks the pastoral; although he sometimes fractures the form and on occasion uses the motifs in a comic vein, he for the most part seems to take the pastoral world quite seriously, employing its famous tranquillity in deliberate opposition to the world of the mind, and also as a vehicle for underscoring the loss of those golden times. And Beckett uses words in his lyrical passages in a special way, depending on them alone to revive a world unreachable now except through language.

In *More Pricks Than Kicks* he alludes irreverently to the "pastoral clamour" of the birds (107) and to a barking dog as "but a single pastoral motiv" he might draw on (115). Two stories—"Fingal" and "Walking Out"—show Beckett utilizing his native Irish landscape as a sort of pastoral backdrop. Indeed in "Fingal" the pastoral functions as protagonist. "One fine Spring morning" Belacqua takes his girl out to the country, where the pair considers the landscape in silence:

> Its coast eaten away with creeks and marshes, tesserae of small fields, patches of wood springing up like a weed, the line of hills too low to close the view. (24)

The entire story is based on the contradictory reactions of Belacqua and the young woman to this landscape. She finds it dull. He finds it magic. "I often come to this hill," he tells her, "to have a view of Fingal, and each time I see it more as a back-land, a land of sanctuary, a land that you don't have to dress up to, that you can walk on in a lounge suit, smoking a cigar" (25). The young woman views all this as nothing but a dream. Belacqua believes that "if she closed her eyes she might see something"—presumably in her imagination—and for himself elects at least "not to try to communicate Fingal, he would lock it up in his mind" (26). Beckett's point is clear enough. What appeals to Belacqua is *not* the literal Irish countryside in front of him, but rather the idealized landscape of the imagination, which he resolves to keep to himself. Belacqua here elects to become a sort of closet pastoralist, withdrawing, like

Marvell, into "a green Thought in a green Shade" ("The Garden," line 48). It is this imaginative escape from harsh reality, coupled with a ferocious confrontation with the same reality, which is Beckett's special contribution to the pastoral form.

In "Walking Out" Beckett uses the pastoral landscape—of course the technique is absolutely conventional—as a reflection of his character's mood. Himself a sort of shepherd, Belacqua one spring evening walks with his dog out to the "bright green grass" of the late Boss Crocker's Gallops. There he pauses, we are told, "not so much in order to rest as to have the scene soak through him" (101). The description of what follows alludes unmistakably and rather humorously to the pastoral tradition:

> Belacqua regretted the horses of the good old days, for they would have given to the landscape something that the legions of sheep and lambs could not give. These latter were springing into the world every minute, the grass was spangled with scarlet afterbirths, the larks were singing, the hedges were breaking, the sun was shining, the sky was Mary's cloak, the daisies were there, everything was in order. Only the cuckoo was wanting. It was one of those Spring evenings when it is a matter of some difficulty to keep God out of one's meditations. (101)

Again, the real landscape is less important to Belacqua—and to Beckett— than his imaginative "pastoralization" of that landscape. The sheep, lambs, larks, hedges, evening sun, blue sky, and daisies are all easily recognizable motifs of the pastoral—"everything was in order." In creating this pastoral scene Beckett goes so far as to borrow some of the self-consciously poetic diction from eighteenth-century poetry, in particular the words "legions" and "spangled," and (at the beginning of the next paragraph) the reference to the grass as an "emerald floor."[1] Of course the diction is not employed altogether straightforwardly. This sort of thing in the *Pastorals* of Ambrose Philips (1748)

> Have you seen the ethereal blue
> Gently shedding silvery dew,
> Spangling o'er the silent green,
> While the nightingale . . .
> (53)

becomes this:

> One fateful fine Spring evening . . . the grass was spangled with scarlet afterbirths, the larks were singing . . .

The grass spangled with dew in Philips's pastoral is spangled with scarlet afterbirths (notice how the painterly emphasis is maintained) in Beckett. Quite cleverly, Beckett keeps true to the pastoral tradition and yet tinkers with that tradition in order to make us smile at the stylistic incongruity. He does not want us to forget that behind the lovely surface of every pastoral, as Frank Kermode has said, is "the knowledge that Nature is rough, and the natural life in fact rather an animal affair" (17). Belacqua discovers the underside of the pastoral when instead of the cuckoo he hears the "crex-crex, crex-crex, crex-crex" of the corncrake—a "death-rattle" instead of a "promise of happiness" (111). In any case, the aesthetic near-perfection of the scene prompts Belacqua, as it has so many landscape poets, to mention God.

In *Murphy* Beckett similarly develops the concept of withdrawal into pastoral tranquillity, and the tranquillity is similarly qualified by the author's irrepressible humor. Riding a bus to Hyde Park, Murphy shuts his eyes and asks the conductor to tell him when they reach the Marble Arch: "By closing his eyes he could be in an archaic world very much less corrupt than anything on view in the B.M." (95). When he gets to Hyde Park, Murphy, overcome by the problem of which of his biscuits to eat first, falls forward on his face on the grass and is roused only by the approach of one Miss Rosie Dew (morning or evening dew is a staple of the pastoral, and "rosy dew" actually appears in Pope's *Pastorals*), who asks him to have the goodness to hold her doggie while she feeds the poor dear sheep.[2] Is Murphy dreaming all this? Are Rosie Dew and the sheep not in Hyde Park at all but only residents of Murphy's highland imagination? Beckett, typically, has blurred the boundary between the so-called real world and the dream. In any case, Miss Dew moves among the sheep with two heads of lettuce while Murphy (like the pastoral poet) is confined to the role of observer.

> The sheep were a miserable-looking lot, dingy, close-cropped, undersized and misshapen. They were not cropping, they were not ruminating, they did not even seem to be taking their ease. They simply stood, in an attitude of profound dejection, their heads bowed, swaying slightly as though dazed. Murphy had never seen stranger sheep, they seemed one and all on the point of collapse. They made the exposition of Wordsworth's lovely "fields of sleep" as a compositor's error for "fields of sheep" seem no longer a jibe at that most excellent man. (99–100)

Like most living things in Beckett's world, these sheep seem to be decidedly on the decline and quite unimpressive successors to the skipping flocks of the pastoral tradition. But similarly dilapidated sheep (untended, reflecting their master's grief) appear in the pastoral elegy, and Beckett's description is reminiscent of one in *Lycidas*:

> The hungry sheep look up, and are not fed,
> But swoln with wind, and the rank mist they draw,
> Rot inwardly, and foul contagion spread . . .
> (lines 125–27)

Perversely, however, Beckett's learned joke based on an interpretation of a line in Wordsworth's "Intimations of Immortality" (much debated in the pages of *Notes and Queries* at the end of the nineteenth century) serves to remove us from the truly bucolic.[3] But while we have looked on with rather ironic detachment, Murphy has romanticized the prospect—recollected it in Wordsworthian tranquillity—and been virtually swept away by his vision. He, we are told, had been "absorbed in this touching little argonautic [the word is carefully chosen], and above all in the ecstatic demeanour of the sheep" (100), with whom he feels "in close sympathy" (104).

In *Molloy* Beckett returns to the symbolic landscape he toyed with in "Walking Out" and in *Murphy*. Here, however, there is far more emphasis on the tranquillity of the scene than in these early experiments. It is appropriate that the pastoral should appear in both halves of this double novel, serving as poetic respite for both Molloy and Moran in their respective quests. As Murphy vaults into the pastoral by way of a Hyde Park trance, so Molloy awakens from a tortuous sleep to discover himself watched by a shepherd (who carries a crook) and his dog. Again, is this a dream? Molloy says that typically, when he wakes, "in my eyes and in my head a fine rain begins to fall, as from a rose" (remember Rosie Dew), and that he can rather easily see and understand the first things that present themselves (28). He quickly identifies the sheep and their "anxious bleating" and asks the shepherd, "Where are you taking them, to the fields or to the shambles?" The question is tantamount to asking whether these are poetic sheep or real sheep raised for slaughter. But the shepherd goes on his way without a word (he does whistle to his dog) and Molloy is left alone, watching the "little procession" recede and the mist close in as expected: "All that through a glittering dust, and soon through that mist too which rises in me every day and veils the world from me and veils me from myself" (29). We can be sure that *something* of importance has occurred here. The interlude leaves Molloy with anxiety about the destination of those sheep. Furthermore, he has been unable to permeate the insular world of the pastoral. Perhaps only a dream, the magical little idyll was provocative in its evanescent perfection and now seems lost forever. Molloy remains behind to continue his frustrating search for his mother, although for a moment at least he has been permitted to observe a pastoral tranquillity—not to experience it—with a clarity which the rest of his day cannot possibly match.

Moran's similar interlude (it occurs not in the morning but at dusk) seems on Beckett's part almost a doubling back in order to pick up the fuller significance of this little scene.

> Stop, I said to my son one day. I had just caught sight of a shepherd I liked the look of. He was sitting on the ground stroking his dog. A flock of black shorn

sheep strayed about them, unafraid. What a pastoral land, my God. Leaving my
son on the side of the road I went towards them, across the grass. (158)

Moran's reaction to the scene is quite profound:

> I came finally to a halt about ten paces from the shepherd. There was no use go-
> ing any further. How I would love to dwell upon him. His dog loved him, his
> sheep did not fear him. Soon he would rise, feeling the falling dew. . . . I longed
> to say, Take me with you, I will serve you faithfully, just for a place to lie and a lit-
> tle food.

Moran watches as the flock moves happily away, the sheep huddled comfortably together, snatching nibbles of grass, the dog contentedly wagging his
tail: "And in perfect order, the shepherd silent and the dog unneeded, the little flock departed" (160). Like Molloy, Moran admires the tranquillity and
harmony of this Wordsworthian shepherd's life, and he goes even further
than Molloy, expressing his desire to live with him; he desires, that is, to partake of the inviting peacefulness of the pastoral, although Molloy's question
(is this poetry or real life?) and the poetic style of both passages have hinted
that this world may exist only in literary tradition. When the flock moves off,
Moran is left in an all-too-real world, and he soon falls to bickering again
with his son. Molloy and Moran may not have gained much from their pastoral observations. Beckett's reader, however, should have: by introducing these
descriptions of an impermeable but delightfully rudimentary Arcadia into a
far more intellectual, altogether more frenzied world, the author has introduced a wider perspective. This juxtaposition of the complex and the simple
is a strictly conventional use of the pastoral tradition, as, for example, in *The
Tempest,* or in John Hawkes's *Second Skin.* "The central meaning of pastoral,"
says Hallett Smith, "is the rejection of the aspiring mind" (10).

   In *How It Is* the best that can be hoped for are "a few images on and off in
the mud earth sky a few creatures in the light," and the pastoral is the
source of several of these fragments. Here we are not far from Wordsworth's *The Prelude:*

> I see by glimpses now; when age come on,
> May scarcely see at all; and I would give,
> While yet we may, as far as words can give,
> Substance and life to what I feel, enshrining,
> Such is my hope, the spirit of the Past
> For future restoration.
>
>   (Book XII, lines 281–86)

The conventional springtime scene comes together most fully near the beginning of Beckett's novel, where over a four-page stretch the pastoral narrator

attempts to assemble a scene out of the bits and scraps of memory, which unfortunately begin to dissolve before he can complete the scene. I have lifted the following phrases out of context in order to suggest the existence of a complete mosaic somewhere behind the several fragments:

> sometimes in this position a fine image fine I mean in movement and colour blue and white of clouds in the wind sometimes some days this time it happens this day in the mud a fine image I'll describe it . . .

> I look to me about sixteen and to crown all glorious weather egg-blue sky and scamper of little clouds . . .

> the colours that deck the emerald grass if I may believe them we are old dream of flowers and seasons we are in April and May . . .

> this immensity of verdure and emergence little by little of grey and white spots lambs little by little among their dams what else the bluey bulk closing the scene . . .

> swinging of arms silent relishing of sea and isles heads pivoting as one to the city fumes silent location of steeples and towers . . .

> we are again dwindling again across the pastures hand in hand arms swing heads high towards the heights smaller and smaller out of sight . . .

> some animals still the sheep like granite outcrops . . .

> blue and white of sky a moment still April morning in the mud it's over it's done I've had the image the scene is empty a few animals still then goes out no more blue I stay there . . . (27–31)

Beckett refers elsewhere in *How It Is* to "the golden age the good moments the losses" (47). Imaginatively, this image of the golden age of boyhood is assembled, piece by piece, before our very eyes.[4] While the *Ur*-image may of course have its roots in Beckett's personal experience, he has, by using the familiar motifs of a conventional pastoral scene, enabled his reader to participate in the process of memory. April, May, blue sky, white clouds, green pastures, flowers, lambs, dams, and expansive hillsides are the recognizable props. (Conventionally, the natural beauty of the country is here opposed to the "fumes" of the nearby city.) Like Dylan Thomas in "Fern Hill," Beckett has called up for us a literary image of some long-gone Edenic boyhood ("honoured among wagons I was prince of the apple towns"), and re-created the image in a highly poetic language which makes that golden time come alive once again: in particular, "egg-blue sky," "scamper of little clouds," and "deck the emerald grass" (recall the "emerald floor" in *More Pricks*) are all consciously poetic phrases, and the words "verdure" and "bluey" are lifted from the large body of poetic diction common to eighteenth-century poetry.[5]

While unoriginal, these words and phrases are most emphatically *not* used ironically, for they arrive trailing their golden pasts, and the metaphors are fresh enough to be a welcome relief from the deserts of uninflected prose in which they blossom. Beckett is doing in *How It Is* what writers of pastorals have always done—employing beautiful metaphors and pleasant-sounding words to convey an appreciation for nature and a nostalgia for a simpler time. Then, having established this scene near the beginning of the novel, he can in the pages that follow allude back by way of a mere phrase (like "patches of blue") or even a single word (like "blue," "azure," or "sky") to this image no longer fully recoverable.

Ill Seen Ill Said (in this context the title assumes special significance) shows the pastoral to have receded yet further. The sparse "sun clouds earth sea patches of blue" of *How It Is* (132) has dwindled in this pastoral elegy to "rags of sky and earth" (51). The old woman of this story repeatedly traverses the "zone of stone" surrounding her cabin in order to reach the pastures which lie beyond that stone, always carrying flowers to place on a worn grave bearing an enigmatic inscription.[6] Just whose tomb this is—a husband's or lover's or the woman's own tomb—is left nicely ambiguous, and the stones surrounding the cabin (encroaching ever further into the pastures) seem to represent the old woman's decline into the inanimate. It is worth noting, however, that stones in the pastoral tradition have always posed a threat to the sometimes limited vegetation as well as to the safety of the flock.[7]

The narrator in this work (the shift away from the first person makes the pastoral seem more distant) would appear to be a sort of meticulous but enfeebled landscape painter, daubing a bit of color here, questioning what belongs there, everywhere encountering difficulty in summoning the old woman's pastoral memories onto the canvas. Surely it is no coincidence that pastoral poets (Spenser, Milton, Pope, and Thomson come to mind) have frequently relied on painterly imagery in depicting their landscapes.[8] But here is the pathetic fallacy in reverse; the landscape is not so much reflecting the woman's sadness as causing it. Thus such lines as these from the November eclogue of Spenser's *The Shepherd's Calendar*:

> All Musick sleepes, where death doth leade the daunce,
> And shepherds wonted solace is extinct.
> The blew in black, the greene in gray is tinct,
>   The gaudie girlonds deck her graue,
>   The faded flowres her corse embraue.
>   O heavie herse,
> Morne nowe my Muse, now morne with teares besprint.
>   O carefull verse.
>
> (lines 105–12)

are transformed into these in *Ill Seen Ill Said:*

> In the way of animals ovines only. After long hesitation. They are white and make do with little. Whence suddenly come no knowing nor whither as suddenly gone. Unshepherded they stray as they list. Flowers? Careful. Alone the odd crocus still at lambing time. (10)

The familiar pastoral scene is all but departed. The sheep (the notion is not unusual in the tradition) wander unshepherded. The poet-painter in the next section interjects this self-conscious rationale:

> There had to be lambs. Rightly or wrongly. A moor would have allowed of them. Lambs for their whiteness. And for other reasons as yet obscure. Another reason. And so that there may be none. At lambing time. That from one moment to the next she may raise her eyes to find them gone. A moor would have allowed of them. In any case too late. And what lambs. No trace of frolic. White splotches in the grass. (11)

With perverse logic, the poet-painter explains that there had to be lambs in this scene because come spring there had to be lambs to remove from the woman's view. And he proceeds first to deny the lambs their customary frolic and then their aliveness, referring to them as mere "white splotches."[9]

In any case, having once established the pastoral scene, if only by allusion to what is *not* there, Beckett dismantles it piece by piece: thus on subsequent pages we hear of "withered flowers" (15), "miscalled pastures" (26), "withered crocuses" (29), "drooping grass" (29), and "limp grass strangely rigid" (42). Of course lamenting vegetation is a frequent motif in the tradition, and withered trees and drooping flowers appear in Pope, withered ferns and leaves in Thomson, withered flowers in Shelley. And typically these few remaining props are themselves removed. "Fled is the blasted verdure of the fields," rhapsodizes Thomson ("Autumn," line 998). "No more sky or earth" (31), says Beckett, and finally: "No more lambs. No more flowers" (45).

Beckett's technique is reminiscent of Pope's in *The Dunciad*, where even amidst the gloom at the end of Book IV there are faint echoes of the world of Pope's youthful pastorals:

> In vain, in vain,—the all-composing Hour
> Resistless falls: The Muse obeys the Pow'r.
> She comes! she comes! the sable Throne behold
> Of *Night* Primaeval, and of *Chaos* old!
> Before her, *Fancy*'s gilded clouds decay,
> And all its varying Rain-bows die away.
>
> (lines 627–32)

"Gilded clouds" and "varying Rain-bows" both hark back to Pope's own previous allusions to the Golden Age in his pastorals. Similarly, the lamentation in *Ill Seen Ill Said* is not only for the woman's lover, or simply for her own departed youth, but also for the poet-painter's own ebbing powers of imagination. Pope and Beckett both dramatize themselves as victims of the relentless darkness and what Pope (a few lines later) calls its "uncreating word." This is what they as writers fear most. Only Beckett (there may be some surprise here) ends on the more positive note. Pope concludes: "And Universal Darkness buries All." Beckett hesitates: "No. One moment more. One last. Grace to breathe that void. Know happiness" (59).

Beckett's deep indebtedness to the pastoral tradition is indisputable. He has borrowed from that tradition not only the conventional motifs but also the pathetic fallacy which predominates in the tradition, the diversity of mood (from the comically idyllic in *Murphy* to the seriously nostalgic in *Molloy* to the elegiac in *Ill Seen Ill Said*), and any number of specific images, themes, and words. Behind this various borrowing lies a belief in the writer's power to beckon through language to a departed or even purely fictional Golden Age. As Pope says in *Windsor Forest:*

> The Groves of *Eden,* vanish'd now so long,
> Live in Description, and look green in Song.
>
> (lines 7–8)

Or Yeats in "The Song of the Happy Shepherd," which he placed first in his *Collected Poems:*

> The woods of Arcady are dead,
> And over is their antique joy
>
> . .   .   .
> Words alone are certain good.
>
> (lines 1–10)

Through art the poet enables us to rise above the mundane realities of the present and to discern the remnants of a happier, more beautiful, more harmonious time. Beckett at least partially accepts the aesthetics inherent in the pastoral and which we associate with the Renaissance and the Neoclassical Age. Martin Battestin has termed this "the redemptive function of artifice" (60).

Our unwillingness to acknowledge the value of the pastoral impulse in Beckett—or, more broadly, the lyrical impulse—may stem in part from our understandable assumption that his relentless questioning of the very roots of artistic expression has rendered any sort of literary form (especially one as conventional as the pastoral) inoperative or at best ironic. Beckett's jokes at the expense of language and its conventions certainly suggest an unfertile soil for his pastoral crocuses. But there are several features of both the tradition and Beckett's aesthetics that make this coming together not as unlikely as it seems.

Pastoralists and their readers have always been conscious of the artificiality of the genre. The rustic life of the poet-shepherd described in the sophisticated language of a highly poetic, conventional form: this contradiction has existed at the core of the genre since the beginning. The pastoral is best understood as the subject of itself, for the poet's lines themselves, like the precarious beauty they describe, seem always on the verge of collapse. "The fascination of pastoral language," says Richard Cody, "is the difficulty of coming to a just appreciation of what the poet does not say" (161). This self-consciousness inherent in the genre has surely been part of its fascination for Beckett.

By everywhere undermining the connection between language and reality, Beckett has deliberately run words aground, leaving them no longer usable as signs for meanings beyond themselves, but oddly free to express meaning by reference to other words. Thus Beckett's lyrical style is no more devalued than his hyperbolically rationalistic style. Once the referential function of language has been exposed as a sham, the lyrical is put on an equal footing with the less than lyrical. And once that occurs, the pastoral claims high priority because it refers back to previous uses of poetic language and thus draws into itself the glories of those old words. The truth of poetry as poetry is one thing Beckett has *not* found it necessary to jettison. He can't go on, but he does so by the power of words alone. The language of Beckett's minimalist fiction can, by definition, cut away everything but language. And once language is accepted as relying not on external "reality" for its significance but is understood rather as the source of its own meaning, the more poetic, more conventional use of it lends at least a linguistic significance to what is said. We *need* the lyrical in Beckett. Those sparse passages suggest that language has somehow gathered itself together, echoing old words and old forms, and managed for a moment to arrange itself meaningfully—then lapsed again into its mechanical laying down of word and phrase, signifying nothing. "The blue celeste of poesy" (as it is called in *Lessness*) is in itself a kind of sanctuary from the myriad permutations and combinations which lead nowhere. The lyrical functions throughout Beckett's fiction as an allusion back to what, linguistically and literally, once was, or should have been.

Notes

1. Cf. the poetical uses of "expanse" and "bright" earlier in this same paragraph. Numerous examples of "legions" are cited by Arthos, 235–37. In addition to the example of "spangling"

cited below, cf. Herrick, "Corrina's Going A-Maying," in Kermode, line 6: "The Dew bespangling Herbe and Tree"; and Pope, "Autumn," line 99: "falling Dews with Spangles deck'd the Glade." See also the uses of "emerald" cited in the *OED*, plus "green emerald" in Thomson, "Autumn," line 155.

2. Pope, "Summer," line 69: "Here Bees from Blossoms sip the rosie Dew." Incidentally, I find no reference to sheep in Hyde Park per se. But cf. Morton, 263: "I remember once falling into a conversation with a foreigner in the Green Park [roughly adjacent to Hyde Park]. . . . 'Look,' he said, 'Sheep are grazing all around us, right in the middle of Picadilly. It is something, that no one could have imagined or believed. Don't you call that extraordinary?' I had to agree that it was."

3. Wordsworth, line 28: "The Winds come to me from the fields of sleep." See *N&Q* 7 (2 March 1889): 168; 7 (4 May 1889): 357; 7 (25 May 1889): 417; 8 (3 August 1889): 89–91; 8 (9 November 1889): 369–71; and 9 (12 April 1890): 297–98.

4. These pages bear some resemblance to eighteenth-century "prospect" poems, which at times seem to be poetic descriptions not of landscapes but of landscape paintings. Cf. Thomson, "Spring," lines 350–53:

> Meantime you gain the height, from whose fair brow
> The bursting prospect spreads immense around;
> And, snatched o'er hill and dale, and wood and lawn,
> And verdant field. . . .

5. Cf. "immensity of verdure" to Thomson's "immensity of space" ("Summer," line 1706) and "blue immense" ("Autumn," line 1356). "Bluey" is used by Southey (cited in the *OED*) and by Philips (34), and is based on the seventeenth- and eighteenth-century habit of coining two-syllable adjectives by adding a *y* to an extant, monosyllabic adjective.

6. "At crocus time it would be making for the distant tomb" (16). Beckett may here be alluding to the *et in Arcadia ego* tradition in the visual arts; cf. Panofsky.

7. Cf. Virgil, Eclogue I, 7: "Happy old man! So these lands will still be yours, and large enough for you, though bare stones cover all, and the marsh chokes your pastures with slimy rushes." Interestingly, in *How It Is* even the sheep are said to be "like granite" (31).

8. For just one example, see Thomson, "Spring," lines 475–76: "Ah, what shall language do? ah, where find words / Tinged with so many colours. . . ."

9. Things were less bleak in *Company:* "Next thing you are on your way across the white pasture afrolic with lambs and strewn with red placentae" (35). Cf. Thomson, "Autumn," lines 658–59: "In boundless prospect—yonder shagged with wood, / Here rich with harvest, and there white with flocks!"

HERSH ZEIFMAN

"The Core of the Eddy":
Rockaby and Dramatic Genre

In a recent review of the five Beckett plays currently running in New York, critic John Simon issued a provocative challenge. Calling these late Beckett plays "soporifics" and "exhausted exhalations," Simon wrote: "I would . . . urge the scholars and critics who continue to rhapsodize about these hackle raisers and eyelid lowerers to look into their hearts, then look into my eyes and say they really enjoy *Rockaby* and its ilk, as one can enjoy even such very bleak works as *King Lear*, wherein the basic constituents of drama are not abandoned" (Simon, 96–97). Stout-hearted and steely-eyed, I take up the challenge. *Rockaby* is hardly *King Lear*, of course, nor was it meant to be, but it *is* a play, and a very moving one. This charge that Beckett is not writing plays, that he has abandoned "the basic constituents of drama," has dogged Beckett's theater from the beginning. Thus *Waiting for Godot* was viewed by many early critics as totally undramatic—a nonplay in which, to quote Vivian Mercier's tongue-in-cheek description, "nothing happens, *twice*" (*Beckett/Beckett*, xii). What some critics, though not Mercier, failed to realize was that Beckett was not abandoning the basic constituents of drama but redefining them. A great deal is "happening" in *Godot*, although not in traditional theatrical terms; the very fact that nothing happens *twice*, for example, is, on one level, the something that happens. As Tom Stoppard, one of the many contemporary dramatists who have acknowledged a profound debt to Beckett's theater, has noted: "At the time when *Godot* was first done, it liberated something for anybody writing plays. It redefined the minima of theatrical validity. It was as simple as that. [Beckett] got away. He won by twenty-eight lengths, and he'd done it with so little—and I mean that as an enormous compliment" (Hayman, 6–7).

On the surface, it is not difficult to see how Simon was misled into concluding that Beckett's recent dramatic works have abandoned drama. When the lights fade up on *Rockaby*, we see a woman (W) dressed in black—"Prematurely old. Unkempt grey hair. Huge eyes in white expressionless face" (7–

23)—sitting in a rocking chair. Soon she begins to rock, and, as she rocks, she listens to an offstage voice (V) telling a story about an old woman who wound up her days rocking in a rocking chair. Superficially, nothing "happens" even once in *Rockaby:* we see a woman, rocking away, listening to a tale—a tale that is narrated rather than dramatized, and is thus presumably closer to the genre of fiction than to drama. This narrated tale lies at the heart of most of Beckett's late plays, determining the new variation on the Beckett "pseudocouple" these plays most frequently depict: a speaker and a listener. In *Not I*, for example, the speaker is represented simply by a disembodied, spotlit Mouth, pouring out a torrent of frenzied words into the surrounding darkness, while an Auditor, in the double sense of his name, both listens to and implicitly assesses the validity of her account. In *Ohio Impromptu*, we have Reader and Listener, "*[a]s alike in appearance as possible*" (*Rockaby*, 27), the one reading a story from a book on the table in front of him, the other listening attentively. And in *Footfalls*, both May and V, the offstage voice of her mother, tell stories—though whether either in fact listens to the other during their respective monologues is a moot point.[1]

The significant shift in this pattern in *Rockaby* is that both speaker and listener are the same person—literally, and not just perhaps symbolically as in other Beckett plays. The play features two characters but a single actress: V is W's own recorded voice. The closest parallel to this in Beckett's recent drama is *That Time*, in which the onstage listener, called Listener, hears three separate voices (A, B, and C), three separate stories, all of which are his own. These voices apparently lie outside Listener's control, arriving unbidden and unwelcome; in *Rockaby*, on the other hand, W specifically calls her voice into being. Four times in the play she commands "More," and four times V obeys, narrating yet another chapter of the story. Such measure of control may remind us of Beckett's early radio play *Cascando*, in which the central character, Opener, repeatedly invokes Voice and Music to tell their story with the words "I open. . . . And I close" (7–19). In *Ohio Impromptu*, Listener similarly exercises some control over the story being read to him: by knocking once on the table, he signals Reader to stop and reread the previous sentence. And in *What Where*, V, the voice of Bam represented on stage by a small megaphone at head level, demonstrates the greatest control of all. Godlike, he creates an entire "world"—lights, characters, story—with the words "I switch on." Deciding from time to time that his creation is "not good," he can instantly return to the void ("I switch off"), correct his errors, and create anew.[2]

In addition to this issue of control of the voices, *Rockaby* differs significantly from *That Time* in terms of the pronoun used throughout the voices' stories. The voices in *That Time*, uniquely in Beckett's late drama, speak in the second person: "that time you went back that last time to look was the ruin still there where you hid as a child" (28). This is not quite first person, of course, not quite an acknowledgment that listener and voice are one. As Voice C accuses Listener at one point: "did you ever say I to yourself in your life come on now . . . could you ever say I to yourself in your life" (31). Still, it is not as fully distanced as third person, which is how most characters in Beckett's late drama refer to their lives—either because the pain of their existence is too intense to be faced directly and so must be displaced on a fictional creation, or, as Linda Ben-Zvi has forcefully argued, because Beckett's characters are trapped in the prison of a Mauthnerian "schismatic self," unable "ever to merge the inner and the outer parts of the ego."[3] Thus Mouth in *Not I*, whose "vehement refusal to relinquish third person" (14) gives that play its title: "what? . . . who? . . . no! . . . she!"[4] Thus May in *Footfalls*, a character who has not quite been born, who only *may* exist, who wears, according to Beckett, "the costume of a ghost,"[5] transmuting her pain into the fictional persona of Amy, an anagram of her name, a ghostly projection whose story May repeatedly insists is fiction: "Amy—the daughter's given name, *as the reader will remember*" (*Ends and Odds: Eight*, 47). Thus the Reader in *Ohio Impromptu*, who goes May one further by literally reading his third-person narration from a book. Thus the Speaker in *A Piece of Monologue*, who immediately distances himself from his tale with his opening sentence, "Birth was the death of *him*" (*Rockaby*, 70), and who twice specifically questions the pronoun "he" (76, 78).

And thus V in *Rockaby*. The voice we hear is W's own, telling what is presumably her own story—but telling it, typically, in the third person, a story about "she." And what is this autobiography-turned-fiction about? The story V tells, the story W summons forth, is a bedtime story, though in a horribly ironic sense. As the title of the play suggests, the story is a lullaby, crooned at bedtime to soothe a child to sleep.[6] (*Rockaby* evokes both the rocking movement of a cradle and the beginning of a popular lullaby: "Rock-a-bye-baby on the tree top.")[7] And, as with most lullabies, it is *about* sleep itself—in this case, eternal sleep, the sleep of void, the sleep of death. It is the sleep evoked by Hamm in his *Endgame* chronicle: "In what condition he had left the child. Deep in sleep. . . . But deep in what sleep, deep in what sleep already?" (53). And the sleep of the unseen V in *Footfalls*, calling out to May from the dark: "I heard you in my deep sleep. (*Pause.*) There is no sleep so deep I would not hear you there" (33).

The lullaby V croons is divided into four movements, four "verses," each movement preceded by W's imploring "More." As in classical Greek tragedy, the story begins just before its end, just before its "catastrophe":[8]

    till in the end
    the day came
    in the end came

close of a long day
when she said
to herself
whom else
time she stopped
time she stopped

In the lullaby's first movement, the protagonist decides it is time she stopped "going to and fro, all eyes," searching "for another / another like herself / another creature like herself / a little like." In the second movement, she retires instead to her room, sitting at her window with the blind up, though still searching, "all eyes / . . . for another / at her window / another like herself / a little like." But this search too proves futile, as she acknowledges in the third movement: not only does she never see a face at a window, she never even sees a blind up: "all blinds down / never one up / hers alone up." So, in the fourth and final movement, she abandons her search, lets down the blind, descends the deep stair into the old rocker, "mother rocker / where mother sat / sat and rocked," and rocks away "with closed eyes, closing eyes," having become "her own other":

so in the end
close of a long day
went down
down the steep stair
let down the blind and down
right down
into the old rocker
and rocked
rocked
saying to herself
no
done with that
the rocker
those arms at last
saying to the rocker
rock her off
stop her eyes
fuck life
stop her eyes
rock her off
rock her off

Like most lullabies, the story V narrates is in verse. As Enoch Brater has noted: "*Rockaby* is Beckett's first play in which the language is not merely poetic, but a poem complete in itself" (*Light*, 346). It is a poem without punctuation, beginning mid-sentence without a capital letter and ending, appropriately on the word "off," without a period. In between, we hear a remarkably small number of words—simple words for the most part, generally monosyllabic, but often weighted with extraordinary poetic density. The phrase "behind the pane," for example: V uses it when she speaks of possibly seeing a face at one of the windows ("behind the pane / famished eyes / like hers"). In the theater, however, the word "pane" echoes with deliberate ambiguity: we understand "pane" to mean window glass, but we also simultaneously hear its homonym ("behind the *pain*"). This small number of words is then repeatedly combined and recombined, providing the lullaby with its distinctive metronomic beat—thus, for instance, the opening phrase of each movement: "till in the end," "so in the end," "till in the end," "so in the end." Significantly enough in this lullaby of ending, the phrases most frequently repeated are "time she stopped" and "close of a long day." So hypnotic is the restricted lexicon, so powerful are the verse rhythms of the language, that the shocking intrusion of "fuck life" near the very end of the monologue resonates not simply because of the unexpected obscenity, but because we suddenly hear two words not previously used by V in her litany of repetition—words, moreover, which form a teasing near-rhyme for the lullaby's closing phrase: "fuck life / . . . rock her off." (In his French translation of *Rockaby*, Beckett sacrifices some of the shock for the sake of a smoother rhyme. "Aux gogues la vie," while still startling, is less obviously explosive than its English counterpart, but it helps close the play on a deliberately sustained end-rhyme: "berce-la d'ici / aux gogues la vie / berce-la d'ici / berce-la d'ici."[9] The double rhyming couplets subliminally inform us, as at the completion of a Shakespearean blank-verse scene, that the end has indeed arrived.)

By focusing almost exclusively on V's monologue, what I have been describing up to this point has been primarily a verse narrative, dramatic only in the sense that a monologue by Browning might be considered "dramatic." And yet, *Rockaby* is not at all a Beckettian version of "My Last Duchess"; it consists of much more than simply V's monologue. Beckett has carefully crafted his lullaby into a specifically theatrical work, a work in which verse and narrative are transformed into drama. The story V narrates is a lullaby turned threnody, its movement a contraction and descent—a journey from the outside (a "going to and fro" in search of another) to the inside (a retreat into the room and a more passive variation of that search) to a still deeper inside (the abandonment of the search through a descent into the solipsism and oblivion of a rocking chair). And it is precisely this movement which the play itself, as distinct merely from its story, encapsulates. We may not actually see the protagonist moving from street to room to rocking chair, but the trajectory of her movement is nonetheless essentially enacted before us. There are two parallel journeys being traced in *Rockaby*—one of them *narrated* in V's monologue, the other *dramatized* in the very shape and texture of the play as theatrical performance.

Central to this dramatization is the onstage presence of W, dressed in black, rocking herself to death. One full revolution of her rock encompasses one printed line of verse (Brater, *Light*, 346): the lullaby's poetic rhythm is given its metaphoric metronome in a theatrical analogue. The rocking *is* the poetry. It is also the dramatic symbol for the arc of V's narrative, a movement from light to darkness, from youth to age, from cradle to rocking chair, from lullaby to threnody. As a title, *Rockaby* thus evokes not only the narrative flow of V's lullaby of death but its theatrical representation: the constant onstage rocking of a rocking chair. (Beckett's title for the play in his French translation captures all these associations brilliantly: *Berceuse* means simultaneously cradle, lullaby, and rocking chair.) W's rock is a rock of ages, a rock *through* ages. In effect, she rocks herself into her mother, not simply because her rocking duplicates the description of her mother's rocking in the narrative, but because the rocking chair itself becomes the matrix in which she seeks dissolution: "into the old rocker / *mother rocker* / . . . those arms at last" (my emphasis). And the arms of her "mother" literally enfold her: Beckett directs that the rocking chair have "[r]ounded inward-curving arms to suggest embrace." W's rocking, then, is a merging with her mother at the most basic level: a return to the womb, an embrace with death, a journey into nothingness.

It is a journey undertaken, however, with startling courage. Dressed in black W may be, but the image is not entirely funereal: "Black lacy high-necked evening gown. Long sleeves. Jet sequins to glitter when rocking. Incongruous frivolous headdress set askew with extravagant trimmings to catch light when rocking." On one level, the journey is clearly terrifying, a descent into the void, but there is more than a touch of bravado in those sequins, that headdress, the "best black" of a woman rocking toward death as if into the arms of a lover—a consummation devoutly to be wished. Thus Billie Whitelaw, the sublime performer of *Rockaby*, marking her rehearsal script with brief, sometimes cryptic notes to herself, wrote near the end of her script, "Strongest drive toward death," followed by the single word "Hurray!" (Gussow, 21).

Nor is W's rocking toward death only a visual image. Four times we hear her cry out "More," and four times rock and death-rattle monologue respond by beginning their identical journeys, drama and narrative intertwined. Like a child begging for just a few minutes more, a few verses more—anything to delay going to sleep—W's spoken command "More" initiates the lullaby that is *Rockaby*. For W, however, the "More" is deeply ironic; instead of postponing sleep, the story's progress will, as she well knows, propel her toward it. In *That Time*, B speaks of "just another of those old tales to keep the void from pouring in on top of you the shroud" (31); in *Rockaby*, the "old tale" is designed specifically to usher in that shroud. It is a tale, after all, about stopping—seven times W joins with V in intoning the phrase "time she stopped."

Speaker and listener *do* interact verbally in this play; the apparent monologue is in fact a form of dialogue.

But the ultimate transformation of verse narrative into drama in *Rockaby* occurs in the very structure of the play as performance. On the narrative level, V's monologue is divided into four sections, each section describing a progressive diminution, a *cascando*, a descent into silence and immobility. And this is precisely what we see and hear dramatized onstage. As the story winds down, so too does the stage picture: narration and theater image coalesce. Thus, after each section, Beckett notes that the light becomes a little fainter; each "More" from W sounds a little softer;[10] her "time she stopped" voice-overs likewise grow progressively softer, until in the final section W is silent throughout (a visual analogue of V's decision in the narrative to cease speaking to herself). V's last dozen lines in this final section similarly become gradually softer. And W's eyes, in section 1 "now closed, now open in unblinking gaze," remain increasingly closed through sections 2 and 3 (a visual analogue of V's narrative "let down the blind"), and "closed for good halfway through [section] 4." (Exactly halfway through section 4 we hear the lines "with closed eyes / closing eyes"; here stage picture literally coincides with verbal narrative.) At close of play, W sits blind, mute, completely unmoving. As the lights start to fade, there is a long pause when only her face is lit. In that faint light we see her head slowly sink and come to rest, a final visual analogue of the narrative's quest for oblivion: "till her end came / in the end came / . . . dead one night / in the rocker / in her best black / *head fallen*" (my emphasis). If "time she stopped" has been the recurrent leitmotif in this lullaby of stopping, we now fully comprehend the double meaning of that haunting and ambiguous phrase. For W's decision that it is time to stop is dramatized in the end by her *stopping time:* daughter merges into mother; rock is stilled; voice is silent—there is literally no "More." (Compare the similar movement in *That Time*, which opens with the words "that time" [28] and closes with the words "no time" [37].) The slow sinking of W's head thus functions as the punctuation mark noticeably absent from the text of the play seen only as verse narrative. For the "text" of *Rockaby* is ultimately a *theater* text, and so the play ends appropriately with a dramatic period. "Reckoning closed and story ended":[11] verse-narrative journey and dramatic journey have reached their identical dead end.

Such journeys by no means imply, however, an *artistic* dead end. Beckett's recent, ever-more-minimalist drama continues the process of paring away, of refining and redefining the basic parameters of dramatic genre—so much so that, looking back now on a play like *Godot*, one becomes positively giddy with the relative lavishness of Beckett's vision. Donald Davis, after appearing in the New York production of *Catastrophe* and *What Where*, commented that, next to them, *Waiting for Godot* "looks like an MGM musical" (Carey, 1). And yet, Beckett's late drama is still undeniably drama. The genre has not been refined out of existence; if anything, it has been refined even more clearly *into* existence. What Beckett wrote of the artist in his 1931 book on Proust has become equally true of the dramatic assault on traditional dramaturgy characteristic of Beckett's plays themselves. "The artistic tendency," Beckett noted, "is not expansive, but a contraction. . . . The only fertile research is excavatory, immersive, a contraction of the spirit, a descent. The artist is active, but negatively, shrinking from the nullity of extracircumferential phenomena, drawn into the core of the eddy" (*Proust*, 47–48). By progressively stripping his plays of all superfluities, by drawing in more and more closely to the core of the eddy, Beckett has steadily chipped away at the genre of drama so that what now remains is precisely its core: genre reduced to its very essence.

Notes

1. Beckett's original manuscript of *Footfalls* was succeeded by five separate typescript revisions, labeled by Beckett TS1, 2, 2A, 3, and 4 (all of which are in the Beckett Archives at the University of Reading). In the first British edition of *Footfalls* (London: Faber and Faber, 1976), which, with some exceptions for reasons unknown, appears to have been based on TS3, V suggests in her monologue that she is emanating from May's mind: "*My voice is in her mind. . . .* She has not been out since girlhood. (*Pause.*) *She hears in her poor mind, She has not been out since girlhood*" (11; my emphasis). In his final version of the play (TS4), Beckett eliminated the underscored lines; neither the first American edition of *Footfalls*, in *Ends and Odds: Eight New Dramatic Pieces* (New York: Grove Press, 1976), nor the second British edition of *Footfalls*, in *Ends and Odds: Plays and Sketches* (London: Faber and Faber, 1977), includes the lines.

2. I am quoting from the notes I took while viewing the New York production of *What Where* in June 1983.

3. Linda Ben-Zvi, "Samuel Beckett, Fritz Mauthner, and the Limits of Language," 194. See also Ben-Zvi's "The Schismatic Self in *A Piece of Monologue*," *Journal of Beckett Studies* 7–17.

4. This refusal occurs five times in the text (15, 18, 21, 22, 23), the last being the most vehement of all: "what? . . . who? . . . no! . . . she! . . . SHE!"

5. Quoted in Walter D. Asmus, "Practical Aspects of Theatre, Radio and Television: Rehearsal Notes for the German Première of Beckett's *That Time* and *Footfalls* at the Schiller Theater Werkstatt, Berlin," trans. Helen Watanabe, *Journal of Beckett Studies* 2 (Summer 1977): 85.

6. Although V's lines are not, of course, literally sung, they have a deliberately musical rhythm. In D. A. Pennebaker's and Chris Hegedus's film of *Rockaby*, we see Billie Whitelaw rehearsing the piece under the watchful eye of director Alan Schneider. As she begins chanting the lines, one hand instinctively flutters to an imaginary beat, "conducting" the words. "I haven't got the feeling yet," Whitelaw notes at one point. "I'm not playing the right music." See also Mel Gussow, "Billie Whitelaw's Guide to Performing Beckett," *New York Times*, 14 February 1984, 21: "After [Beckett] reads a play to [Whitelaw], they will often read it together, and each will automatically begin to flutter a hand in rhythm with the words. 'It's become sort of a joke between us,' she said. 'We both sit there conducting each other.' In rehearsal, Miss Whitelaw will do that characteristic hand movement by herself, and in performance, secretly, she will continue to flutter a foot or a toe."

7. According to Bartlett's *Familiar Quotations*, the lullaby is attributed to Charles Dupee Blake (1846–1903).

8. Donald Davis, playing the Director (D) in Alan Schneider's New York production of *Catastrophe*, pronounced "catastrophe" ("There's our catastrophe") with the accent on the first syllable and the final *e* silent—thus emphasizing the Greek etymology of the word in its primary definition: "The change which produces the final event of a dramatic piece; the dénouement" (*SOED*). See *Catastrophe*, in *The New Yorker*, 10 January 1983, 27.

9. Beckett creates the rhyming couplets by eliminating the phrase "stop her eyes" in the French translation of the ending.

10. In Billie Whitelaw's performance at the premiere of *Rockaby* in Buffalo (8 April 1981), the final "More" became simply a strangled, inchoate cry, barely decipherable as a specific word.

11. The sentence is Hamm's, very near the end of *Endgame* (83).

ANGELA B. MOORJANI

The *Magna Mater* Myth in Beckett's Fiction: Subtext and Subversion

That every text repeats other texts, which repeat still other texts, and so forth ad infinitum, is nowhere more dramatically evident than in Beckett's writing. Indeed, the dizzying abysmal structure of his novels, which heaps fragment upon fragment upon fragment, provides no foundation or end that might anchor or limit the text. Of the novels' reverberating myths, this essay examines the subtexts related to the *Magna Mater* and explores how they function within the fiction.[1]

Of the many attitudes writers can take to the subtexts they manipulate, Beckett's is almost without exception ironic or antagonistic. The many texts his fiction quotes directly or indirectly are rewritten, mocked, superimposed one on the other, only to be erased. Beckett's demythologization thus joins his other debunking activities, which, in contesting language from within language, genre conventions from within genre, and mythic categories from within myth, are, as Roland Barthes would have it, what writing is all about (16–17). In the process, readers are challenged to question one after the other the categories that make up their conceptual universe, the archaeology of the mind, to reflect on the consequences of the old ideologies, and to hear the whispered call of something as yet untried. Within a dialogic dimension, then, in Beckett's fiction the infinite store of stories that readers bring to the reading process is subverted along with the rest as a web of illusions.

The following discussion of the *Magna Mater* fragments concentrates on *Molloy* (1951), whose mythical reverberations have long been noted, and on *Mal vu mal dit* / *Ill Seen Ill Said* (1981).[2] The narrator of the first part of *Molloy* carefully stages what he calls his "irréel voyage" (22) / "unreal journey" (16) toward his mother as a descent into the psyche, the poetic descent into the underworld. The narrator/writer, then, after fraying a path into the embedded archives of the mind, transcribes the tracings of multiple inner texts made up of layer after layer of inscriptions. Such textual travel/travail brings to mind similar inner autobiographies, not least of which Dante's *Commedia*, that other journey through the mind's book toward the celestial rose and divine light, those partial translations of the ineffable.

The first inner landscape of *Molloy* features a bare white road at evening undulating through pastures in which cows are chewing. The town and the sea are not far off. After a brief stay in the town and a night passed in a ditch, on approximately the third day Molloy runs over a dog and, having entered its owner's domain, remains there for a year or so before continuing his wanderings. The description of this one-year cycle in Sophie-Loy-Lousse's garden bristles with mythic allusions and functions as a micronarrative reduplicating the narrative that surrounds it. Embedded within Molloy's inner journey to his mother, then, is the mythic realm of a maternal divinity.

The triple-named Lousse calls to mind a whole cluster of deities, among them the Greek lunar trinity of Artemis, Selene, and Hecate, particularly the latter, associated with the waning moon. The triple-bodied Hecate is the mother of witchcraft and the goddess of death and rebirth, who with her hounds guards the gates of Hades. Dog sacrifices were offered to her at crossroads. The key, the dagger, the dog, and the cross were among her symbols (Spretnak, 65–77, Jung, 369–71). One need only recall the long description of the moon, Lousse's sorcery evoking Circe along with Hecate, the mysterious garden gate, the death and burial of the dog, the knife and cruciform kniferest Molloy takes from the house, to recognize Hecate within Lousse.

In *Symbols of Transformation* (179), the first version of which appeared in 1912, Jung links Hecate to the bad mother and the sphinx, a role the haglike Lousse plays by keeping Molloy captive in her underworld prison and by preventing his journey to his mother. That she also saves him from being torn to bits by the surly crowd that gathers after the dog's death, that she loves and nourishes him in her paradisiacal garden, point to Lousse as the good mother, blending the negative with the positive.

The repeated allusions to the dead dog as Lousse's child, whom Molloy replaces, suggest, however, the Greco-Asian *Magna Mater*, predating classical myth by thousands of years, whose divine child, in imitation of the seasonal cycle of growth, decay, death, and rebirth, suffers death or a descent into the underworld and a return to life. The Sumero-Babylonian Ishtar and Tammuz, the Phoenician Astarte or the Cypriote Aphrodite and Adonis, the Phrygian Cybele and Attis, the Egyptian Isis and Osiris, and the Greek Demeter and Persephone and later Dionysus are all versions of the Great Mother and her dying and resurrected child. Outranking her child in importance, this *Magna Mater*, the embodiment of creative power, controlled birth, vegetation, and fertility and taught humanity law and divine worship. Among her emblems were the dove, the lion, and the fish, and she was associated with life-giving waters (James, 186, 237f.). Although Beckett could have thought of any or all of the above myths, or of others still, certain elements found in the Lousse episode would make it appear that the Cybele-Attis rites as portrayed by Frazer in *The Golden Bough* are the text to which he alludes, a connection first pointed out by Aldo Tagliaferri (53). According to Frazer, one of several versions of the legend has Attis, the son and lover of Cybele, bleed to death after castrating himself under a pine tree (264). Frazer glosses this as an attempt to explain the presence of eunuch priests, whom he describes as "unsexed beings in . . . Oriental costume," in the service of the divinity (265–66). Other writers have pointed out that such self-mutilation was motivated by the desire "to secure complete identity with the Goddess" (James, 167). The main festival of Cybele and Attis, which took place at the vernal equinox, consisted of bringing a pine tree wreathed with violets into the *Magna Mater*'s sanctuary, for these flowers "were said to have sprung from the blood of Attis, as roses and anemones from the blood of Adonis" (Frazer, 267). Frazer speculates that it was during the ecstatic death and resurrection rites around the tree that the self-emasculations took place, adding that the mutilated worshippers would thereafter put on female attire (268–70).

In returning to Beckett's novel, we find Lousse burying the dog Teddy, whose divine nature is hinted by his name signifying "gift of god," under a larch, whose green needles appear speckled with red, while Molloy contemplates ridding himself of his testicles: "J'avais donc intérêt à ce qu'ils disparaissent et je m'en serais chargé moi-même, avec un couteau ou un sécateur, n'était la peur où je grelottais de la douleur physique et des plaies infectées" (52). / "So the best thing for me would have been for them to go, and I would have seen to it myself, with a knife or secateurs, but for my terror of physical pain and festered wounds, so that I shook" (36). This passage, of course, is an example of Beckett's self-destructive texts, for no sooner identified with Attis, Molloy becomes an anti-Attis. Further hints, however, link him to the Cybele myth: he awakens in Lousse's house shaven of his beard, dressed in a frilly pink nightgown, served by an Oriental, and feeling like a sacrificial victim. When he leaves Lousse's garden at the end of a year, when the weather is warm, multicolored flowers are growing on Teddy's grave. These details and Molloy's continued identification with the buried dog point to the motif of the year-god, particularly Attis and Dionysus, and to Lousse as a Great Mother of birth, death, and rebirth. Of Lousse's garden Molloy tells that it appeared to change very little "abstraction faite des menus changements dûs au cycle habituel des naissances, vies et morts" (78) / "apart from the tiny changes due to the customary cycle of birth, life and death" (52). That he merges with this garden's life in a mythic return to the womb of the Earth-mother emphasizes his oneness with the *Magna Mater*, a oneness evident in his symbolic emasculation and in the blended names Molloy/Loy and Mollose/Lousse. He is as it were reabsorbed in the mother awaiting rebirth.

At the same time, though, as we have seen, Molloy is the son-lover of the mother goddess. That, as a consequence, he identifies Lousse both with his mother, Mag, a blend of "Ma" and "hag," and with another triple-named crone Ruth-Edith-Rose, an anagram of "Eros," does not prevent him from thinking that she is perhaps male or at least androgynous, an observation echoing the dual gender of Cybele and of the earliest-known divinities (James, 166). An androgynous *Magna Mater* and her hermaphroditic child, moreover, question and confound the rigid male/female polarities of patriarchal religions, which devalue the female principle. From an archetypal perspective, this androgynous image shifts Lousse beyond the *Magna Mater* into the primordial archetype in which opposites are undifferentiated (Neumann, 7–8).

In linking Lousse to the lunar triad and the *Magna Mater*, we have far from exhausted this fragment's intertextual reverberations, for in Sophie Lousse, there are also echoes of the gnostic Sophia or divine Wisdom in female form. That Beckett playfully manipulates Gnostic concepts has been pointed out by a number of commentators, although not in relation to the Sophia myth (Morot-Sir, 81–104; Busi, 76f.). For the Gnostics, Sophia combined the attributes of the Greco-Oriental moon, mother, and love goddesses into one figure, encompassing the whole spectrum from the most spiritual to the most sensual. She was known accordingly as "Sophia-Prunikos" or "Wisdom the Whore" (Jonas, 176–77). That the ancient Sumero-Babylonian Ishtar was similarly called both "Queen of Heaven" and "Harlot" shows that the blending of spirituality and sensuality was a constant of goddess worship (Langdon, 81f.). (In relation to Beckett, one cannot help but think of *Murphy* and the novel's punning reference to Celia as a celestial whore.) The dove, which became the symbol of the Gnostic Sophia in her role of Holy Spirit, provides a further link to the ancient Mother and Great Goddess (Walker, 951).

In returning to Beckett's Sophie Lousse, we find that the elements linking her to Sophia are treated with particular ridicule. Lousse, whose soliloquies Molloy finds harder to understand than her parrot's obscenities, in which the word *putain* ("whore") stands out (37, 55), is a travesty of Sophia-Prunikos. The French word for "parrot," *perroquet*, moreover, is close enough in sound to "Paraclete" (Holy Spirit) to make me suspect a multilingual pun.

Certainly, *Molloy*'s ironic treatment of Sophia and of the *Magna Mater* she represents parallels the Gnostic attitude toward her, for Gnosticism—or more precisely, the older Syrian-Egyptian or emanationist Gnostic tradition—makes the distinction between an unknowable, unnamable, and hidden divinity, on the one hand, and the divinity's degraded emanations, the creators of an evil world, on the other. Among these creators comes first the androgynous Sophia, followed by a demiurge born of her and commonly identified with the biblical Yahweh.[3]

In order to clarify the parallels between the Gnostic bisexual creation myth and *Molloy*, it is necessary to situate the Lousse text in the two-part novel. As we have seen, in chronicling a mother quest within a mother quest, the Lousse fragment is embedded, indeed more or less centered, in the main narrative of the novel's first part, which, in turn, is contained in the novel's second part, featuring a patriarchal order. The second part repeats the first by rewriting its maternal discourse in terms of the paternal.[4] Since the female order is thus everywhere traceable within the male, just as the mother-identified Molloy is within the father-identified Moran, the novel's second part is an example of an androgynous text or palimpsest.

Once the formidable *Magna Mater*/Sophia figure of part 1 has been rewritten as a tyrannical *Pater*, a parody of Yahweh, in part 2, however, these two discourses, echoing the multiple mythic representations of the female and the male, are equally subverted by the narrators. The androgynous nature of the text, giving equal status to the maternal and paternal law, which we might prefer over the uniquely patriarchal, does not end the quest. All totalizing solutions, archetypal or otherwise, are rejected, for the quest, one of an infinite series, spirals on to the unnamable. Thus, at the end of his self-narration, Moran no longer identifies the voice he hears with the paternal Logos, and Molloy, rejecting the maternal law (Loy/law), listens to the small voice telling him to leave Lousse's garden. It is this anonymous call that might free them perhaps from the violent maternal and paternal inscriptions of the past and undo writing's ties to a degraded creation mystique.

And finally, as is well known, the narrators proceed with a more drastic negation, that of their own discourses and by extension of the texts they contain, all of which they dismiss as lies, as fictions of fictions, which like all language are the faulty translations of what cannot be named.

The fictions, visions, or transcriptions that the narrators of *Molloy* produce during their journey through the psyche are, however, not so easily blotted out. So that thirty years or so after *Molloy*, the landscape and figure of *Mal vu mal dit* evoke the Lousse fragment and its multiple subtexts. As in the first part of *Molloy*, the landscape is pastoral, containing unshepherded white cows, in whose form the divine mother is frequently pictured. The sea is nearby. The garden, however, is replaced by a circular area of stones, within whose nonexistent center stands a cabin. The deathly whiteness of stone and snow in the light of the moon increasingly invades the terrain. The unnamed old woman, a silhouette of white and black like so many recent Beckettian figures, alludes particularly to Ishtar, the ancient Great Mother. Like the *Magna Mater*, Beckett's silent apparition is linked to the planet Venus as the morning star, associated with the moon, attended by male guardians, here a cyclical or zodiacal twelve, linked with a stone pillar or menhir (replacing the sacred tree), has the fish as an emblem, and flowers a mysterious tomb (Langdon, 53f.). She is foremost a *mater dolorosa*, the mother sorrowing for her lost lover and child (here recalling the divine shepherd Tammuz) during the desolate seasons of the year. As a *mater dolorosa*, she evokes Mary, the mother of

Christ, to whose sacrifice this as most Beckettian texts makes direct reference, and with which Beckett associates his own birth.

Unlike the narrator of *Molloy*, whose tone is mocking in relation to Lousse and whose comments playfully undermine the discourse he is producing, this later narrator's tone varies from panic to weary sadness at the tenacity of the illusory maternal trace, which like all the other figments of the mind, all lying traces of lying traces, is the "ill seen ill said" transcription of the still unnamable.

These Beckettian texts, then, in displacing the usual male/female oppositions, in subverting the mythic network imprisoning female and male, and in contesting language from inside language, join with contemporary theoretical critiques of self-presentation, as so well exemplified by Hélène Cixous in *La Jeune Née:*

> Hommes et femmes sont pris dans un réseau de déterminations culturelles millénaires d'une complexité pratiquement inanalysable: on ne peut pas plus parler de "la femme" que de "l'homme" sans être pris à l'intérieur d'un théâtre idéologique où la multiplication des représentations, images, reflets, mythes, identifications transforme, déforme, altère sans cesse l'imaginaire de chacun et rend d'avance caduque toute conceptualisation. (152)

> Men and women are caught up in a network of millenial cultural determinations of a complexity that is practically unanalyzable: we can no more talk about "woman" than about "man" without getting caught up in an ideological theater where the multiplication of representations, images, reflections, myths, identifications, constantly transforms, deforms, alters each person's imaginary order and in advance, renders all conceptualization null and void. (Marks, 96)

Notes

1. "Subtext" is here defined as "an already existing text (or texts) reflected in a new one" (Taranovsky, 18). For a discussion of the concept, see Rusinko.

2. Since both *Molloy* and *Mal vu mal dit* were first written in French, I shall quote in French, adding the English translation immediately after. For references to other mythic subtexts in *Molloy*, see Moorjani, 96–120.

3. This cosmogony is described in the *Apocryphon of John*, written in about A.D. 95, and since the second century one of the most widely known Gnostic tractates. For the text of the *Apocryphon*, see Robinson, 98–116; for further discussions of Sophia, see Rudolph, 72–84, and Pagels, 57f.

4. To illustrate how the second part of *Molloy* rewrites its maternal subtext, one might mention that Molloy's wrangling over the distribution of his sixteen sucking stones (maternal-substitute objects) reappears in the second part as Moran's preoccupation with sixteen irreverent theological questions of a patriarchal nature (Moorjani, 114). For an analysis of the intricate relation between the two parts, see Moorjani, 39–48, 99–118.

LINDA BEN-ZVI

Phonetic Structure in Beckett:
From Mag to Gnaw

In describing his relentless movement "worstward," the narrator in Beckett's most recent fiction suggests, "Add a—" but immediately cancels the idea. "Add? Never," he states with opprobrious display (22). Beckett's personae don't add; they subtract. Like their creator, they move in ever narrowing fields with fewer variables to range and rearrange. For example, in *Worstward Ho* the physical body becomes "bones," a state prefigured at the end of *Ill Seen Ill Said:* "not another crumb of carrion left" (59). No oversized head with tufts of hair, no mismatched testicles or splayed feet, just skeleton. And of that other repository of woe—the head—there too only "remains of mind," no longer affixed to a proper name, Molloy or Malone; to a personal pronoun, I or he; or a given locale, "ivory dungeon" (*Texts for Nothing*, 78) or "unspeakable globe" (*Ill Seen Ill Said*, 58).

Barely visible in these remains are the traces of images fleshed out and full in preceding works. A father telling his son a nightly tale of a Joe Bream or Breen in "The Calmative" and *Texts for Nothing*, reduced to a walking pair of undetermined sex in "Enough," becomes in *Worstward Ho* "barefoot plodding twain" (28), headless, legless, brush-stroked torsos. Diminished too in recent works are those two palliatives of life for Beckett's people: arithmetic and laughter. Mathematics that Molloy believed could "help you know yourself" (30) becomes for the speaker in *Company* only a generalized "help in time of trouble" (40). And of humor: "no trace. None any more," the narrator in *Ill Seen Ill Said* says (55).

Yet the speaker is not accurate. Although diminished when compared to its prominence in preceding Beckett works, humor can still be seen—albeit ill-seen—in recent writing, just as traces of body, mind, and imagery are still discernible even in the most severely limited forms. One element of Beckett's genius is precisely his ability to jettison more and more material of traditional literature and drama, and to make of the remains, the bones, an art that gains power in accordance with its refinement of materials. As each new work appears, we marvel at the narrowing terrain, swear the limits have been reached, and marvel anew as the little becomes even less in the following attempt. The clear direction toward an ever retreating point was set by Beckett early in his career when he accepted Democritus's premise that "Nothing is more real than nothing" and took upon himself the challenge of shaping that "nothing" in his art, a challenge doomed to failure but attempted again and again in the writings he has produced.

Nowhere is Beckett's drive for lessness more apparent than in his language. To speak and say nothing—the "nothing" that underlies speech—has been his characters' dream and their torment. The Unnamable describes the dilemma of them all:

> This voice that speaks, knowing that it lies, indifferent to what it says too old perhaps and too abased ever to succeed in saying the words that would be its last, knowing itself useless and its uselessness in vain, not listening to itself but the silence. (307)

In Beckett's plays the problem is less acute. There characters may wince, shrug, stand mute, be;[1] but in fiction, if they are to exist at all, they must exist in a world of words. They must speak even if they speak of silence. Therefore, the problem for Beckett, particularly in his fiction, has been to find verbal "bones," some remains that bear traces of the forms that preceded them and hints of their own desired surcease.

Although the Unnamable at the end of his story commits himself to going on, Beckett was aware of the burden of that declaration. In 1956, describing the impasse he faced after completing the trilogy, Beckett said:

> For me the area of possibilities gets smaller and smaller. . . . At the end of my work there's nothing but dust. . . . In the last book, *L'Innommable*, there's complete disintegration. No "I," no "have," no "being." No nominative, no accusative, no verb. There's no way to go on.

The fictions that follow the trilogy are marked by Beckett's awareness of the difficulty—seeming impossibility—of going on. Building on the "dust" and "disintegration" that precede them, Beckett experiments with new graphological and syntactic forms, omitting paragraphs in one work, punctuation in another, destroying logical sentence structure. Even their curious tripartite titles—*Texts for Nothing, How It Is, All Strange Away, Imagination Dead Imagine*—reflect ambiguity: Are they texts about nothing or texts for no purpose? Is imagination dead or are we exhorted to imagine anew? The answers must be tentative, for clues are few. The reader's uncertainty traversing these curious skullscapes parallels the uncertainty of the personae and perhaps of the writer, seeking ways to move out of the impasse his earlier works created.

Among the many experiments with language and form that Beckett attempted during the 1950s and 1960s, one that has received little notice is his manipulation with phonemes. Simply defined, phonemes are the primary linguistic units, both vowel and consonant, that indicate distinctive features in a given language, phonetics the science which studies the objective characteristics of human sound making, phonology the sound system of different languages.[2] Although usually represented by letter symbols, phonemes are not letters; they are sound categories. Beckett's manipulation of phonemes is not the familiar use of assonance and alliteration to produce "a noticeable effect"[3]—what Marjorie Perloff, for instance, so skillfully described in her article "Between Verse and Prose: Beckett and the New Poetry," where she cited the repeated use of spirants in the opening of *Ill Seen Ill Said*. Rather, in the fiction after *The Unnamable*, Beckett calls attention to the manner, place, and voicing of speech sounds, plays with sounds, and shifts from sounds of strong articulation to those of progressively weaker force, these patterns used as linguistic parallels to the thematic structures of his writing. As Beckett's terrain becomes fixed within the skull, the mouth and its accompanying articulating apparatus become more prominent, as the sounds they emit become stiller: from the strong voiceless sounds to weaker voiced sounds, from phonemes of ejaculation called plosives or stops to those of hissing expulsion of breath called fricatives or spirants.

The chart diagrams the three principal ways linguists describe consonant phonemes: by their manner, their place of articulation, and their voicing:

Manner of Articulation	State of Glottis	Bilabial	Labio-dental	Inter-dental	Alveolar	Palatal	Velar
Plosive or Stop	−voi	p			t		k
	+voi	b			d		g
Fricative or Spirant	−voi		f	θ	s	š	
	+voi		v	ð	z	ž	
Affricate	−voi					č (ts)	
	+voi					ǰ (dž)	
Nasal	+voi	m			n		ŋ
Lateral Liquid	+voi				l		
Retroflex Liquid	+voi				r		
Glide	+voi	w				y	
	−voi						

Associated with articulation is the question of force of sounds, whether they are made with a relatively strong degree of muscular effort and breath, identified as fortis or tense, or by a weaker force, indicated by the term lenis or lax. In English the fortis/lenis correlation moves in the following way, as indicated by the column marked *state of glottis:* from voiceless to voiced plosives, from voiceless to voiced fricatives, through the other manners of articulation to the voiceless glide, and then—ultimately—to silence. Beckett's direction has always been toward silence; therefore, the sound patterns he employs in his fiction following *The Unnamable* move perceptibly from fortis to lenis, from dominant plosives to fricatives. This diminution of sound is a corollary of the diminution of the variables in his works: from a walking, talking, named persona to a gelatinous ball; from unnamed voice to Mouth, in the 1972 play *Not I*, a gaping hole spewing out barely audible sounds.

Beckett has long demonstrated an interest in at least three qualities of sound: pleasure—Krapp savoring the sound of "spool" with the same relish he savors his bananas; power—Molloy obliterating his "Ma" by effacing the signifier with the final phoneme /g/, thus turning Ma into Mag; and ambiguity—the source of the puns and word games so central to Beckett's writing. While Beckett plays with sounds from his earliest writing—"Whoroscope" is predicated on the pun—in his writing after *The Unnamable*, sound becomes more than play or embellishment; it becomes progressively an important concomitant to his thematic purposes.

In *Text 13*, the last of the *Texts for Nothing*, the unnamed speaker, describing himself as "a head and its anus the mouth" (119), realizes that he is not going to escape the "farrago of silence and words" (100) that engulfed the avatars that preceded him. He says, "There is nothing but a voice murmuring a trace. A trace it wants to leave a trace, yes, like air leaves among the leaves" (133). The forms of the verb *to leave* and the noun *leaves* are identical in phonemic structure, and their juxtaposition provides an example of the type of wordplay Beckett employed often in earlier writing. There seems no attempt to have the sound ambiguities parallel the stated theme—to murmur a trace. However, near the conclusion of the same text, the simile gives way to a metaphor that produces a more complex image: "the screaming silence of no's knife into yes's wound" (135), an image Beckett found of sufficient importance to choose as the title of his collection of shorter prose, 1945–66. At first glance the image is clear: the thrust of nullity into surety, a thrust that is silent. But here Beckett is aided in structuring his image of the silence that cannot be articulated by phoneme play. First he offers the phonetically identical pairs "no" and, one line later, "know," thereby fusing negation and knowledge. Both "wound" yes. But Beckett does not stop with meaning alone. He shows the soundless form the recognition of nullity takes by also coupling the word *no* with *knife*, thus drawing attention by the presence of the silent *k* in *knife*, the trace of the absent *k* in *know*. In linguistic terms, a letter unpronounced has no phonemic existence. A letter unpronounced therefore does not designate a phoneme; it designates only silence. Thus by his manipulation of phonemes, Beckett is able to indicate absence underlying presence, silence underlying sound, while at the same time illustrating the point that knowledge cleaves to negation, and both undermine certainty. The phrase is an example of Beckett's use of phonetic possibilities to reinforce his ideas. Here, instead of creating a literature of the "Unword" as he described to Axel Kaun,[4] Beckett is experimenting with the "unletter," the graphic and phonetic bones of the "unword," the basis of the soundless literature he seeks.

Besides utilizing the articulatory nature of phonemes, Beckett also indicates in *Texts for Nothing* acoustic influences. In *Text 5*, the speaker begins by saying, "I'm the clerk, I'm the scribe" (91). He makes clear that the texts he has been weaving are not his own. "I say it as I hear it" (93). Instead of a narrator telling his tale, Beckett has created a storyteller that is himself being told, a narrator narrated. The connection between an invisible mouth and a waiting ear becomes central, and the sounds that blur the communication— the buzzes, hisses, pure noise—are serious obstacles in the way of the narrative for "the ears straining for a voice not from without" (91). These difficulties in the transmission of speech sound from mouth to ear continue in the next fiction, *How It Is.*

Texts for Nothing ends with the word "murmurs," a communicative impasse similar to that experienced by the Unnamable. This time, however, Beckett did not attempt to go on in his fiction. Ten years separate the *Texts* from *How It Is.* In the interim he wrote three stage and three radio plays.[5] When he did return to fiction in 1960, the phonemic and phonetic structures introduced only tentatively in the preceding fiction are given greater structural significance in *How It Is.*

The novel—if we can call it that—is Beckett's most insistently linear work: before Pim, with Pim, after Pim, a straight line of discourse "languidly wending its way eastward," the direction that a reader travels across the line of the text. In many ways the work is about the possibility of narrative linear discourse and the possible structuring of such a narrative. The markers along the straight line that the unnamed speaker constructs are phonetically paired words, presented as names of characters: Pim/Bem/Bom, Pam/Prim/Krim/Kram, and the dog Skom/Skum.[6] In *Murphy* and the trilogy Beckett had shown a preference for euphonious names beginning with *m*; but in *How It Is* the relational nature of the chosen names seems to form a structure that parallels the narrative form.

It was one of the central premises of the linguist de Saussure that phonemes in themselves have no meaning; they only signify in relation to other phonemes or sounds. For example, it is through our ability to distinguish *Fred* from *bed* or *fed* that we can distinguish phonemes and use them in meaningful combinations. That is, it is only through a phoneme's contrastive and combinatorial or paradigmatic and syntagmatic potential that we can recognize it and adduce from this primary unit more complex syntactical levels.

In *How It Is* Beckett structures his narrative around the anticipated meeting of the speaker and Pim, and the eventual replacement of Pim with Bom. To reinforce this narrative movement and displacement, Beckett carefully chooses names that allow him to indicate paradigmatic and syntagmatic structures through the Pim/Bom alignment. Their phonetic structures are contrastive and combinatorial, just as their narrative roles are both contrastive (as tormentor and tormented) and combinatorial (part of an unending line, or only three that wend their way eastward). Pim and Bom are what linguists would call near-minimal pairs, with two elements altered: the initial plosive sound /b/ for /p/ and the vowel sound /o/ for /i/. They are also both created from the same syllable structure formula: consonant vowel consonant. These associations appear to parallel what Beckett does in the narrative when he divides his work into three parts—beginning middle end—and insists on the integrity of the tripartite structure.

Yet almost immediately in part 1 of the novel, the speaker indicates that the carefully delineated form will not work, that after Pim arrives nothing will be clearer, that after he leaves nothing will change.[7] In the same way, after offering a relational connection between Pim and Bom, Beckett introduces another pair, Krim and Kram. In linguistics, just as /p/ /b/ are paired as voiceless-voiced, so too are /k/ and /g/. If the syllable structure and the phonetic structure were in fact relational, from one pair to the other, we would expect Krim/Grom rather than Krim/Kram. What Beckett seems to be doing is setting up a linguistic system for transferring names syntagmatically by adding sounds, using syllable structure to make the transference look like rules, and then purposely not following the implied formula. In short, he is doing on the phonetic level what he does on the narrative level: insisting on linearity and order and then almost immediately sundering the very structure he so carefully creates. Unlike the phonetic and sound structures of puns that are purposeful and logical, the phonetic patterns that Beckett suggests in *How It Is* destroy the very possibility of structure, just as his insistence on linearity destroys the possibility of the narrative form itself in this work.

Beckett is also able to employ specific phonemes in his paired names *Pim* and *Bom* to indicate other relationships within his novel. Whereas both /p/ and /b/ are plosives, /p/ is voiceless, as the signified Pim is, while the phoneme /b/, like Bom, is voiced. Also, Pim appears first in the narrative order, followed by Bom. In the fortis/lenis correlation, on the straight line to silence, a voiceless plosive has phonetically greater strength of articulation than a voiced plosive, just as the voiced plosive /b/ is stronger than the even weaker voiceless spirant /s/ that will proliferate in the next work, *All Strange Away*.

The central image of *How It Is*, a man scratching his words on a fictive surrogate—or on himself—has been used by two other twentieth-century writers:

James Joyce in *Finnegans Wake* and Franz Kafka in "In the Penal Colony." In Joyce's novel the image is used to reach an entirely different conclusion. In *Finnegans Wake*, Joyce's Shem the Penman, using his own body as the only foolscape available, writes upon himself and produces "mood-moulded cycle wheeling history." Beckett's unnamed "I" scratches his roman capitals on Pim's back, but finds after Pim that he is alone, still without voice, unable to structure his experience. His scriptural exercises bring him closer to those described by Kafka in "In the Penal Colony," where language provides no enlightenment, only gratuitous pain and senseless death. Joyce, using a similar image of self-effacement, finds coalescence; Beckett—like Kafka—finds failure.

With the hoped-for linear structure a dead end, Beckett turned in 1963 to *All Strange Away*, his most phonetically self-conscious work, where the spatial replaces the temporal, and phrases such as "no sound," "murmurs," are repeated; voiced and voiceless binary oppositions are suggested; spirants are mentioned by name and are emphasized; and their form of articulation—turmoil or turbulence of the wind in the mouth producing hissing sounds—is described. The work marks Beckett's shift from dominant plosives to the lesser velocity of fricatives or spirants that recur in great number toward the conclusion of *All Strange Away* and in subsequent writings.

All Strange Away takes its point of departure from an image in *How It Is*: a mouth, lips clenched, teeth and gums hidden, to which the speaker poses a question: "Where am I flown?" The answer seems to be within a skull, where the personal pronoun *I* dissolves into an unstated *you* and the "gibberish garbled six fold" is reduced to "ten words fifteen words like a fume of sighs when the panting stops." To mark this reduction of scope and sound, Beckett once more makes use of phonetic imagery.

On the walls of the enclosure "five foot square, six high, no way in, none out," appear the "tattered syntaxes of Jolly and Draeger Praeger Draeger" (7). The triad names echo the name-play of *How It Is*—three initial plosives, two voiced and the middle one voiceless. The images do not remain on the walls, however; they are soon canceled, and in place of the dominant plosives Beckett begins to employ fricatives or spirants to mark the growing silence. The shift toward the lenis is accompanied by the diminished dimensions of the space—finally two foot cube—and growing light that subsumes the figures within, first a man and then a woman the speaker calls Emma.[8]

Lines such as "for old mind's sake sorrow vented in simple sighing sound" and "no other sounds than these and never were that it is than sop to mind faint sighing sound for tremor of sorrow at faint memory of a lying side by side and fancy murmured dead" indicate that Beckett is self-consciously employing fricatives or spirants to reinforce his theme, the desired move toward soundlessness. He even calls direct attention to his manipulation within the text:

Glare back now where all no light immeasurable turmoil no sound black soundless storm. . . . All gone now and never been never stilled never voiced all back
whence never sundered unstillable turmoil no sound. . . . Fancy dead, try that
again with spirant barely parting lips in murmur and faint stir of white
dust. . . . (62–63)

His shift to spirants can be explained by their diminished energy on the
fortis/lenis scale and by the fact that they provide Beckett with an auditory
equivalent to the ocular world of growing whiteness he describes in *All
Strange Away* and the two following works, *Imagination Dead Imagine* and
Ping. Acoustically, the characteristic feature which marks fricatives is called
"white noise" because on a spectrograph, a machine that measures the
speech-wave spectrum, the /s/ appears almost as a solid, devoid of individuality since it covers the whole band within a continuous section of the spectrum. By using spirants, Beckett is able to reinforce the ever-encroaching, all-
obliterating whiteness that invades the world of his fiction.

Finally, to indicate the centrality of sound in *All Strange Away*, Beckett offers a dominant image that clearly represents this shift to murmured "bones"
of language. When he places Emma within the ever-narrowing cube, he
places in her hand an object, a rather puzzling object: "a small grey punc-
tured rubber ball or ball from a bottle of scent." The important fact seems
not which it is but the similar function of both. Three times in the text Beckett describes the same motion: "squeeze firm down five seconds say faint hiss
then silence then back loose two seconds and say faint pop." The motion and
the accompanying sounds suggest both plosives and spirants, and Beckett accompanies the description with words such as "voiced," "voiceless," "no
sound," "all sound," and even a specific reference to spirants. But in true
Beckettian fashion, he goes even further in the vocal chain, back to the source
that makes sound possible: the lungs. The squeezed ball, like the lungs, is
ingressive and egressive, fills and empties; it is capable of creating hissing
and popping. From these breath patterns words are eventually formed and articulated. The image and accompanying action upon it thus become iconic of
the entire action of sound formation and indicate once more Beckett's unre-
mitting attempt to reduce language to its "remains" and then to silence. *All
Strange Away* thus ends with the desire expressed in the text, "Well say a
sound too faint for mortal ears to hear." Not a word but a sound is emitted.

In more recent works Beckett has continued to play with phonetic structures and sounds. In *A Piece of Monologue*, the opening sound patterns of the
first paragraph trace the actual way a baby learns to talk; in *Company* the persona is called H Aspirate Haitch, the name a play on sounds, and in *Ill Seen Ill
Said*, as Perloff mentions, the spirants provide a structure for the opening stro-
phe. Most recently, in *Worstward Ho*, near the end of the novel, Beckett uses

the word *gnaw*. This time the /g/ does not efface the word—as it did in *Mag*—but is silent, absent, allowing the "naw" or "naught" to stand undeterred.[9]

In answer to a query, Beckett has said, "Of modern linguistic philosophy I know next to nothing";[10] yet his writings indicate that he is at least highly sensitive to the possibilities of phonemes and phonetic structures as devices to reinforce the themes of his work. Just as Beckett is not a linguist, he is also not a mathematician, but that fact has not kept him from playing with numbers in order to provide "bones" for his writing. In Beckett's continuing journey "worstward," phonemes, like numbers, have offered a skeletal underpinning to hold up an ever more compressed world, a world of the mind that still requires form but has long since abandoned conventional devices that support literatures going in the other direction.

Notes

1. It was Alain Robbe-Grillet who, when writing about *Waiting for Godot*, observed: "And their situation is summed up in this simple observation, beyond which it does not seem possible to advance: they are *there*, they are on the stage" (*From a New Novel*, 115).

2. For assistance with the discussion of phonemes and phonetic principles, I wish to thank Professors James Garvey and Richard Warner, Colorado State University.

3. In discussions of assonance and alliteration, *The Princeton Encyclopedia of Poetry and Poetics* stresses their use for stylistic effects and sound organization, but not for structure.

4. In one of Beckett's earliest and most detailed descriptions of his intentions in writing, he wrote to his German friend Axel Kaun: "As we cannot eliminate language all at once, we should at least leave nothing undone that might contribute to its falling into disrepute. To bore one hole after another in it, until what lurks behind it—be it something or nothing—begins to seep through; I cannot imagine a higher goal for a writer today." Beckett called such writing "literature of the unword" (Reprinted in *Disjecta*).

5. During the period from 1950 to 1960 Beckett wrote *Fin de partie* and *Acte sans Paroles 1* (1956), *Krapp's Last Tape* (1958), *Embers*, and *Acte sans paroles II* (1959). It is possible that because of his experiences with the stage, Beckett was able to move away from the impasse that *Texts for Nothing* presented to him. *How It Is* becomes the demise of the narrative of time, and the next prose work, *All Strange Away*, introduces a fiction of place—complete with costume changes, curtains, shifting positions, direction from without—that may have been a carryover from Beckett's experiences with theater and radio in the 1950s.

6. I am assuming that Bom is pronounced /bam/ (rhymes with "mom") and not /bom/ (rhymes with "home"), since I assume the pronunciation follows the analogy of the English orthographic system. Also, what I am saying about the sound structures in *How It Is* will alter in the French translation *Comment c'est*.

7. Punctuating the narrative of *How It Is* is the recurring phrase "something wrong there." It is uttered five times in part 1, three times in part 2, and nine times in part 3. Were the narrative formula to work, part 3, "after Pim," should have fewer doubts than either preceding section. Just the opposite seems true. Only in Part Two, while Pim is present, is doubt assuaged. After Pim leaves, nothing is made clearer; "how it is" is still unsettled.

8. The central action of *All Strange Away* is the folding of bodies—first a man's and then a

woman's—in a box that continually changes dimensions. There may be a suggested analogy between these laborious movements and the movement of the tongue in the mouth as it produces sounds, or even of the vocal box or vocal triangle formed by the inner mouth as it works in articulating sounds.

    9. In *What Where* (1983), Beckett also continues his play with euphonious names. The characters are called Bam, Bem, Bim, and Bom.

    10. Letter received from Samuel Beckett, 2 September 1979.

PART 4

Transpositions for Stage and Screen

TOM BISHOP

Beckett Transposing, Beckett Transposed: Plays on Television

A number of Beckett's dramatic works have been produced for and shown on television. These include works written specifically for the small screen, theater pieces adapted for television, and theater pieces filmed for television presentation without specific adaptation.

Since *Eh Joe*, written in 1965 and aired originally in 1966, Beckett has become increasingly interested in the new medium and has himself directed all the works written especially for TV. Meanwhile, many other dramatic pieces have found their way to TV productions in the United Kingdom and West Germany and, to a lesser extent, in France and the United States.

These various Beckett plays on television present several forms of transposition or transmutation: (1) stage plays adapted to television; (2) Beckett's German television stagings, following initial BBC productions; (3) two versions of a single dramatic script, both directed by Beckett; and (4) intertextual approaches in recent works that refer to previously utilized images and techniques. (This last category admittedly stretches the notion of transposition, but it provides examples too interesting to pass over.)

The purpose of this essay is to examine examples of each of the above categories in order to analyze the nature of the transmutations, especially when operated by Beckett himself. We will not deal with stage productions shown on television with little or no adaptation, since these are not in any sense examples of transpositions (e.g., *Oh les beaux jours* in France and *Happy Days* on BBC).

1. *Play Adapted to Television.* Undoubtedly the most interesting and most significant example in this category is *Not I*. It is a true transposition from one medium to another with differences so substantial in nature that one may consider that the 1977 TV version altered the 1972 stage play significantly. The direction of the BBC version was signed by Anthony Page, but Beckett participated so closely in the production that he must be considered at least to

have had a share in the direction. Not only did he approve the important transpositions made, but he is now known to feel that the BBC version is the best rendering of his play—in a way, the definitive one.

These changes concern, first, the space occupied by Mouth and, second, the absence of the Auditor.

Most striking is the total invasion of all visible space by Mouth. On stage, the most startling nature of the play had been the stunning isolation of a sharply defined mouth singled out by a pinpointed spotlight in the vast darkness of the stage. (This was true in the New York creation of *Not I*, directed by Alan Schneider with Jessica Tandy, in the French staging by Jean-Louis Barrault starring Madeleine Renaud, and in the London production with Billie Whitelaw, but not always in a number of later productions.) On television, the Mouth is not counterpointed against the darkness; it literally fills the entire screen. It is more *there* than any object or thing usually viewed on a TV screen. It is *there* not only in the obvious, crucial sense of capturing the screen during the entire fifteen minutes of *Not I*, it is *there* in a phenomenological sense, embodying that "thingness" so dear to Sartre—like the chestnut tree in *Nausea*, the Mouth is endowed with extraordinary immanence.

Watching *Not I* on the small screen is riveting, mesmerizing, and physically painful—or at least those are my own reactions, unchanged after some forty viewings. That mouth, those lips, those teeth, that tongue are obscene because they are so very present, because, too, their constant frantic movement gives them an independence of life that is quite near unbearable. And Billie Whitelaw's teeth, brilliant against the darkness, enthrall and very nearly paralyze us. Accordingly, the televised *Not I* is impossible in color; although shot in color, the print had to be abandoned in favor of the black-and-white rendering, for the mouth and tongue were too much to bear in red.

In the theater, the Mouth had achieved a different kind of presence, another sort of riveting attraction. Tiny in the vastness of a stage, sharply white and red against the pitch darkness, it triumphed over its surroundings, obliterated them, and forced us to stare at it entranced, as one gets overwhelmed by the glare of a headlight incandescent in the night. On the screen, that effect would have been impossible; what was substituted for it—the total occupation of our field of vision—was the best solution for the other medium. (Of course, *that* solution would have been impossible on a stage.)

The second factor in this transposition is the role of the Auditor—and it presents a serious problem. The Auditor is no superfluous figure in *Not I* . . . as if one could really imagine a superfluous character in a Beckett play. His is a very important role: his very presence links the Mouth to a human reality and introduces a semblance of dialectic, albeit a silent one. The Auditor's presence also structures the stage space, forcing us (allowing us?) to change the focus of our vision several times, deflecting it at times from that hypnotizing Mouth. His unusual size, his strange elevation, counterpoint the minuteness of Mouth and its location in a void to produce an eerie spatial relationship that serves the play admirably.

More important, the Auditor's reactions, his apparent regret and eventual resignation at Mouth's unwillingness to relinquish the third-person narration and to speak in the first-person singular, bring a telling though unvoiced echo to Mouth's discourse and give particular texture and tension to the repetitions of "what? . . . who? . . . no! . . . she!" In the Paris production, originally in Barrault's small theater, the Petit Orsay, the stage was too small to accommodate the Auditor. Reluctantly, Beckett, who had collaborated with Barrault on the production, agreed to do away with him. It proved to be a regrettable loss for the play. When the play was later moved to the larger theater at Orsay, the Auditor was (re)introduced.

On television, the situation was quite different. The spatial relationship could not have been maintained between Mouth and Auditor. Since Mouth could be made to fill up the entire screen, the Auditor would have been a visual intrusion; using two different camera shots would have meant yielding the constant, magnetic presence of Mouth. As transposed to TV, *Not I* becomes, reasonably, Mouth's play totally—the dialectic had to be sacrificed and rendered implicit. The result is certainly one of the most astounding quarter hours of television ever conceived.

2. *Beckett's German Television Versions.* Three dramatic pieces make up this category: *Eh Joe, . . . but the clouds . . .* , and *Ghost Trio.*

Eh Joe, Beckett's initial venture into television, was first aired by the BBC in 1966, directed by Alan Gibson, with Jack McGowran and Sian Phillips; subsequently, Beckett directed two different productions of *Eh Joe* for Süddeutscher Rundfunk. There are several differences, but not marked ones, between the original BBC presentation and the later German ones. The quality of acting is striking in all three. Neither Jack McGowran on the one hand nor Heinz Benent on the other falls into the potential trap of overacting by indulging in facial tics while listening to the voice in the skull. To achieve simplicity and credibility in this role is not nearly so easy as it may seem, since the actor is reduced to listening, to reacting with only his face and body, as the camera inexorably zeroes in on him. If these splendid actors succeeded, such has not always been the case in TV renderings of *Eh Joe* in other countries. Excellent actors in the title role, guided by outstanding directors, have disappointed with twitching, sweating, and straining.

There is not too much to choose from between the British original and the two Beckett-directed German versions. One element to note is the smile at the very end, when the voice has receded and stopped. McGowran and Mendel grimace a smile of relief at this point in obvious satisfaction that the Voice has stopped its tormenting, at least for the evening. No such smile is visible on the face of Benent (to Beckett's great dismay). One may note in passing that the printed text makes no reference to a smile or to any reaction at the conclusion of the piece. The stage direction reads only: "(*Voice and image out*)." As to that voice, there are some differences: Sian Phillips speaks in a husky whisper, while Beckett obtained in German firmer, louder voices, more demanding in their insistence but perhaps less insinuating.

Technically, Beckett's two German versions are more satisfying—the lighting is much sharper, the camera work, as executed by Jim Lewis, who has worked on everything Beckett has directed on German TV, more crisp. The British version is 6 minutes shorter than the German ones—19 minutes compared to 25—but that does not mean that *Eh Joe* drags in Beckett's direction. As points of comparison, one may mention that the French TV production lasted 25 minutes also, while an American one lasted a long 34.

Since the subject here is transpositions, it seems appropriate to mention that in the past few years *Eh Joe* was adapted to the stage in two American productions (at the Beckett Festivals in New York in 1978 and in Paris in 1981) and more recently in a French-language production in Paris. It is the first Beckett television play to be adapted to the stage. Of course there are by now many examples of other generic metamorphoses: *Krapp's Last Tape, Happy Days, Not I, Waiting for Godot* on television; the stage play *What Where*, which Beckett was to direct for German TV in 1984 (but had to postpone until 1985); the by-now countless stage versions in various languages of Beckett prose texts, starting with the memorable Mabou Mines production of *The Lost Ones*; the transformation to the stage (again by Mabou Mines) of the radio play *Cascando*; and the TV version of another radio play, *Tous ceux qui tombent* (*All That Fall*), on French television, directed by Michel Mitrani.

More fascinating than the case of *Eh Joe* is the contrast between the British and Stuttgart versions of *Ghost Trio* and . . . *but the clouds*. . . . These two plays were presented by BBC together with *Not I* under the collective title *Shades*. *Ghost Trio* and . . . *but the clouds* . . . were directed by Donald MacWhinnie, and *Not I* by Anthony Page, with Beckett's close collaboration. Süddeutscher Rundfunk presented the same threesome under the title *Schatten. Geister Trio* and . . . *Nur Noch Gewölk* . . . were directed by Beckett, while *Not I*, the last of the three, was shown by the Germans in the BBC English version.

Beckett's German version of *Ghost Trio* is quite close to the earlier BBC production, though perhaps a bit less crisp, the male figure somewhat more hazy, the cassette player less distinguishable. The only striking difference involves the appearance of the Boy. In the BBC version one cannot fail to be struck by the Boy's marvelous luminosity. In the German production, the Boy's lovely smile has been replaced by a sad, dark negation, a shaking of the head that spins off less rich (and clearly negative) overtones than the brief, positive blond presence in the English production. The change gives a vastly different tonality to the nature of the memory.

...but the clouds... presents divergences between the English and German versions more interesting than *Ghost Trio.* The crucial camera shot of the Protagonist in the process of remembering, so fuzzy as to be barely recognizable in the BBC tape, is crisp and clear in the Stuttgart direction by Beckett. It is likely that Jim Lewis's camera work is again responsible for added clarity. Having worked with Beckett for a long time, Lewis seems to understand Beckett's needs intuitively. Not only are the shots clearer in the German version but the movement of the Protagonist is also sharper, more intelligible.

Another change involves the quotation from Yeats's poem *The Tower*, which is spoken by the Protagonist at the end of the play. Since not only the title *...but the clouds...* but the collective title *Shades* come from that quotation, it naturally occupies a key role in the work. In the original BBC version, Beckett included only the last four lines of *The Tower:*

> ... but the clouds of the sky
> When the horizon fades;
> Or a bird's sleepy cry
> Among the deepening shades.

In fact, Beckett intended the last fifteen lines of the poem (the last stanza) to serve as his quotation—and in the German version of the play, he does indeed include the longer selection—but he felt that the poem is so well known to English-speaking audiences that anything more than the last four lines would be too explicit ("I didn't want to dot all the i's," he said to me). Following the German production with its full fifteen lines, Beckett came to regret the shortened version in the original production and stated that he would now use the entire quote if he were to do it over. The last stanza of *The Tower* does indeed shed a richer light on *...but the clouds...:*

> Now shall I make my soul,
> Compelling it to study
> In a learned school
> Till the wreck of body,
> Slow decay of blood,
> Testy delirium
> Or dull decrepitude,
> Or what worse evil come—
> The death of friends, or death
> Of every brilliant eye
> That made a catch in the breath—
> Seem but the clouds of the sky
> When the horizon fades;
> Or a bird's sleepy cry
> Among the deepening shades.

Ironically, the long quotation in German is of little help, because the Yeats poem is not very happily translated. A new translation of the final stanza for the purpose of *. . . Nur Noch Gewölk . . .* might have been a better solution.

Nowhere has Beckett used the television medium more perfectly than in *. . . but the clouds . . .*, and especially in his own German version. It is a beautifully devised and designed work, with its splendid depiction of the process of memory, its lovely pensive mood coupled with gentle irony in the recapitulation of the Protagonist's movements and statements. In Stuttgart, Beckett produced a clarity and simplicity of shots, a perfect modulation of voice quality, in what is probably his best work as television director so far, combined with his most sensitive writing to this date specifically for the medium.

3. *Two Versions of a Single Script: Quad, Quad I*, and *Quad II*, Beckett's most abstract pieces, seem to stand quite apart in his TV work, and in his work in general. He terms *Quad* "A piece for four players, light and percussion," and he refers to the figures in the piece as "players."

Quad (or *Quadrat*, the German title for this dialogueless work recorded in Stuttgart and subsequently rebroadcast by BBC) has a "scenario" shooting script of merely two typewritten pages. It is the exploration of possible permutations of four variables in movement, color, and sound on a square surface, along prescribed paths, while avoiding the middle of the playing area (referred to as point E, with points A, B, C, and D denoting the four corners of the area). Beckett described the "problem" to be solved by the work as: "Negotiation of E without rupture of rhythm when three or four players cross paths at this point. Or if ruptures accepted, how best exploit?" In fact, the ruptures were not accepted in the final version, and the avoidance of E, whatever the permutations of movement, remains as the central organizing principle. Beckett's footnote explains that "E supposed a danger zone." Perhaps we are to read a measure of meaning into the abstraction after all? What is clearer than the answer to this question is that in *Quad* Beckett draws on his lifelong passion for mathematics.

Beckett went to Stuttgart in the spring of 1982 in order to create what is now known as *Quad I. Quad II* is, as it were, an afterthought, an exercise and a variation on a theme in which Beckett reshapes the initial material into a different form in order to see what would happen. What *Quad II* yields is fascinating, particularly as contrast. Where *Quad I* is in color (*mirabile dictu*—Beckett's first use of color television . . . a spare, lovely, *necessary* use of color), *Quad II* is shot in black and white, and its movement is slow and deliberate in contrast to the somewhat mocking speed of *Quad I*. Furthermore, in *Quad II* there is no percussion, and the shuffling sound of the players is the only soundtrack. (One cannot help but think of *Footfalls*.) Finally, whereas *Quad I* consists of four variables—a full exploration of all the possible combinations of four players—*Quad II*, for the obvious imperative of duration, given the slowness of movement, depicts only a single set of permutations and not the full four. The resulting contrast between the two is very clear indeed: two very different moods.

4. *Intertextual Approaches in Recent Works.* This category may stretch the notion of transposition; nevertheless *Nacht und Träume* presents some fascinating examples of intertextuality. *Nacht und Träume* was directed by Beckett in Stuttgart in 1982 and aired by Süddeutscher Rundfunk the following year. It has no dialogue; the only words heard are those of the last seven bars of Schubert's well-known Lied. The 10½ minutes of the videoplay depict a dreamer and his dream in which he himself is central. It is a gentle dream, twice repeated, in which the dreamt self is comforted by dreamt hands that touch him, give him drink, wipe his brow, and finally join his hands in a clasp. In the first dream, the dreamer is visible dreaming, together with his dreamt self; in the second, the image of the dreamer fades during the dream, leaving only the dreamt self on the screen. When the second dream fades out, *Nacht und Träume* ends.

The figure of the dreamer recalls the protagonists of *. . . but the clouds . . .* and *Ghost Trio;* one may even be reminded of the figures in *Ohio Impromptu.* In his quality of dreamer, the protagonist is especially close to *. . . but the clouds . . .* , down to the materialization of the dream on the screen. But *Nacht und Träume* is more ambitious technically in its depiction of the dreams. Each dream is portrayed in a diffused, milky light (termed a "kinder light" by Beckett in the script) as opposed to straight lighting for the nondream sequences, and the dream is shown in a sort of bubble, first at the top of the screen and eventually on the entire screen. The dreamer himself is at times part of the dream. On another level, the use of the Schubert Lied "Nacht und Träume" recalls the use of Beethoven's "Ghost Trio" in the TV play of that name.

Some of Beckett's very recent pieces, *Quad* on television and *Catastrophe* and *What Where* on stage, seem to be opening up new directions yet again in the evolution of his work; *Nacht und Träume,* on the contrary, appears to link up with themes and techniques of Beckett's work on television in the seventies.

RUBY COHN

Mabou Mines' Translations of Beckett

When Samuel Beckett was in Berlin in 1976 to direct *Damals* and *Tritte*, the German translations of *That Time* and *Footfalls*, he accepted an invitation from English-speaking actors he had never met. He agreed to look not at a performance but at settings of their Beckett adaptations of *The Lost Ones* and *Cascando*, which were not intended for live performance. Confronting the clutter on Astroturf, the setting for *Cascando*, he queried with surprising good humor: "You *have* adapted it, haven't you?" He said "adapted" and not "translated," but the Mabou Mines—for they were the English-speaking actors—were engaged in a kind of translation. Beckett himself is a dedicated translator, and four Mabou Mines translations to the stage are dedicated to Beckett, however provocative they may be to the Beckett scholar.

Mabou Mines are Nova Scotia coal mines near which a New York City-based theater company rehearsed during one humid summer. The name is redolent of hard work and hidden wealth, which is what the group wished to convey by its name, resolutely *not* mentioning theater, for Mabou Mines was in revolt against the dominant Western theater esthetic, in which an actor impersonates a character for a passive spectator. In that revolt they conscripted two playwrights, Brecht and Beckett. They performed no Brecht plays, but they absorbed his theory of epic, or, in their word, *narrative* theater, in which a story is conveyed with little or oblique impersonation. For over a decade they have blended Brecht, Beckett, and a palette of special skills.

During the 1970s Mabou Mines' artistic director was Lee Breuer, who, like many of our own students, first heard of Beckett in a classroom—a UCLA French class. In 1958 he hitchhiked to San Francisco to see the Actor's Workshop production of *Waiting for Godot*—the same production that played San Quentin Prison. He and his actress-wife, Ruth Maleczech, left school to join the Actor's Workshop, where they met actor Bill Raymond, then a spear-carrier of the avant-garde, and JoAnne Akalaitis, then a Stanford student working in the office. The young people were poverty-stricken during the day, but they were richly stagestruck at night. Would-be playwright Breuer wanted to nourish his writing by inventive directing, and his first major assignment was *Happy Days.* In his binary mind's eye—an eye for which he later received great praise—Winnie was an aging flapper of the Jazz Age, but he did not dare realize that outrageous marriage, as he did in his recent gospel *Oedipus.*

In 1966 the Breuers went to Europe and were surprised to stay five years, soon working with the nucleus of what was to become the Mabou Mines. In 1967, in Paris, they renewed their friendship with JoAnne Akalaitis, and met her husband, composer Philip Glass. Theater exercises at the American Cultural Center introduced them to another Westerner, actor Fred Neumann, who had learned his craft in the Army during World War II, and who had been drawn to Beckett since seeing the original French production of *Godot* in 1953. Since Fred's wife, Honora Ferguson, wrote for the French review *Réalités,* they made the acquaintance of her British colleague, David Warrilow, who had understudied Nagg's role in a British production of *Endgame.* Akalaitis, Breuer, Maleczech, Neumann, and Warrilow felt hemmed in by Stanislavskian personalization, and yet they were cool to Brechtian epic acting. A performance breakthrough came in 1968, when a pregnant Ruth Maleczech and a nursing mother JoAnne Akalaitis hid their respective conditions to enroll in a Grotowski workshop in Aix-en-Provence. Back in Paris, they evolved an acting approach that Breuer called Mr. Outside (Brecht) combined with Mr. Inside (Grotowski). Beckett's *Play* and *Come and Go* became the linchpins of new theater constructions by the still-unnamed group. Under Breuer's direction, they performed these plays strictly according to Beckett's scenic directions, or interspersed with Glass's music; they played with mirrors, ventriloquism, taped loops, video inserts.

They celebrated Christmas 1969 by forming a company, and they began the new decade in New York City. In their thirties by this time, some of them parents, with no illusions about swift success, they played in galleries, museums, and gymnasiums. All the company members were present at all rehearsals, earning their living precariously so that—and they would be embarrassed to hear me state it so baldly—their art could remain pure of commerce.

By 1975 the Mabou Mines sported an avant-garde reputation but no bank account. While drudging away at their respective jobs, they effervesced collectively at the prospect of an all-Beckett program—the two short plays that had nurtured their esthetic, and the recitation of a prose text that would provide scope for their antistentorian, antiempathy, narrative attitude to theater. After haphazard dipping into Beckett's lyrics of fiction, they selected *The Lost Ones* for a reading by Warrilow. Its descriptions, calculations, and ratiocinations presented a challenge to telling a story.

Beckett's paragraphs alternate between the elements of a cylinder-world and the movements of its 205 inhabitants, "each searching for its lost one." As Warrilow read and reread the sixty-three-page text, he inadvertently memorized long sections, and he found the book a hindrance to his lecture-demonstration of a two-foot-high cross section of cylinder with its population of half-inch celluloid dolls. At the same time Breuer and designer Thom Cathcart conceived an audience environment comparable to Beckett's "solid rubber or suchlike."

Shoeless, the spectators enter a dark foam-rubber cylindrical space in which tiers of foam-padded steps are built from floor to ceiling. An ugly sulfurous glow emanates from the sides of the steps, but spotlights follow Warrilow around the cylindrical playing area. Electronic music by composer Glass approximates the text's "faint stridulence as of insects." Cutting Beckett's text by a third, Warrilow graduates from a dry and seedy academic clinically observing the small cylinder to a naked human essence who draws an equation between the tiny celluloid dolls and ourselves, but his involvement deviates, mesmerizing us to its changes. In various dull lights, playing mainly on audience right, he recites Beckett's text, his voice a resonant stringed instrument. After about half the playing time, but quite late in Beckett's text, as the temperature rises in *our* fetid cylinder, Warrilow removes his clothes to enact the several torments of the cylinder's inhabitants. During a blackout his voice softens for the vanquished woman called the North; lights then reveal a nude actress, "her head between her knees and her legs in her arms." In a graceful movement that departs from Beckett's description, she lifts her face and slowly spreads her arms and legs. She freezes for a moment, then returns to Beckett's head-down position, vanishing in another blackout.

Warrilow on the playing-floor shines a pencil-light on two tiny dolls, then on one "if a man." After dark finally descends in the theater, Warrilow's voice chants from the exit—"if this notion is maintained." For nearly an hour the Mabou Mines—actor, plants in the audience, little cylinder, and cylindrical environment—have maintained this notion with hypnotic intensity. *The Lost Ones* is one of the first of many translations of Beckett's fiction to the stage.

The 1975 Mabou Mines Beckett program was unexpectedly reviewed in the popular press. Jack Kroll hailed it in *Newsweek:* "Mabou Mines has captured the eerie elegance of Beckett's testament of death-in-life as the destiny of a race that has worn out its spiritual capital." Breuer wrote to Beckett, whom he still hasn't met: "When we closed on schedule after three weeks it was quite clear the program could have run a couple of years." He requested Beckett's permission for what had developed into something quite different from a reading, which Breuer explained in his letter as "a reading of writing—not a staging of events written of." He concluded the letter: "Please be assured that our respect for you and your work is such that if you clearly disapprove there is no alternative for us but to drop completely any idea of ever performing it again. We plead our cause but would not dream of contesting your decision." Beckett did not reply, performance of *The Lost Ones* continued to 1982, Warrilow performing in French or English in cylinders built for the occasion.

On the sidelines of *The Lost Ones* was JoAnne Akalaitis, who imbibed the energy radiated by the production and wished to disperse Beckett energy to all the actors in the company. After helter-skelter reading, she fixed on *Cascando* as her instrument. Totally ignoring Beckett's directions for the radio play, she drew upon Mabou Mines actors' exercises to compose a score for a range of voices in a fisherman's house in a Nova Scotia winter, which seemed to her the Celtic edge of the hemisphere. In that fictional corner of a no-man's-land, actual Mabou Mines actors would perform tasks centered on simple objects; task and voice deliver energy.

Fred Neumann in company exercises had imitated the explosive voice of his friend Kenneth Burke, which seemed to Akalaitis perfect for Opener. She heard Music as a cello, and Glass provided the score, although he was no longer her husband and no longer in the company. Akalaitis assigned Beckett's longest part, Voice, to five actors, only one a woman—pregnant Ellen McElduff. Raymond and Warrilow traced the mishaps of Woburn, but all the actors set their words to the rhythm of their tasks—Neumann shaving, Warrilow knitting, Raymond carving wood, McElduff playing solitaire, Cathcart painting, others building a house of cards. In their winter isolation, the idled fishermen had one frail proof of an outside world—a 1920s radio over which Ruth Maleczech parodied excerpts from the BBC version of *Cascando*. This quasi-chaos on stage subdued Beckett's lines to the performance on Astroturf, a winter dream of vegetation, and *Cascando* on stage channeled JoAnne Akalaitis's energy into directing other theater pieces.

Inevitably, artists as gifted as those of the Mabou Mines have their disagreements. In 1978, when company meetings were sour, Neumann wanted to pour some Beckett on troubled waters, and he envisioned *Mercier and Camier* as a vehicle for Warrilow and Raymond, under his direction. By the time Neumann received Beckett's permission—and he did—Warrilow had withdrawn from the company, but he nevertheless consented to play the Narrator on video and Watt on audio. Neumann then cast himself as Mercier, and called upon Terry O'Reilly for the several secondary roles of the novel, which he reduced to some fifty typed pages.

Like other neophyte directors today, Neumann conceived in high tech. Moreover, he followed *The Lost Ones* pattern of enclosing the audience in an environment. Surrounded on three sides by a narrow, unevenly rising Plexiglas road, the spectators sit on risers under a canopy of white cloth, as though in a mammoth covered wagon. Front and center is the main playing area and at its center a doorway. Above that doorway, only occasionally visible, is Helen's room. At ground level, on audience left, is a revolving scrim door; at audience right is a small window offering a glimpse of a distant city. Among the technical feats of Neumann's *Mercier and Camier* were slides projected on the long sides and revolving door, a Narrator on television, real rain pouring down the center doorway, real water in the stage canal, a colored film in Helen's room, a duet of laughs like a musical scale, a café waiter serving drinks while noiselessly skating, a movable harpsichord on which Harvey Spevak played specially composed music by Philip Glass. For about half the performance, Mercier, Camier, and their encounters cleave to the front stage. Then the "pseudocouple" make six starts up the rough narrow road but finally return to the stage by the murky canal.

Neumann's narrative production follows Beckett's plot selectively: after a rainy entrance, Mercier and Camier trade insults with O'Reilly as watchman. They take stock of their meager possessions and set out on their voyage. After a brief detour to Helen's home—a velvety room just above the Spartan doorway—they journey empty-handed. When Camier leaves to fetch Mercier a cream-horn, the latter is accosted by two children in black oilskins, played by Neumann's sons. Mercier and Camier board an invisible train. While moving slides convey the passing countryside, Mercier and Camier sit under the side window on a bench in the compartment they share with O'Reilly as a grotesquely masked Madden. The three beat out a complex train rhythm, but Madden comes front and center for his monologue. Then, from the bog at stage front, the couple again negotiates the arduous road. They occasionally converse when close together, but more often when they are far apart, shouting over our heads, across the width of the theater. When they bludgeon a constable to death, we see it in the small window as a Punch and Judy show.

It is mainly in what he calls the Epilogue that Neumann strays from Beckett's text. While the Narrator—Warrilow on television—launches into the last lap of their journey, Terry O'Reilly as a waiter carries the seated harpsichordist to a café table at stage front. This deflects audience attention from Neumann and Raymond, who, at the far corners of the road, don white robes and carry shepherds' crooks. Trudging toward the stage for the last time, they meet Warrilow as Watt on the revolving scrim, and we hear him on voiceover: "Fuck life." When they are alone again, the rain sounds musically. Camier leaves Mercier after some two hours of Mabou Mines special effects in this most elaborate of their Beckett adaptations.

After Neumann's high-tech directorial debut, he yearned to be simply a solo Beckett actor, and after a brief flirtation with *From an Abandoned Work* fell durably in love with *Company*. While playing in *Lulu* in Boston, he committed *Company* to memory—all of it. Even while memorizing, Neumann contrasted the lyrical passages of the second-person memory voice with the ratiocinative third-person voice that is unable to affirm anything *but* its voiceness. The problem was how to stage these voices.

Neumann was initially lured by blandishments at MIT—laser beams, video sculpture, disembodied heads—but he soon heeded Beckett's advice: "Keep it simple, Freddie." Despite simplicity, however, this late text bewildered uninitiated spectators, as evidenced by this published note of a West Coast journalist: "William Beckett's company, a New York theatre group, will make its West Coast debut . . . in a production of 'Mabou Mines.' "

When Neumann and his wife sat opposite one another in their living room, he decided to move that simplicity to the stage—one chair for each voice and a lamp between them. In production, the chairs became rocking chairs, and a wooden crate supported the lamp. Behind them Neumann placed three large white disks, about ten feet in diameter, at once the zeros dear to Beckett, an abstraction for the eyes and mouth openings also dear to Beckett, and parabolic reflectors for intricate light changes. The vast wardrobe of the New York Shakespeare Festival Theater disgorged a greatcoat, worn boots, a shapeless hat, and a rubber-tipped stick. This time Philip Glass provided a string quartet, to be heard during pauses, and not, as in previous pieces, to accompany Beckett's words.

Although Beckett's basic and repeated image in *Company* is of one alone on his back in the dark, Neumann does not assume the supine position until the end. We first see him smoking in a rocking chair, back to us, musing about voices. After the first "Quick leave him," Neumann abruptly shifts to the other chair, facing us with eyes closed for the you-voice. He becomes an old codger in the suppositions of "Yes I remember . . . Yes I remember . . . Yes I remember." And the mercurial light plot remembers Beckett's harmony of voice and light, even to the Miltonic darkness visible. Beckett's discontinuous narrative is translated into blackouts by the addition of several "Quick leave him"s.

Paradoxically, however, "that same flat tone" mounts in anxiety. With the introduction of the "deviser of the voice and of its hearer and of himself," Neumann vigorously strips the stage. First one rocker is tossed off, then the other, then the lamp. The crate becomes his seat when the voice imagines a fly, which Neumann, hunched over and crosseyed, pinpoints at the rubber tip of his stick. Soon the box becomes a hutch for the hedgehog horror. By the interval, Neumann paces and rages before the accusing disks, reasoning repetitiously with high verbal velocity.

After the interval he slows to a weary walk for a long paragraph blending human life into the seasons, both ever "withershins." In the summerhouse love scene, a seated Neumann faces Honora Ferguson as the nameless She, in a turn-of-the-century hat and long shapeless dress. When she vanishes, her shadow remains on one disk: "That dead still." After sitting, pacing, kneeling, straining, Neumann lies down for another memory of a love scene. "She murmurs, Listen to the leaves," and a colored abstraction of leaves appears on the three disks.

Increasingly, Neumann enacts the actions described in the text. Citing the crawl, he comically crawls, impeded by his coat, followed by his enlarged shadow various on the three disks. In a sudden verbal sprint, Neumann ponders imponderables: "Could he not conceivably create while crawling in the same create dark as his creature." Standing for the last time, Neumann leans on his staff, then lifts it to make a clock of the center disk: "round and round the second hand now followed and now preceded by its shadow"—as the creating speaker has been shadowed by his creature. Neumann's tall frame shrinks. Back to us, he sits on the floor, "now huddled and now supine," but finally supine, head close to us, music silent "Alone," in this piece called *Company*.

And can we speak finally of a *company* attitude toward Beckett texts on the part of these three Mabou Mines directors? First and foremost, like Beckett himself and unlike most American directors, they are obsessed with form, although they translate Beckett's forms into their own. Again like Beckett, they persist against all odds in telling a story, and the telling—their staging—virtually devours the story. Still again like Beckett, they smile through pain— Breuer's mix-and-matches, Warrilow's fastidious ironies, Akalaitis's maniacal tasks, Raymond's nimble witticisms, Neumann's resolute hesitations. Unlike the theatereality of Beckett's own late plays, theirs "stink of artifice," enclouding us in modern technology. And yet they lure us to listen to Beckett's words in polyphonic voices. Though we are sensually seduced, we are also challenged to think by this group that grew up with conceptual art. From a secure academic perch, it is easy to scoff at these translations, but the Mabou Mines are aptly named; their work yields a brilliantly impure Beckett ore.

SUSAN BRIENZA

Sam No. 2: Shepard Plays Beckett with an American Accent

> And we were listening to some jazz or something and he sort of shuffled over to me and threw this book on my lap and said, why don't you dig this, you know. I started reading this play he gave me, and it was like nothing I'd ever read before—it was *Waiting for Godot*. And I thought, what's this guy talking about, What is this? And I read it with a very keen interest, but I didn't know anything about what it *was*.
>
> —Sam Shepard interviewed by Kenneth Chubb

We all know the play, as if by heart: a desolate set with a few props, two down-and-out men suggesting a comic physical/metaphysical dichotomy, and nothing happening at least twice. The two bums play, banter, imagine, repeat, reverse, philosophize—all in race-then-halt speech patterns. There is some memory loss, some love/hate ambivalence, and some stage business with hats. Later, another couple enters from the wings, and it performs a drama within the drama; then the short piece ends, swallowing its tail. We are all familiar with *Waiting for Godot*, and that is why we are also at home with the play just described—Sam Shepard's *Cowboys #2*.[1]

Within a few years of reading Samuel Beckett's most famous work, Shepard, then a young off-off Broadway dramatist, wrote this early play, produced in 1967, that translates *Waiting for Godot* into a distinctly American context. While the *Godot* imprint on *Cowboys* is apparent at first exposure, a detailed comparison allows us to see all the transmutations and to understand the many dramatic correspondences between Sam No. 1 and Sam No. 2. Shepard's prop is not the classical tree and path but an American road barrier with a blinking yellow caution light; his bums, Chet and Stu, are cowboys *sans* cow or horse, drifting between the desert and the freeway—or rather they are contemporary men, perhaps actors, playing at Old West cowboys (Cohn, *New Dramatists*, 172). Chet's ode to breakfast foods rivals Gogo's discourse on radishes and turnips, while Stu's lamentations about the land parallel Didi's thoughts about the mental terrain. Both pairs delight in games, usually word puzzles, to fill the time, for instance, seeking the appropriate simile to complete a sentence: in *Godot* the tramps try variations on "the dead voices are like . . ."; in *Cowboys* the bums repeat, "the dark clouds are like . . ." Also, physical games of pretending and acting make the wait bearable: the players balancing as trees in *Godot* and sliding in imaginary mud in *Cowboys*. While Gogo and Didi stay in character as they perform various skits, changing routines as they get bored, Shepard's cowboys shift from their original young selves to aging prospectors with old voices and gestures (adopting two different names, Clem and Mel), either to evade a fearful reality or to obey the command of off-stage whistles (as in Beckett's *Act Without Words I* and *II*).

Time, space, and language are out of joint for both sets of characters. Chet declares that the Red Valley they are inhabiting looks identical to Red Valleys in many another state; then Stu fractures time when he explains that he is doing jumping jacks *today* because his feet fell asleep *yesterday*. Prose in Shepard's play can be as multivalent as *Godot*'s opening phrase, "Nothing to be done": when one cowboy yells to the other "Hey! Come back!" he means come back downstage from upstage, come back to the continuation of the main script away from a digression, come back from the fantasy old man persona to the normal role, and finally "Come back to me, I'm lonely." At the end, Shepard translates the scene of the unaware Gogo sleeping while the wiser Didi strives to banish nightmares to a symmetrical one with the innocent Stu lying still in the sleep of death while the brighter Chet tries to ward off nightmarish vultures. Finally, enter Man Number One and Man Number Two (a citified copy of the primary couple); they mirror the ages and heights of Stu and Chet much as Pozzo and Lucky reflect the power balance of Didi and Gogo. Numbers One and Two read in monotone voices from hand-held scripts the first several lines of the play, thus imitating the circularity Beckett embeds in *Godot* and that he would later perfect for *Play*.

Cowboys #2 is not, however, simply a derivative piece of metatheater; it is a *Godot*-like play transposed into an American key and thereby made new. While Beckett ponders man's place in the universe through the actor's plight on stage, Shepard locates man's niche in the vastness of the United States with its physical and cultural wasteland. Thus the exhausted material of vultures encircling a dead man in a desert, a Western cliché, prompts Shepard's survivor to shout at the sky, "This ain't no joke, you shitty birds! What do ya think this is? TV or somethin' " (240). Even background effects have thematic import, charting the industrialization of America as they gradually shift from farm sounds to city noises: crickets, dogs, and rain, to the hammer and saw of construction, to car honks and highway racket. *Cowboys* #2 is the first of many Shepard plays to mourn the loss of the land, the American West, and the larger-than-life American hero. But neither God nor little god exists, and there is nothing to wait for, so Shepard's tramps can hardly discuss Christ or the four gospels; all they can do is play, sometimes imitating cowboys and, inevitably, Indians. Their ghostly, imagined Indians remind us of the dispossessed in America and make us realize that the two modern cowboys here are similarly displaced, disowned. The confrontation of Americans with a forbidding, uncharted, unsocialized landscape finds a dramatic counterpart in the situation of a few lonely characters on a mostly bare, desolate stage in the settings of Beckett and Shepard. (The latter sometimes equates a decaying land with a dilapidated house, as in *Buried Child* and *Curse of the Starving Class*.) In other plays by both writers, the stage becomes a shelter or refuge outside of which looms an indifferent or hostile wilderness, literal or figurative, as in *Endgame* or Shepard's *Action*—two apocalyptic dramas where provisions are depleted and four characters tell stories about the death of the cosmos as they wait, enclosed by four walls, strangely outside of time, for an ending.

One wonders why Shepard fit his themes about cowboys into the shape of *Godot* when so many American dramatic models were at hand; one preliminary answer might be that the unscholarly Shepard simply happened upon Beckett's work and did not pause to study Miller and Williams. But this response would be too facile: deeper affinities appear between the two Sams the further one looks. During interviews, Shepard invokes Beckett's name in admiration and explication. When asked, for example, whether he sets out to write plays of particular lengths, he replied, "The term full-length to me doesn't make any sense, because people call a two-act or a three-act play, or a play with a certain number of pages, a full-length play, but I think it's ridiculous, because . . . well, Beckett wrote *Come and Go* and it's five pages long but it's full-length, whereas some of O'Neill's . . ." (Chubb interview, 10). These are Shepard's ellipses, and his truncating the sentence—a verbal tossing up of the hands—implies an exasperation with the question of length and with full-blown three-act tragedies that paradoxically lack the weight and power of Beckettian miniatures, an impact gained through silences, patterning, and imagery.

Discussing *Geography of a Horse Dreamer*, Shepard considers the artist's unnamable and mysterious uncovering of his theme that occurs during creation; in so doing he recalls the first Sam when he described art as a "poetical excavation" that advances toward "the ideal core of the onion":

> Every play is a discovery. You create a framework, this time it is crime, and leave something open in the hope you will discover something. Whether it has a name to it I don't know, but with a really great writer like Samuel Beckett, every time he writes he is approaching a certain kind of secret. As he approaches it the audience is approaching it too. As soon as you name it you kill it. There is no question of naming and having it at the same time. ("Underground Landscapes," 8)

In fact, many of Shepard's statements about his philosophy of art, about the process of composition, the role of the artist, and the nature of character echo Beckett's hypotheses offered in "Three Dialogues," in interviews, and in

Proust. Beckett saw himself, like Proust, as a nonrational sort of writer; and then, with Irish exaggeration, he takes this observation one step further:

> I'm working with impotence, ignorance. I don't think impotence has been exploited in the past. There seems to be a kind of esthetic axiom that expression is an achievement—must be an achievement. My little exploration is that whole zone of being that has always been set aside by artists as something unuseable—as something by definition incompatible with art.
>
> I think anyone nowadays who pays the slightest attention to his own experience finds it the experience of a non-knower, a non-can-er (somebody who cannot). (Interview, "Moody Man of Letters")

Just as Beckett as "impotent" artist felt that he, unlike Joyce, was writing out of ignorance rather than from mastery (especially for *Waiting for Godot*), so Shepard says of his early plays: "I didn't have any idea about how to shape an action into what is seen—so the so-called originality of the early work just comes from ignorance" (Chubb interview, 5).

Yet the impulse to continue writing motivates both. Beckett claimed that the modern artist's preferred subject should be "[t]he expression that there is nothing to express, nothing with which to express, nothing from which to express, no power to express, no desire to express, together with the obligation to express" ("Three Dialogues," in *Disjecta*, 139). Similarly, Shepard declares that "Writing is born from a need. A deep burn. If there's no need, there's no writing" ("Visualization," 56). Beckett's writer/characters as well as the author himself experience this need as inner voices dictating a message, whispers demanding a scribe; and Shepard also hears voices as he begins to compose: "In my experience the character is visualized, he appears out of nowhere in three dimensions and speaks. He doesn't speak to me because I'm not in the play. I'm watching it" ("Visualization," 50). In particular, the impetus for *The Tooth of Crime* was an insistent tempo of language: "It started with hearing a certain sound which is coming from the voice of this character, Hoss . . . a very real kind of sound that I heard" (Chubb interview, 11). Echoing Beckett's dramatic dialogues in the fictions *Texts for Nothing* and *The Unnamable*, conversation between "I" and "he" and "I" and "them," Shepard depicts one state of composing: "I begin to get the haunting sense that something in me writes but it's not necessarily me" ("Visualization," 54). Besides feeling an internal compulsion, both dramatists often feel driven by an external extorter of speech, literalized in the plays. Shepard's writer/characters are often tortured, tricked, or blackmailed into writing—sometimes by criminals; they are "artists or dreamers who are forced at gunpoint to be creative" (Hayman, 177). One difference in the midst of similarity is that, while both dramatists focus on the writer as prey, Beckett's suffering artist is Christ-figure as innocent victim dying a slow crucifixion with no redemption in sight (think of the regal and bleeding Hamm or the nailed white body in *Ping*). Shepard's artists and rock messiahs, however, are corruptible men menaced by typically American forces, e.g., 1930s-style gangsters. Still, kidnapped or imprisoned writers in *Melodrama Play*, *Angel City*, *Geography of a Horse Dreamer*, and *Cowboy Mouth* recall Beckett's Molloy ordered to produce a report, Pim tortured into expression in *How It Is*, Lucky enslaved and forced to recite, the creatures in *Play* goaded into speech by a spotlight, and the prisoner-writers threatened turn and turn about in his recent play *What Where*.

Beckett and Shepard agree on the aims of drama as strongly as on its motivations and processes: both playwrights gravitate away from realism and complexity, toward poetry and simplicity. When corresponding with Alan Schneider about *Endgame*, Beckett wrote: "When it comes to journalists I feel the only line is to refuse to be involved in exegesis of any kind. And to insist on the extreme simplicity of dramatic situation and issue" (Cohn, *Disjecta*, 109). In 1974 Shepard expressed a desire for the sort of minimalism Beckett has been perfecting since 1954: "I'd like to try a whole different way of writing now, which is very stark and not so flashy and not full of a lot of mythic figures and everything, and try to scrape it down to the bone as much as possible" (Chubb interview, 16). This aim materialized in plays with uncluttered sets, fewer characters, and cleaner action. Beckett's conception that a true artist works out of nothingness, through the subconscious, in a descent toward the self, tearing away all but the essential, appears to be translated into analogous terms by Shepard:

[A writer] has to come back to the point where he feels he knows nothing at all about the heart of what he's after. He knows a great deal about things like: timing, rhythm, shape, flow, character(?), form, structure, etc., but still nothing about the real meat and potatoes. So he begins again. He strips everything down to the bones and starts over. And in this is where he makes his true discoveries. (Marranca, *American Dreams*, 211)

Here Shepard's questioning of the term "character" hints at how untraditional his characterizations are intended to be; even though Shepard's people never quite lose touch with reality or escape the bounds of realism as Beckett's creatures do (except in *Action*, which has a few "absurd" elements), they cannot be viewed as conventional dramatic personae because they are always self-consciously playing a role.

In approach and technique, then, these two playwrights are converging. In subject matter they also concur: initially Beckett had carved out as his artistic domain the "whole zone of being" that other writers neglect, and gradually Shepard too has focused his plays on the processes of thinking, talking, and imagining. Recently Sam No. 2 rejected the outdated materials of experimental theater and reached this conclusion:

> The only thing which still remains and still persists as the single most important idea is the idea of *consciousness*. . . . For some time now it's become generally accepted that the other art forms are dealing with this idea to one degree or another. That the subject of painting is seeing. That the subject of music is hearing. That the subject of sculpture is space. (Marranca, *American Dreams*, 212; my italics)

His implied assumption is that the subject of his own art form, drama, is writing. Many of Shepard's plays (like Beckett's) are about language, story-telling, style; for instance, *True West* takes scriptwriting as its subject, and the two brothers here become co-authors in the process of composing. Still, this play is mostly *about* being a writer; it has not achieved that essential embodiment of content into form where the play *is* that something of writing itself (to paraphrase Beckett on Joyce). On a deeper level than Shepard's *True West*, a study of the dual nature of the writer and his double role in society, Beckett depicts the public and private artist as well as the raw materials of the actual medium (words and music) in the radio play *Cascando* (Homan, 134–36).

Besides their equal fondness for metadrama, the younger Sam also suggests intensified kinship with the elder Sam in his specific themes and typical characters, each dramatist tracing the solitary being, a speck in the void who reaffirms his existence and worth through speaking and performing. As he faces an enormous physical or metaphysical wasteland, the Beckett/Shepard character whispers in the dark, talks to overcome loneliness, tries on roles to locate the true self, and muses about his position in society and the universe. Back in *Godot*, Lucky describes Man wasting and pining despite the existence of a personal God; Pozzo declaims about the fleeting time of Man on this bitch of a planet; and Didi combines these topics as he soliloquizes about man's relationship to Man, to God, and to Time. In *Cowboys #2* Stu's long monologue on time and modern man decries environmental as well as spiritual decay: civilization overtaking orchards, the once-proud peacock (read "American cowboy") reduced to scattered tail feathers gathering dust in sedate vases.

The rambling speech that ends *Cowboys* (moving through lemon groves and peacocks to sheep and chickens) displays another inheritance from Beckett, a blending of the genres of fiction and drama by the insertion of narratives within plays, flowing monologues within staccato dialogues. Hamm uses three different voices, one for conversations with Clov, one for narrating his chronicle, and one for conversation with himself; Pozzo alternates between "prosaic" and "lyrical" tones for his set speech on night. Shooter in Shepard's play *Action* carries on the legacy of Hamm, as actor and storyteller

(McCarthy, 5), when he relates pieces of his past. In general, Shepard's characters love and live to tell stories, and in *Angel City* this is most explicit, where "a documentary voice" is required, spoken into a self-consciously hand-held microphone specified in the stage directions, "to amplify the narration sequences." For Shepard, as for Beckett and Pinter, these narratives do not halt the forward movement of the plot; rather the story gradually suggests or reinforces or *becomes* the plot (Morrison).

Rarely does the Beckett or Shepard monologue reduce to mere exposition: while Hamm's chronicle may (or may not) reveal the true background of his predicament, it offers *him* a way of creating and re-creating the self as he tries to end his game yet again. This same function of story to define the self, or to justify the nonself, appears in *Footfalls*, and an obsessive four times in *Not I*. Winnie tells distorted fictions in *Happy Days* in order to distance herself from a painful past, to escape a hopeless present, and to heal herself psychologically through retelling. Narrative as ritual—either to transcend mundane reality, to exorcise a history, or to transform a present—is pervasive in both dramatists, perhaps most prominent in Beckett's recent *Ohio Impromptu*. In Shepard's *Unseen Hand*, when one speech is delivered backward word for word (recalling the linguistic reversals in *Watt*), the spell imposed by the original speech is undone. Frenzied monologues, more restorative than narrative, become rites or prayers in Shepard's most mystical plays—*La Turista*, *The Holy Ghostly*, and *The Unseen Hand*—rites spoken by medicine men, either ancient or futuristic, in which language has the force to curse, to cure, to kill, to transmute, or to reincarnate.

Through language alone, Shepard stands near Beckett as one of the greatest contemporary playwrights, with his facility for reproducing the jargons and rhythms of American speech: of cowboy, rock star, disc jockey, valley girl, farmhand, film exec, private eye, gangster. Ronald Hayman has chosen our second Sam as the dramatist who most successfully continues the tradition of linguistic richness on stage: "Shepard, in fact, has the best claim of any writer since Beckett and Genet . . . to being a poet of the theatre" (163). More than one reviewer of Richard Schechner's production of *The Tooth of Crime*, his verbal masterpiece, complained that the audience missed some of the rough yet lyrical lines of the dialogue because it was asked to change seats so often in the Performance Group's environmental set. Yet every sentence in this and many other Shepard plays (as in Beckett's drama) carries poetic, ritualistic import. In the following speech, part of a stylistic duel, we hear the new rock idol Crow put down and one-up the aging hero Hoss with the weapon of words:

> The marks show clean through. Look to the guard. That's where it hides. Lurkin'
> like a wet hawk. Scuffle mark. Belt mark. Tune to the rumble. The first to run.

The shame kid. The first on his heel. Shame on the shame kid. Never live it down. Never show his true face. Last in line. Never face a showdown. Never meet a face-off. Never make a clean break. Long line a' losers. (98)

While diction and rhythms differ markedly in Beckett and Shepard, both poet/playwrights demonstrate supreme verbal control. Shepard's language in his short speeches as well as his long monologues (often termed "arias" by critics) dances across the stage, since Shepard uses "words as living incantations and not as symbols" ("Visualizations," 53). In performance, his plays offer nonverbal images within pictures and music and more charged words that "hit the air between actor and audience," drawing us into a sacramental circuit. Beckett works more quietly and simply, with minimal props, no loud spectacles, fewer family situations to create raging conflict, and, lately, with often a lone character and perhaps another voice, encircled only by darkness or light. This visual starkness naturally implies increased emphasis purely on language itself, as in *Rockaby*, with its incantatory litany of lines accompanied by the movement of the rocker to suggest both lullaby and dirge:

> let down the blind and down
> right down
> into the old rocker
> those arms at last
> and rocked
> rocked
> with closed eyes
> closing eyes
> she so long all eyes
> famished eyes
> all sides
> high and low
> to and fro
> at her window
> to see
> be seen
>   (*Collected Plays*, 281)

The power of language on Beckett's and Shepard's stages is amplified by other powerful elements—color, image, music, and play—with the younger Sam fusing all elements equally and the older Sam focusing more on the word.

In a review of Shepard's early work, *La Turista*, Elizabeth Hardwick praises the "verbal energy" of the text, specifically the "ruling image" of "turista," meaning simultaneously traveler, Montezuma's revenge, America's sickness (67–68). Yet the beginning and ending of the play are purely visual (like *Happy Days*, with Winnie buried in what is no longer a motherly earth and burned by her hellish light): against a bright orange and yellow set, we are introduced to Kent and Salem (cigarette brand names for added satire) with their painfully sunburned skin, their red badge of tourism; and we are finally left with a cartoonlike outline of Kent's body as he leaps through the upstage wall. (We almost expect to see "Pow!" and "Zam!" bold-lettered on the backdrop.) For the one-act *Red Cross*, because the props, set, and costumes are all dazzling hospital white, when the characters first come on stage, the audience is visually surprised by "a new color—skin-color!" (Levy, 96). But flesh color on white isn't nearly as shocking as blood red on white, the image of a literal red cross we get at the end of the wife's fantasy about skiing to her death: "All you'll see is this red splotch of blood and a whole blanket of white snow" (102). After much dialogue about heads bursting and about bedbugs sucking one's blood, all the verbal and visual images coalesce at the end of the play when the husband slowly turns around to expose a rivulet of red blood streaming down his forehead. (This sight is as startling as the final tableau of Beckett's *Rockaby*, where, after the repetition of the words "rocked" and "stopped," a dying woman's head slumps forward.) For *Red Cross* it is as if the speeches about bleeding and dying, the sterilized white set, and the cumulative action of scratching combine together shamanistically to cause the husband's red cross of blood to form in the final frame.

Fond of concluding his works with tableaux, Shepard reveals that his plays often originate with a picture, for instance, a man in a bathtub for *Chicago* (Chubb interview, 6). Like Beckett, he values the three-dimensional qualities of the stage, the mental *space* of the imagination: thus the man in *Chicago* roams in his mind, re-creates sounds, voices, and scenes, as does Beckett's Henry in the radio play *Embers*. Shepard seeks to produce theater through the "other forms" of music, painting, sculpture, and film. This suggests why his theatrical images are so forceful, why his dramatic themes derive from the transmutation of a central image or symbol—most commonly a prop, like the funeral urns in Beckett's *Play*. The empty refrigerator in *Curse of the Starving Class* becomes an ever-present metaphor for the physically and spiritually impoverished family whose father furnishes only a bag of artichokes—absurdly impractical and insubstantial food. Tens of stolen toasters in *True West* symbolize both the macho life of the thief and the suburban stability he covets, while the large wafers of toast provide a false Communion between two brothers. In the elusive early play *Icarus's Mother*, an airplane (a modern Icarus) writes in the sky "E equals MC squared" as it cryptically and menacingly suggests the nuclear terror that this equation makes possible. The sleazy Los Angeles characters in *Angel City* acquire fangs and green slime as their decadence and greed increase, producing an effect as visually and morally horrifying as the human-into-animal metamorphosis in Ionesco's *Rhinoceros*. For a highly ritualistic play, *Operation Sidewinder*, Shepard moves one creature through several symbolic transfigurations: the godlike sidewinder snake, visible or audible during most of the drama, begins as a totem of evil and sexual aggression, gathers force as the military's computer (technology as God), and culminates as the hero of an Indian snake dance, and thereby as an agent of redemption. Often forfeiting conventional dramatic action, climax, and resolution, Shepard plays accumulate structure and strength with a series of images. One of the closest Beckettian analogs here is the play *Come and Go*, in which the names and hats of the three women, the crisscrossing of their hands, and their ringed and patterned movements express as much as their lines. Beckett's stark black/white opposition can allow for Manichean ramifications in *Krapp's Last Tape*, can suggest the light of the skull against the darkness of death in *A Piece of Monologue*, or can provide recursive and self-reflexive structures in *Ohio Impromptu*. More efficient in his use of dramatic tools than Shepard, Beckett can make a single object serve several functions: Krapp's tape recorder becomes prop, symbol, stage business, plot device, narrative strategy, and companion all in one.

If the first Sam excels in compressed verbal and visual imagery, his namesake flamboyantly uses music to evoke an emotional response in an audience. Much more adventurous with music than Beckett, who prefers subtler effects like the continuous sound of the sea in *Embers* or the ironic "Death and the Maiden" song in *All That Fall*, Shepard turns music into one of the languages, or indeed one of the characters, of a play. Rock lyrics serve as a modern Greek chorus in *Operation Sidewinder*, voicing society's malaise, supplementing and explaining each preceding scene. Two of Shepard's plays harmonize word and music in equal parts (but without the self-reflexive layer of Beckett's *Words and Music* or *Cascando*): *Tongues* juxtaposes percussion and short phrases of lyrical prose, recalling performances of the fifties beat poets; and the longer, more ambitious piece, *The Sad Lament of Pecos Bill on the Eve of Killing His Wife*, advertised as a New Western Opera, places lyrics about a fallen legendary hero in a score orchestrated for ten instruments, including pedal steel, saw, synthesizer, and fiddle.[2] Although Shepard more boldly experiments and innovates with music, the words and ideas sometimes still derive from Beckett: *Tongues*, a fragmented monologue spoken by a man layering on new selves in a search for his true identity, reads in substance and prose rhythms like a condensed dramatization of *The Unnamable*.

Beckett often adds a single song in order to comment on the theme or atmosphere of a play, like the circular dog ditty in *Godot* echoing the circularity and futility on stage, or Krapp's mournful lament that "night is drawing nigh" to suggest all his lost nights and his fast-approaching final night. But Shepard uses music intermittently throughout a drama, for example, the saxophones and drums in *Angel City* "to heighten or color the action" (Shepard's "Note on the Music," 6). Music intensifies near the end of *Angel City* to accompany the conflict between two battling characters who play two generals, dressed in Oriental robes. When we remember that Beckett borrowed elements from Japanese Noh drama, Shepard's note about this operatic war for civilization becomes doubly significant: "It might be useful for the musicians to listen to some of the recordings of Japanese theater to hear how the actor's voice is used in conjunction with the instruments" (6).

Musical and pictorial terms surface again when Sam Shepard describes the characterization he envisions for *Angel City:*

> Instead of the idea of a "whole character" with logical motives behind his behavior which the actor submerges himself into, he should consider instead a fractured whole with bits and pieces of character flying off the central theme. In other words, more in terms of collage construction or jazz improvisation . . . he's mixing many different underlying elements . . . to make a kind of music or painting in space without having to feel the need to completely answer intellectually for the character's behavior. (6)

The absence of orthodox character motivation, logical action, and dramatic form in his plays creates a flexible area between character and actor. An extreme example occurs in *Icarus's Mother*, for which relationships between the five characters are not specified in the text, so that the actors must define associations through their gestures and dialogue. Even more taxing on both actor and audience, Beckett's *That Time* depicts a "fractured whole" composed of three voices, A, B, and C, who together represent and interweave three phases of the life of the protagonist, a disembodied head.

Shepard as director affords much more scope to his actors than does Beckett, who demands precision in details, like the number of steps to cross the stage, and who advised Billie Whitelaw to imitate his every intonation of Winnie's lines in the Royal Court production of *Happy Days*. For both playwrights, characters are self-consciously and ironically role-playing. Winnie has at least five different voices: her normal one, her tone for scolding Willie, her register for quoting literary fragments, her little-girl whine, and the mode for acting out other scenes from her past. With shifting internal voices, Beckett characters are more liable to duel verbally within themselves than fight physically with others, but on both stages a character is a battleground of many selves.

Peeling back the overlay of American pop culture to the essence of Shepard's people reveals how similar they are to Beckett's, especially in their sense of disjunction between the body and the real "I" (Marranca, "Alphabetical Shepard," 13–17). Both writers attempt to capture evanescent being: what is it that remains after the stories, the games, the roles have vanished? Often their characters occur as male pairs (symbolic of various sorts of duality) with tenuous bonds, with reversals of position, and with props used to transfer power. Most of these creatures feel a need for their existence to be recognized, witnessed, and even a desire to be "verified," a word used in Shepard's self-reflexive play *Action* ("Is there anyone to verify?") and in Beckett's scenic story *Company*, which he has recently dramatized. This notion of witnessing (based on Berkeley's "To be is to be perceived") has become a commonplace in Beckett scholarship and has lately appeared in Shepard criticism (Falk). Conversely, existence is also a burden to be relieved through motion, ritualized game, or performance. While it may be true that "Beckett's method is deeply rationalist and shows minds, however desperate, insistently ordering the games and rituals which piece out their time within the play" and that "Shepard is more impressionistic and allusive in the way he works" (McCarthy, 2), for both their characters, ritual movement offers a way to express feeling, avoid thought, and massacre time. Some Beckett characters, like the pacing May in *Footfalls*, nicely fit this paradigm, and the recent mime *Quad* consists entirely of obsessive feet stepping to drum beats. For Shepard's people, movements such as tap dancing while staying seated in *Action* or the dance of aggression between the two brothers in *True West* may become so stylized that we perceive character transparently as performer—as we also do for Pozzo and Hamm.

Rather than subsuming his personality in a role, the actor must foreground himself *as actor*, each character continuously playing a ham actor like Hamm or a clichéd soap-opera performer like the nameless, schematic Woman 1, Man, and Woman 2 in *Play*. Shepard speaks of "play" as in "kid" ("Visualization," 50), having in mind children's games of pretending; he creates his characters (and encourages his actors, when he directs) to be wildly inventive, adopting different fantasies and voices, and switching roles with record speed. Thus in *Red Cross*, Carol imagines herself as skier and—in a monologue about dangers escalating—kills herself off; then the maid, taking imaginary swimming lessons, verbally drowns herself. In *Cowboy Mouth*, Slim and Cavale "play the coyote and the crow game on their hands and knees" (158); and when this skit reaches a dead end, they ask, *Godot*-like, "Now what'll we do?" (Wetzsteon in *Fool for Love*, 12). Several of Shepard's plays are forthrightly *about* performance: the characters in *Action* are impersonating improvisational actors; the implication of *Tooth of Crime* is that posturing and performing determine heroism; and *Cowboys #2* is a multilayered construction of playing. Here, as we have seen, two young actors on stage portray two young cowboys who then imaginatively become two old-timers; meanwhile two other male voices off-stage play a composite of citified actors/prompters/directors. This serial regression of acting reaches an ultimate state in Beckett's *Ohio Impromptu*, in which a Listener prompts and directs a Reader who reads every night from a large book about a reader who recites every night. Similarly, the players in *Angel City* (who are trying to revise a movie project) periodically speak "as if reading from a script" while their own lines and roles continually change, until at the self-reflexive conclusion the movie producer and his secretary play a boy and girl out on a date, watching a movie.

Going one level further, as did Beckett before him, Shepard compels the audience to play performer or at least participant. In both *Play* and *Come and Go* the players on stage stare straight ahead as if they were watching *us*, while we must rearrange speeches and reconstruct plot as if we shared in the conversation (Homan). In *Buried Child*, as the obviously symbolic ears of corn and stacks of carrots litter the stage, promising and requesting some sort of interpretation, precisely when the audience feels it must know what the vegetables represent, the mother, Halie, asks what it all means. (Perhaps Shepard borrows this self-referential technique from Hamm in *Endgame*, who worries that he and Clov are beginning to "mean something," or from Mr. Shower in *Happy Days*, who demands to know what a woman buried in earth is meant to mean.) In general, the audience's mounting confusion about the entire bizarre family in *Buried Child* is personified in the character Shelly, the outside visitor hazarding inferences and judgments—just as we do—as she learns more about the family history. The audience is explicitly invited to judge in *The Tooth of Crime*, to choose a winner between the two contestants of the rock "dozens"; and so enters a character called Referee, complete with cap and whistle, a dramatization of the spectator's new role. All this again reminds the contemporary theatergoer of the strata of performance within *Godot:* the tramps playing for each other, Pozzo performing a set speech and expecting a critique, Lucky delivering his monologue for Pozzo (to entertain the tramps)—and we as audience sharing the witnessing and waiting.

Even when we have no specific part in a Shepard play, we are active participants in his dramatic world, a cosmos that radiates spokes of exorcism and shamanism (Gelber). Shepard, who glorifies, parodies, and updates our American myths, retains a mythic power himself, a sense of mystery in his plays, to which audiences respond in a realm transcending intellectual understanding, the way we react to the dismemberment of the self in *Not I*, the fading and disappearance of May in *Footfalls*, or the mirror-imaging in *Ohio Impromptu*. Although Beckett is more likely to parody and distort Christian myths (as in *Godot*) or classical myths (as in *Endgame*), and Shepard typically celebrates or mocks myths from popular culture like the worship of the automobile or the veneration of Jesse James, both authors are never far from mythic levels. This second Sam, who says that ideas of dying and of being reborn lie continuously in the cellar of his brain (Chubb interview, 16), provides ritualistic purgations and resurrections for his characters, and ultimately for his American audiences, just as Beckett calms his characters with ritualistic gesture and language and satisfies his audiences with ritualistic repetition and cycles.[3]

Samuel Beckett and Sam Shepard, both writers of poetry, fiction, and criticism, as well as authors of dramas and directors of plays, use powerful words and simple visual images to enact contemporary man role-playing and creating. The result is theater with great mythic depth belying its relatively uncomplicated dramatic surface. Shepard has only lately developed a concern for form, for what he calls "vehicle," for what Beckett calls a "form to accommodate the mess," a concern that the more experienced playwright continuously has in mind during a series of rebeginnings. Shepard used to rebel against revision and was accustomed to multiplying one spontaneous product after another as if demons were chasing him, he recalls. Beckett too has felt controlled by demons, but by the sort who demanded meticulous and exhausting revisions toward perfect forms. The older Sam has so far proven to be far more economical and elegant in his use of theatrical elements: his plays become simpler and shorter as they become richer. Thus for crystalline poetry, tight dramatic structure, and fully integrated symbolism, Beckett is supreme; Shepard, though, has shown a brilliant versatility in his choice of sources (legendary, contemporary, and popular), in amalgamations of various genres and media, and in facility in translating and transforming earlier materials. The cast of characters in *Mad Dog Blues*, for instance, includes a rock idol, a Paul Bunyan, a Mae West—and a drug addict named Yahoudi (the name suggests that he has been reading *Molloy*). For the composition of *Cowboys*, Sam Shepard was directly influenced by Sam Beckett; and many other second-generation playwrights, including Edward Albee, David Mamet, Harold Pinter, and Tom Stoppard, have acknowledged their direct and indirect lessons from the father of contemporary drama.

A more specific issue is how Shepard has absorbed the Beckettian legacy and then transformed it into something original. While also borrowing from Whitman, Emerson, and O'Neill in creative ways, Shepard had to search beyond the heritage of earlier American writers to locate the self-reflexive and circular structures and the spare prose he needed to portray distinctly twentieth-century American themes. America enjoys the rite of self-creation, the individual asserting himself against an overbearing sense of void and absence; and the self-made man finds a natural prototype in Beckett's self-begetting character arguing for his very existence as well as for his artistic identity. The archetypal American hero, whether Old West cowboy or modern rock star, constructs himself through legend, tall tale, song, and posturing—through generative prose and through play. The writer/protagonists on both metatheatrical stages struggle to reinvent the language, and thereby the self, and to fabricate histories and dreams from the nothingness of the imagination, all the while feeling tortured into continued creation against overwhelming social, philosophical, or linguistic odds. Sam Shepard translates the innovative techniques and metaphysical messages of Sam Beckett into an American idiom uniquely his own.

Notes

1. The original, *Cowboys #1*, was lost among a stack of hastily written manuscripts.
2. Shepard's use of music as theme and technique is an entire article unto itself.
3. For more on this, see my article, " 'My Shade Will Comfort You': Beckett's Rites of Theater," in *Samuel Beckett*, Patrick McCarthy, ed. (Boston: G. K. Hall, 1986).

PART 5

Transcreations: Language to Painting

RENEE RIESE HUBERT

From an Abandoned Work:
The Encounter of Samuel Beckett
and Max Ernst

It might seem futile to establish a relation between Max Ernst's oeuvre, known for bold explosive colors and shapes, vast arrays of technical discoveries such as collage and frottage, inexhaustible displays of forms, fantastic, organic, and mechanical, and Samuel Beckett's ever sober and reductive *écritures*, characterized by lucidity and self-defeating struggles with idiom. I would never have dreamed of so risky a venture if Ernst had not established the link by illustrating *From an Abandoned Work*, one of Beckett's works officially labeled as fragment, the incompletion of which is doubly stated by the title: *From an Abandoned Work*. At first glance the illustrated work hardly reveals a clear affinity between the graphic and the verbal. Nonetheless, I shall base my quest for possible verbal/visual relationships on the hypothesis that a painter does not randomly select texts for illustration but is guided by an intuitive, if not conscious, awareness of a problematics that he shares with the writer. Max Ernst in an interview stated that Beckett was the only pessimistic writer of his time whose pessimism did not prevent him from creating. He established that Beckett differed from him in temperament but not in artistic pursuits.

Ernst illustrated many books, including his own poetry. He produced several works of fiction with only minimal recourse to words. He very frequently and sometimes perversely straddled the fence between art and literature. The literature he chose tended to be nonmimetic. He invented for each book a different relation between his graphics and the text and by the same token discarded any conventions on which his previous illustration might have been based. In general, Ernst's translations transgressed the familiar or everyday world. They bypassed the text as a cluster of imagery or as a narrative, however discontinuous it might appear, and focused on the process of its verbal functionings. In one of his first books, *Les malheurs des immortels*, where he participates both as poet and visual artist, he provides a page-by-page con-

MAX ERNST, *La pêche sous-marine*, frottage, 1966. Courtesy Galerie Beyeler Basel.

frontation of verbal and visual collages that block out the syntax of logic and the natural expected order of things. "Discours" and "figure" confront each other on opposing pages, in a double act of defiance against the same type of model. In some of his later books, such as *Logique sans peine* or *Maximiliana*, his plates combined sign and image, often in one and the same ambiguous form. Reader and viewer would not have to engage in separate activities to decode the book. Ernst answered Carroll's queries concerning linguistic logic by the invention of mysterious figures hovering on the borderline of abstractions. These glyphs, born from responses to verbal games and enigmas, translated or transmitted the very nature of their intangible solutions. Such illustrations constituting transpositions or translations of texts, revealing, perhaps deviously, verbal inquiry, have paved the way for Ernst as a reader of Beckett, the author of texts where narrative and dramatic forms undergo a high degree of erosion or reduction, where verbal texture with its overt strategies overwhelms an underlying fiction.

The Manus Presse published in 1969 a trilingual edition of *From an Abandoned Work* accompanied by a plate combining the techniques of aquatint and etching. The single illustration is translated into different color schemes, just as the texts are translated into various idioms. This double translation does not, however, so it would seem, establish analogies between colors and verbal systems. By color shifts, one plate suggests a variation of another, proclaiming at once sameness and difference, a paradox crucial in Beckett's works. Color shifts do not exemplify a different tonality or an optical substitution, but a change of emphasis in the weblike structure of the illustration. The move from color to color not only heralds the move from language to language but also signals stages of activity, if not motion, and in this sense reflects the Beckettian text, which alludes to alternation of arrest and a resumed itinerary, echoing yet distorting an inner search. Although the four illustrations with their repetitive pattern hardly propose an indefinite open-ended series, they would seem to provide a response to an "abandoned" work, a fragment which at one time or other may have generated or been generated by a longer but insistently absent text.

The presence of recurrent, repetitive elements incorporating what might be described as static, but nonetheless monads, could thus establish an affinity between Beckett and Ernst. Such patterns impose a certain reduction which in the case of Ernst and Beckett can be labeled metonymic. Reductionism characterizes Beckett's work through most of its stages. Molloy is a reduction of Moran, removed from any semblance of a middle-class setting and narrated without recourse to conventional techniques of representation. We may view the tree in *En attendant Godot* as a reduction of the outer world in the context of both space and time, or Hamm, in his wheelchair, condemned to a minimum of mobility, as a reduction of human existence and its bound-

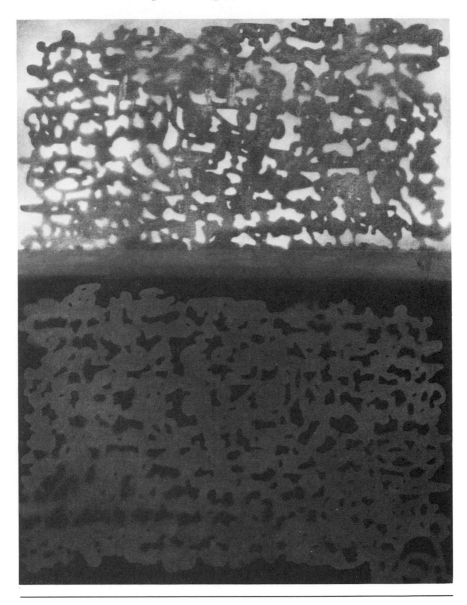

Max Ernst, *L'air lavé à l'eau*, oil on canvas, 1969. Courtesy Galerie Beyeler Basel.

aries. The author often conveys schematized relations in minimal or nonsyllabic language.

Ernst, throughout his career, has created reductive patterns not unlike his illustrations for *From an Abandoned Work*, especially if, at least for the time being, we consider them not as extensions or accompaniments of the Beckett text itself. The weblike pattern stretched across the entire surface, until it is cut off by the frame, compels the viewer to extend it in all directions. Only a circular outline feebly delimiting a region may remotely suggest subdivisions or alternate patterns among the irregular meshwork. Max Ernst frequently repeated an iconographic structure which horizontally divides the picture surface, inscribing on the upper section a circular shape by which the painter intimates a stellar or solar presence. Ernst has painted again and again with multiple variations the same fundamental landscape, the same reduction or scheme which alludes to sky, earth, and sun. He never entered into any precise referential details, into any geographical signs which would enable the viewer to recognize a particular or familiar landscape. In his basic landscape, Ernst has usually avoided any suggestion of a third dimension, though occasionally he did introduce diagonal lines evoking a receding perspective, but only to situate it in a paradoxical relation to the flat sky. His spatial reductionism goes even further, for the viewer cannot unambiguously decipher referentiality to water, air, and earth, as only two spaces are allocated to three elements. They are reduced according to analogy rather than separated by their difference. The present and absent elements become indistinguishable. Their concrete, tangible reality has been displaced as well as schematized.

Ernst frequently repeated his basic landscape while avoiding repetition, insofar as the lower section of his canvas assumes appearances as varied as wallpaper bricks, sea waves, bed quilts, while the circle in the upper section assumes those of fire, ribbons, color blotches, and so on. Each work attains to a remarkable unity by its structure, so that its inevitable surprise effect leads to a new order.

Several of the paintings provide manifestations of the web: "The Impeccable one," "The Birth of Galaxy," "Pacific Clouds," "Flea." Each work renews its shape and texture, geometrical and cell-like patterns alternate, creating magnified shapes; rigorous divisions alternate with natural formations imposed by water, fire, and land. Ernst again and again condensed the activities of the cosmic and the intimate by making them simultaneous. He abolished all proportions which might recall the natural order. The often ironic titles of his paintings reveal paradox and contradiction relevant not only to Ernst's own art but to earlier paintings, parodied by the willful undermining of realism, mimeticism, invoking at least implicitly the authority of inclusion and exclusion. Replacing the older forms of representation, Ernst introduced into his paintings the discoveries he made through collage and montage. However, the weblike texture hovering between the abstract geometrical and the organic cellular does not only appear in the horizontally divided landscapes into which a circular form is inserted. Often the entire painting is invaded by their weblike formation, which varies in transparency and opacity, in color scheme, in density, both from painting to painting and within the same work. To such paintings belong "Almost dead romanticism" and "Midsummernight's Dream," a title no doubt inspired by Shakespeare, where all references to narration and dramatization are substracted. The dream is separated from any type of dream action. The encounter of all elements within the same spatial context completely transforms the recognizable world. The source of light or darkness becomes inseparable from the space illuminated; vibrations which reflect floral, fossil, molecular, and cellular units constantly change, as they interact in their fluidity as well as their crystalline sharpness. Ernst introduces the viewer to a world which undergoes simultaneously the process of creation and deteriorization, of variance and sameness.

The aquatint etchings illustrating *From an Abandoned Work* testify to the same preoccupation as these paintings. We may ask what new elements Ernst introduced on the net-covered surface, where each link differs. The viewer's attention is drawn toward the display of repetition, toward the interplay between the same and the other, and, eventually, toward a possible model and its numerous distortions. The rectangular shapes, pulled in one direction or another, indeed indicate distortion. Everywhere the weblike structure undergoes sustained pressure and tension without collapsing. Forces or motions eagerly manipulate the links without providing the least hope for a possible abatement. As viewers, we cannot step outside the web, for we are condemned to remain transfixed within its net of forces, determining the shapes and tensions of the links. No single direction or force can predominate. Whereas the other works of art so far considered stress contrast, or at least refrain from completely submerging it, as, for instance, the blue and yellow coloration in "Midsummernight's Dream," the contrasts in these etchings have subsided, the circular shape has become elliptic, differing in more than one respect from rounded shapes in Ernst's other works. Moreover, circularity is almost integrated into the surface of the web and requires the viewer's concentrated attention. It no longer represents a schematized sun or moon but takes steps toward pure abstraction.

The Ernstian web has connections with the Beckettian text, liberated from generic allegiances and conventions. *From an Abandoned Work* presents a continuity or condensation marked by the spatial arrangement on the page— words following words, without blank spaces or division into paragraphs. As we follow the course of the lines, we encounter difficulties in stepping "outside" or "beside" the text, much in the same way that in viewing Ernst's web we could not disentangle ourselves from the links, as though our space-bound minds could not envision a point beyond the web.

Once we attempt to examine the fabric of the Beckettian text not as a purely spatial arrangement but as a semantic sequence, we encounter verbal deviations—or as Moorjani says, "subversion of syntactical discourse"—not continuity. The narrator proposes to record his moment of separation from his mother. He sets out to outline the paradox between the son's early morning alertness and mobility, the mother's stillness and gloom. He promises opposition between the one and the other; morning and evening, movement and immobility, does not enable us to steer in a given direction.[1] Every characteristic is deviated. Separated from any defining force, the word itself becomes subverted. The perturbance of the textual surface by wordplay and syntactical substitution produces penetrating effects in the fabric. Because of these very strategies, the text cannot be broken up into separate autonomous units. As the reader progresses, opposition telescopes, undercutting the relations so far established. No linear continuity emerges, either from mother to son, or from house to street. Reader's expectations are aroused, only to be diverted rather than satisfied. Any tangible information is eventually undermined as it is separated from its source and from duration. The reader, from whom meaning and definition constantly slip away, hovers just like the viewer of the etching, on the borderline of the nonrepresentational.

The text imposes and records repeated deviations that withhold linear readings, even of small fragments, yet the text meanders back to words temporarily bypassed and thus constitutes in its own way a web. Inquiries or references to time, its dynamics or stasis, as well as to the spatial context of narration, resurface in the written texture, suscitating renewed tensions. From the initial statement onward the narrator proposes an itinerary in an undefined or undefinable space within a nonmeasurable or indeterminate time.[2] His course being at once interrupted by displacement, but continuous in its effort and endurance, marks its multiple turns, which combine their meshing lines.

Beckett's narrator, however, has no equivalent in Ernst's illustration. The painter omitted allusions to the human agent, no doubt because Beckett's narrator talks to no one. Ernst echoes the emergence of traces replacing planned or predictable patterns never realized. The reader in deciphering the text is caught in meandering segments which produce new verbal distances, encounters, or clashes. On more than one occasion, Beckett's narration returns to the initial statement or initial intent with or without slight modification, reiterating on such occasions the proposed itinerary or reformulating a self-imposed assignment, after having strayed to a certain extent and perhaps diverted or even temporarily confused the reader. But the second and third attempted statements of purpose, by tending toward formulations involving time and space, lead to deviations and unexpected verbal encounters not unlike the knots in Ernst's visual web, e.g., *Let me get on with this day to get it over.* Within the text, time sequences—annual, daily, momentary—abolish distance by sliding into and encroaching upon one other; and, thus compounded, alternations between sameness and otherness graduate to a more deconstructive stage.

Beckett's initial statement posits a beginning which may appear incompatible with Ernst's figure. But the notion of beginning is introduced merely to be denied on more than one account. Indeterminacy sets in as time fissions into past and present. Syntactical inversions, devious transitions, create ambiguity, weaken the terminology of origin, impel the reader to follow a plurality of directions. The expectation of a focused reading goes unrewarded, for concentration is repeatedly thwarted. Thus the following statement by J. Hillis Miller can readily be applied to Beckett: "The language of narrative is always displaced, borrowed. Therefore any single thread leads everywhere, like a labyrinth made of a single line or corridor crinkled to and fro" ("Ariadne's Thread," 74).

In addition to accepting Ernst's web as an appropriate visual rendering of the text, regarded from the perspectives of movement and arrest, of separation and encounter, as a juxtaposition of nondetachable fragments, we can also establish certain analogies between words and image as a process of mental activity and production. Beckett is undoubtedly more engaged in the process of writing as such than of actually telling a particular story. His narrator includes the reader as an accomplice, as an associate, as a playmate ready to be gulled or enlightened. In discussing the making of the text, he displays his failures, his rejections, his impatience: "I shall not say this again—I shall come back—Enough of it." These remarks underline the paradoxical thrust of the text and compound its tensions, while raising the issue and even the threat of abandonment and abysses. The text at moments propels itself along with apparent spontaneity and without manifest control; but it quickly loses momentum by making the reader face stubborn alternations of fettered progression and arrest.

Both Beckett and Ernst refer at least implicitly to textual and graphic genesis, to a becoming and even to a future. The illustrations for *From an Abandoned Work* can be viewed as a grid which, while it defies standard models, points to the artistic process of production, to the Bergsonian opposition between the natural or organic and the mechanical, so characteristic of much of Ernst's art. In *The Red Forest* we discover as already separate elements which in other works, including the etching, overlap in the same space. Indeed the foliage, the red color, and the wood are three distinct components of the painting. The foliage is decoratively introduced, while the wood nailed to the red surface reminds the viewer of a collage, for it assembles two elements: a red surface and a rough, unshaped piece of wood, as well as of a frottage, for Ernst seems to have rubbed the wooden fiber. Decorative art is highly planned, schematized and orderly; the frottage unconscious and, according to Ernst, automatic because it depends on inner pulsations. The Beckett illustration, the grid, not only juxtaposes but combines these paradoxical tendencies without having to reconstruct, except as tiny vestiges, any systematic representation.

Ernst's work is permeated by the discoveries he made with frottage. Surfaces partially or fully covered by lines do not delineate, for they defy geometry or any predictable course while bringing to the surface what has remained hidden to the naked eye. Among the links emerge apparent vestiges of frottage, traces which from above or below work their way into the web, suggesting the basic principle of flux which pervades Beckett's text as he abandons it to return to another equally abandoned fragment or stage.

By introducing frottages, Ernst asserts the continuity of his own art through the manifest presence of the stages of its production. In *From an Abandoned Work*, he signals or directs us toward what lies beyond the surface, beyond the domain of the visible. He displays signs of the unconscious activities of the mind, translated by the gestures of the artist. The deviations so far noted in Beckett's text can also pertain to shifting levels of consciousness. Such shifts may produce discontinuity in the narrative discourse, but they also testify to the opening up of other levels of mental functioning, to the loosening of other strata, themselves in constant displacement. The narrator voices repeated appeals to memory by attempting to bring to the surface and resurrect whatever Lazarus may lie in peace. He solicits at least an intermittent contribution on the part of memory, whose efforts may adumbrate zones of relative opacity—zones reflected in the etching, where the repeated configurations of frottage drown shape and detail in a sea of magnetic lines.

Beckett, in his antimimetic stance, questions memory only to reject it as a source of repetition and representation. The discontinuities of the text echo deviations between past and present, blurred by the interweavings of unconscious libidinal activities. Consequently the narration, amorphous or confused as it may seem, depends on shifts in relation to the very frame it tentatively seeks to assess and to the mental operation which it attempts to clarify. When we scrutinize Max Ernst's web, we assume that, like the changing moon, it occludes another side, and we are driven to speculate on zones closed to normal vision, layers lurking "beyond" and "below" which not only retrace, retrieve, or advance but actually form bends and arches gravitating toward absolute concavity and convexity. We cannot even surmise a lost thread or a dropped stitch. Ernst has appropriately interpreted the multilevel transforming meshwork shaping the Beckettian text in its refusal of any form of linearity, as well as in its uncompromising reductiveness.

Repeatedly, and without resorting to a direct form of mimesis, we can relate a word in the text to the outline of a form in the etching. Ernst's links enclose transparent zones, windows or frames which may allude to artistic production. As their relative opacity fluctuates, as they seem to move to and from the viewer, they eliminate the possibility of a unidirectional or nonreversible perspective. The word "window" functions as a term in the text. The mother looks out of the window serving as a borderline between two worlds which it paradoxically separates and connects. The act of seeing is introduced and, later, reinforced by the encounter of the narrator's eye with that of another, as though to signal resemblance and self-recognition. The window pertains to the distinction—ever dwindling though it may be—between the outside and the inside worlds, a distinction which leads to the merging of the house and the mind or memory, operating as an undefinable storehouse. By means of the word "window," Beckett alludes to distance, proximity, and even encounter and ensures the reduction of space and the telescoping of time. He catalyzes a spectacle or miniscene, which becomes a model constantly repeated and varied throughout the text. In addition to leading to a corresponding image in the etching, the window provides a focus for structural analogies between text and illustration. When the narrator claims he can see "through" his mother, the window no longer constitutes a privileged transparent surface through which images can be perceived. Beckett evokes the psychological dimension of perception, as well as the breakdown of the opaqueness and tangibility of the physical world. The frame, together with the images it contains, gradually becomes indistinguishable.

If the window in the text and the linkage in the etching provide the viewer with changing images, moving in and out of focus as though purposely to confuse, they also introduce a landscape, drastically streamlined, schematized, and reduced. Beckett emphasizes the landscape by several devices, notably an apparent spatial reduction outlined by the broken-up itinerary and the encounter with flora, which gravitates toward and ultimately assumes the shape of a fern, a recurring image in Max Ernst's iconography, e.g., *The Red Fern* and *The Fern Man*. Indeed, the interrelating of human and vegetable shapes had gone apace in the painter's work long before his official encounter with Beckett. In the etching, frottage "fibers" emerging with vestiges of a fern transpose into linear signs and shape Beckett's scaled-down landscape. Ernst's bluish web, where dark clusters and frottage lines vie with fairly transparent cellular areas, pertains to both flora and fauna. In spite of spatial reduction, in spite of the restrictions imposed by the exclusion of a third dimension, a fundamental ambiguity, appearing notably in the equivalence of submarine and celestial areas, pervades the web. In *From an Abandoned Work*, the anthropomorphic presence of ferns and bushes is counterbalanced by a process of dehumanization whereby man assumes animal characteristics, where the bird and the worm combine; whereby flying and crawling are but one and the same activity. Beckett blurs all distinctions of category and hierarchy: man observes the worm which he will soon resemble; the same and the other become even less distinguishable. In both the painter's and the writer's world, the landscape emerges not through the delimitation of geographical areas or spaces but through the establishing and mirroring of relationships.

I mentioned earlier the ellipsoid circle inscribed at the center of the etching as a sort of concession to geometry. It alludes to vision, introduces a change of distance, suggests a potential magnifying force. This circle functions also as a window, as well as a modification of the net or rather of its links. It points toward the self-reflexivity which permeates nearly all of Ernst's works, including his theoretical essay "Beyond Painting," which closes with the definition of his convulsive identity, as well as his many portraits and presentations of Loplop, a subject to which Werner Spies has devoted a recent book. The ellipsoid shape at the heart of the etching—a slightly deviant circle with a barely displaced center—echoes Beckett's techniques. It presents also the highly stylized image of a head, to which we could adjoin some scarcely detectable diagonal lines separating two shadings of color as the ultimate reduction of a shoulder. A streamlined portrait situated within the confines of a minimally defined landscape obliterates the duality of the artist and his world, of the artist and his signs.

Ernst's introduction of a portrait as a superannuated or transformed convention of painting corresponds to Beckett's use of a first-person narrator, whose visibility is threatened throughout the text as he tries to "retrace" his memories, which sporadically suggest the intrusion of a third dimension. These memories confront an identity too elusive to grasp. The self of the narrator is evoked not by spontaneous or felicitous words but by negative manifestations: a sore throat inchoately formulating verbs addressed to and heard by no one, memories which can easily be tampered with, an obsession with whiteness tantamount to the eventual blocking out of live forces. This procedure accounts for the prevalent lack in the text of a central force. In the fragmentation and schematization of identity, the interplay of the first and third persons, the shift from the one to the other without transition, surface with marked intensity.

"You could lie there for weeks and no one hear you, I often thought of that up in the mountains, no, that is a foolish thing to say, just went on, my body doing its best without me" (49). Beckett's final reference to a body living without mind intensifies a cleavage which becomes all the stranger if we situate it in the context of life and death, or more precisely the threat of death in life. In a way, the etching may suggest that this cleavage, however intense it may appear, is not altogether complete. Ernst's web, with its curves and shadows, with its focused and unfocused areas, evokes at least remotely the circumvolutions of the human brain or those mental figments to which Beckett repeatedly refers as though pointing toward the intersection of the material and spiritual, toward what is at once a dominant and an unlimited space. Jessica Prinz, in her "Foirades/Fizzles/Beckett/Johns," mentions Beckett's parody of Cartesianism (484). The final statement in *From an Abandoned Work* can also be interpreted as relevant to the same problematics. But whereas Descartes' discourse features clarity, Beckett's words surface with great difficulty in the fabric of narration.

As in most of his works, Beckett points toward a degenerative process far more than to a regenerative one, to an ebbing of energy simultaneous with a blurring of contours, as well as to the lack of any union between mind and body. In this context, Ernst differs markedly from Beckett. The etching pertains to a combined process of regeneration and deteriorization, but the scales are weighted in a direction opposite to Beckett's. The viewer engages in a game of substitutions and replacements without receiving any directional signals; ebb and flow remain reversible throughout.

By condensation of multiple layers and tracers, by the suggestion of ambiguity and tension, Beckett and Ernst turn referential fragments and representational art against themselves. However, Beckett's allusions to the ineffectiveness of the human mind, his insistence on decline, find no echo in Ernst's visual transposition. The painter, who has above all recognized the technical achievement of the writer, his genius in manipulating language, further undercuts Beckett's text as fiction in order to suggest its metacritical strategies.

Beckett was born fifteen years after Ernst. The impact of his writing made itself felt after World War II. He belongs, according to more than one critic, to postmodernism. He deconstructs various types of discourse: narrative in particular. Throughout his tale, he undermines the signified: "Unremembered— There is no accounting—no two breaths are the same." No context is restored as these utterly reduced fragments come into contact with other fragments without ever approaching any focal point or center. Recognizable word clusters are disturbed by others, perhaps figments of darkness, of the unconscious. Beckett's *écriture* provides a challenge to the text itself.

From an Abandoned Work seems to be an encounter of a postmodernist writer and a modernist painter, resulting in a different concept of illustration as compared to Beckett's *Fizzles*, illustrated by Jasper Johns, an exemplary postmodern venture. Yet Ernst's work can in more than one sense be considered as close to both postmodernism and modernism. His art can be construed as another form of deconstruction, an elusion of meaning. Early in his career, Ernst painted the Virgin spanking Jesus, thus subverting both technically and ideologically representational painting. But frottage constituted a much more radical gesture in putting into question representational art. It blatantly projects disturbing forces which make deciphering for message and meaning defunct. As does Beckett, Ernst diverts the reader who still believes in the shock of recognition by putting into play dissociative forces that set equally at odds the complementary principles of identity and otherness.

Not only do I suggest that Max Ernst's works, especially after World War II, are particularly meaningful as postmodern gestures, but also that postmodernism underlies other surrealist productions. *From an Abandoned Work* provides a point of departure and perhaps even a chart for such an inquiry.

Notes

1. Cf. in this context Enoch Brater, "Still/Beckett: The Essential and the Incidental": "Beckett therefore presents us with an image of stilness which is at the same time an image of movement,

a text which refuses to be decoded because it is forever on the run." *Journal of Modern Literature* (Summer 1977): 15.

2. My point of view differs from Ludovic Janvier's: ". . . un sujet anonyme, mais occupé par sa généalogie, également sujet de l'histoire mais à distance de son texte, et récapitulant dans l'éllipse et la tension trois journées de l'errance et des inquiétudes enfantines qui l'ont fait. Retrouvant une campagne irlandaise peu typée mais reconnaissable, renouant avec des occupations d'humain, le sujet s'éloigne dans cet aveu inachevé du point focal insupportable." *Cahier de l'Herne*, no. 31 (1976): 201.

BREON MITCHELL

Seeing the Unsayable:
Beckett and H. M. Erhardt

In the contemporary *livre d'artiste*, image and text confront each other in a manner far removed from traditional notions of illustration. No longer content to retell a story in pictures, the artist devises a series of reactions to a text which may appear, at first glance, not to be illustrations at all, but rather variations on a theme, a shape, a tone. In such cases, traditional criteria of evaluation seem to tell us little or nothing about what we are seeing. In the nineteenth century, illustrations were considered successful insofar as they managed to portray selected dramatic high points of a narrative convincingly and accurately. By the middle of our own century, such criteria seem among the least interesting we might apply.

Today the artist who presumes simply to substitute his or her own vision of the events and characters in a story for that of the reader treads a path which is well worn, narrow, and largely outmoded. That this has been recognized by almost every major artist of our time is clear from the vast range of styles and approaches to the *livre d'artiste* since the turn of this century. Initially, this very variety posed certain problems for scholars and critics steeped in traditional aesthetic values of book illustration. For what were we to make of an "illustration" which was nonrepresentational, or one which willfully distorted the "reality" of the text, or one which seemed a meditation on structure rather than the elucidation of a narrative incident?

Recent literary theory has come to our aid in this dilemma in more than one respect. Developments in semiotics have provided at least one way in which we can talk fruitfully about text and image as parallel sign systems, each conveying related levels of aesthetic meaning, without falling prey to the temptation of positing parallel effects or means. Intersemiotic transpositions among the arts have been effectively discussed by Claus Cluver, Umberto Eco, and Wendy Steiner, among others. While the semiotic approach may provide a methodology for the analysis of specific modern illustrated books, contemporary reader theory has offered a means of understanding more clearly the range and variety of visual responses to texts in this century. Insofar as the ideas of a Stanley Fish or a Wolfgang Iser have enlarged our notions of how the "meaning" of a text is constituted by the reader, they have also opened up a new approach to the concept of illustration. If we see the artist as a reader of the text to be illustrated, constituting the text by that very act, and participating in its formation by filling gaps at certain points of indeterminacy, we will hardly be surprised at the variety of visual readings which result. Our reactions to these results will, following Fish, depend in part upon the extent to which they fulfill the institutional expectations of a particular interpretative community. Any visual reading of the text, any construction of the text's meaning in visual terms, will prove acceptable insofar as it corresponds to such norms.

The text to be illustrated thus serves as a pre-text for the artist, to be transposed into visual terms which will necessarily offer only one among many possible valid readings. We do not approach a series of modern illustrations, then, expecting to find confirmation of our own reading of the text, and certainly not in the hopes of finding some grand synthesis of possible readings in which an underlying core of ultimate meaning resides. Instead we expect and hope precisely for illumination of another sort. The artist's vision at its best may provide us with an insight into the text which might equally well have been offered by a sensitive literary critic, or by our own rereading had we been blessed with the artist's sensitivity to form, to texture, to a particular constellation of signs. It is in this sense that the venerable concept of the mutual illumination of the arts may take on concrete reality: we *see*, through the eyes of the artist, a reading of the text which might otherwise have escaped us. That text is illuminated with new aesthetic meaning for us. And at the same time, the text is the key by means of which the visual images which confront us are themselves illuminated.

This last point deserves further consideration. Whereas the original text may be read fruitfully without reference to any particular subsequent series of illustrations, the illustrations themselves can scarcely be understood in any larger sense without a knowledge of the text for which they were created.[1] Put another way, the sorts of questions we bring to the text differ from those we bring to the series of images which accompany the text; in the latter case, the questions by means of which we construct the meaning of what we see are inevitably tied to our reading of the text itself. We read the illustrations *through* our reading of the text, which alters and enlarges our sense of what the visual images mean. It is of course possible to regard the illustrations as independent works of visual art, and if they do not succeed on that level, there is little likelihood that they will be redeemed by their context. But it would clearly be perverse to ignore the text if we wish to understand the illustrations fully.

Such general considerations might be tested at any one of the numerous intersections of modern art and literature in our time. But here, as so often, the works of Samuel Beckett offer a particularly rich field for investigation. In calling into question the very possibility of telling a story, his works call into question as well all traditional notions of illustration. Seeing the unsayable would seem to be a particularly difficult enterprise. Yet Beckett's works have called forth a richer and more varied response among contemporary artists than any other single writer of our time, conjoining both modernist and post-modernist concerns.

Perhaps the most significant and extended confrontation of any artist with Samuel Beckett has been that of Avigdor Arikha, whose works are well known to most Beckett scholars. For that reason I have chosen here to discuss the work of a less well-known West German artist, H. M. Erhardt, who illustrated four texts by Beckett between 1965 and 1971.[2]

H. M. Erhardt was born in 1935 in Emmendingen im Breisgau, West Germany. He studied at the Academy of Art in Karlsruhe with Wilhelm Schnarrenberger and H. A. P. Grieshaber. Since 1961 he has been living in Karlsruhe, with frequent stays in France. Erhardt first came into contact with the world of Samuel Beckett in 1963, when he saw Deryk Mendel's productions of the pantomimes. In 1964 Erhardt provided the stage decor for the Schillertheater production of Beckett's *Play*. In the fall of that same year he met Beckett in Paris and discussed his illustrations for the Manus Presse edition of *Act Without Words I and II*. Over the next seven years he also created original graphics for editions of *Come and Go*, *Ping*, and *Watt*. Each of these Erhardt books offers a distinctly different vision of a Beckett text. Recognizably the product of a single sensibility, they nevertheless display a surprising range of techniques and temperament.

Act ohne Worte (1965) startles the reader first of all by its monumentality, the sheer physical size of the book standing in clear contrast to our expectations in light of the relatively short mimes it contains. Before even opening the oversized volume we are challenged by a view of the texts which seems to claim for them a status far beyond the average reader's expectations.

In one sense it seems particularly appropriate to select a play without words for illustration, and Erhardt's involvement with set design seems a sufficient explanation for his interest in texts that can only be fully realized in stage production. Yet even this first venture into Beckett's world is marked by a tension between representation and abstraction which is symptomatic of much of modern book illustration. On the one hand, the very nature of the theater is to show characters in action; on the other, the essence of Beckett's art is to break down our conventional expectations and reduce that action to its bare essentials. Erhardt reacts to this tension between reductive abstraction and concrete presence by dividing the visual field of each double-page spread in two: on the left we are given realistic line drawings of stage props—

H. M. ERHARDT, linocut for *Act Without Words I*, 1965. Courtesy Manus Presse.

a pair of scissors, a watch, a comb—while on the right, far more powerfully, and filling the entire space of the page, we have the linocuts which depict the pastel grays, browns, and black of the stage as seen through Erhardt's eyes. That latter reading of Beckett's world is itself subjected to constant revision from page to page, and the same tension between abstraction and representation is rendered in shapes and forms which constantly oscillate between sacks and formless figures, blocklike boxes and gray-black balls. Faced with such forms, we may share the confusion of Tetty and Mr. Hackett when they first encounter Watt: "Tetty was not sure whether it was a man or a woman. Mr. Hackett was not sure that it was not a parcel, a carpet for example, or a roll of tarpaulin, wrapped up in dark paper and tied about the middle with a cord." In these mysterious and obsessive shapes we may recognize the characters and action of the text, but only if we read them through the text itself. In themselves they remain opaque signs which may hint at meaning but can never reveal it.

In the 1968 edition of *Come and Go*, this tension between abstraction and representation has been clearly resolved: the seven etchings which accompany the trilingual text of Beckett's play create an intriguing series of permutations of three perfect spheres within a sphere. The tour de force by means of which these horizontally arranged circles are given shape and volume through variations in light and shade is admirable in and of itself. As an independent series of visual meditations on the relationship between the second and third dimensions, between the circle and the sphere, between light and darkness, these etchings lay serious claim to our attention. As a commentary and reflection upon Beckett's text, however, they reveal important layers of signification beyond their purely graphic appeal.

If in *Act Without Words I and II* Erhardt was primarily drawn to the blurred line between living bodies and inanimate shapes, he clearly sees[3] *Come and Go* as a play dominated by an almost musical structure. Permutation, symmetry, balance: a tension between stasis and motion, between silence and the briefest of spoken phrases, lends this 127-word microdrama a power far beyond its length. Erhardt's visual reading of the play reflects precisely this power in its concentration on the tension between the stasis of the individual etchings and the sense of permutation and change in the series itself, the exact order of which is carefully insisted upon by means of a visual table of contents inside the front cover of the box which holds the book. The poignant exchanges of Flo, Vi, and Ru, three old women who have passed through and beyond life without realizing it, and for whom only memories remain, is thus reduced to a rhythmical geometric discourse from which all color fades, a music of the spheres. A partial reading indeed, but one which goes to the core of Beckett's method.

Nor is Erhardt's reading of *Come and Go* limited to purely structural considerations. When, at the close of the play, Flo, Vi, and Ru hold hands "in the

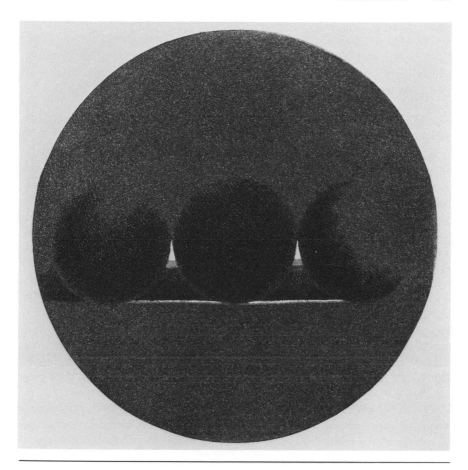

H. M. ERHARDT, etching for *Come and Go*, 1968. Courtesy Manus Presse.

old way," the complicated interlacing of their arms allows Flo to imagine again the wedding rings they dreamed of as young girls. Her final line, "I can feel the rings," serves as an epiphany of failed hopes, particularly when Beckett's printed notes to the play make clear that "no rings [are] apparent." This special moment would seem to defy the creation of a visual analog, given the strict limitations Erhardt has set for himself. Yet without violating the internal coherence of his own aesthetic strategy, he manages to find a simple solution in which image and meaning are merged perfectly. In his seventh and final illustration, Erhardt prints three identical solid circles, side by side, black on black, in bas-relief. The logic of the series itself forces us to read this final illustration as a continuation of the spatial permutation of the three spheres which we have already come to equate structurally with Flo, Vi, and Ru, now side by side at the end of the play, as the lights in the house are extinguished. At the same time we can literally feel the raised impressions of the rings, which in theory would not otherwise be apparent, since they have been printed black on identical black. The sign system of the spheres thus merges perfectly with that of the rings, uniting character and concept in a single tripartite image that brings Erhardt's series to a close with the force of a beautiful concluding move in chess.

Beckett's *Ping* offered Erhardt another sort of challenge in 1970. Surely among Beckett's most difficult texts, *Ping* combines and recombines itself repeatedly, forming a "verbless incantation . . . an artifact woven of permutation, repetition, and emptiness—not unlike *Comment c'est* to the ear, but very different to the eye" (Cohn, 1973: 250). The solid unbroken block of the text itself contrasts sharply with the almost empty whiteness of the text: "traces blurs light grey almost white on white." In this narrative without action, thematic variation and permutation once more provide a musicality of language typical of much of Beckett's later work. Yet Erhardt turns aside completely from any attempt to render this incantatory effect in visual terms. Instead his imagination is seized by the "bare body white on white invisible," "white feet toes joined like sewn heels together right angle invisible," situated in a world of "traces blurs signs no meaning light grey almost white." In *Come and Go* Erhardt sought to find a visual balance between stasis and motion. In *Ping* he seems intrigued by the tension between the task of expression and the desire for silence.

The eight white-on-white raised impressions in blind (*Blindpragungen*) which accompany *Ping* alternate in no strict pattern between five compositions which are clearly related to parts of the body "joined like sewn" (see illustration), and three which consist of the barest traces that surround that body. These latter visions resemble nothing so much as white bacteria and bacilli on a white ground, an impression which is strengthened by the one plate impression that is not rectangular: a perfect circle through which we see with a sharpened eye, as in a microscope, the vanishing signs of Beckett's hermetically sealed universe.

In *Ping* the structuralist reading of *Come and Go* is thus abandoned in favor of a minimalist reading which comments upon the limits of art itself: as language approaches silence, as all narrative action ceases, as vision blurs in a textual world of whiteness, Erhardt effaces all color, reduces line to lineless contour, substitutes touch for sight in an art for the blind, in a series of blind impressions.

In 1971 Erhardt returned to Beckett, this time with eight original etchings for *Watt*, issued as a portfolio of prints without text. It would be difficult to imagine a greater contrast than that between the concrete, detailed world of Watt and the shrunken, subdued images of *Ping*. None of the works which

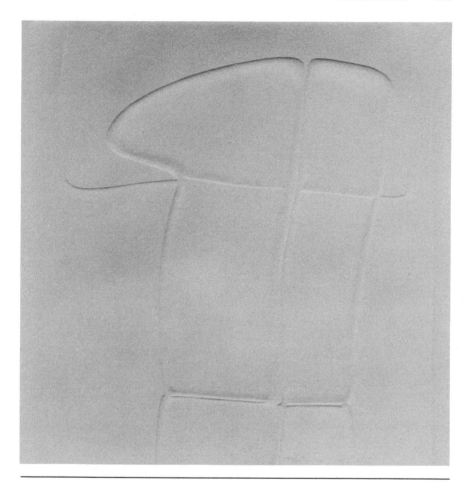

H. M. ERHARDT, Impression in blind for *Ping*, 1970. Courtesy Manus Presse.

Erhardt had previously illustrated must have so pulled the artist toward telling a story, toward concrete representation, in short, toward a more conventional mode of illustration. Here, for the first time, Erhardt chose to confront a full-length novel rather than a minimalist text. Here, for the first time, he was face to face with a total world against which to match his own.

No printed text is included, a fact which in itself alters the whole feel of the enterprise. The artist's world is given a primacy unmatched in the earlier works. The etchings are identified by a series of two-word titles: Watt arrives, loves, rests, speaks, looks, listens, thinks, leaves. In spite of this emphasis on doing, the plates themselves are all, so to speak, still-lifes, in which little or no

H. M. ERHARDT, "Watt loves," for *Watt*, etching, 1971. Courtesy Manus Presse.

action is evident. As if no single style, no single approach, no single visual reading of the novel would be adequate, Erhardt abandons the internal stylistic unity which had characterized each of his previous series of illustrations. Now his etchings range from linear abstraction in "Watt thinks," to solid forms in "Watt hears," from a figurative treatment of the speaker/listener couple in "Watt speaks," to total geometric abstraction in "Watt arrives." Appropriately, "Watt sees" offers us the only plate in which we do not see Watt, but rather his view of the stars through the window.

But if we did not know we were looking at Watt, we would seldom be sure what was Watt and what was not. (Knott, appropriately enough, is not in evidence.) We experience again the shift in perception from the abstract to the representational, which is typical of the insight that our reading of the text brings to our reading of the image.[4] Take, for example, the forms to be found in the second illustration in the series (see "Watt loves"). Had this etching been entitled "Composition II" and placed in an exhibition with Erhardt's other works, it would have blended in perfectly. Yet when invested with the title "Watt loves," and viewed in the context of this series, it takes on quite specific narrative qualities.[5] The two major forms, sexless as they are, begin to seem male and female, with sexual congress not totally out of the question. A closer look at the text of *Watt* transforms the shape below them to a chair, and convinces us that Erhardt has chosen and read this passage with care:

> Then he would have her in the kitchen, and open for her a bottle of stout, and set her on his knee, and wrap his right arm about her waist, and lean his head upon her right breast (the left having unhappily been removed in the heat of a surgical operation), and in this position remain, without stirring, or stirring the least possible, forgetful of his troubles, for as long as ten minutes, or a quarter of an hour. . . . But Mrs Gorman did not always sit on Watt, for sometimes Watt sat on Mrs Gorman. . . . Further than this, it will be learnt with regret, they never went, though more than half inclined to do so on more than one occasion. (140–41)

Erhardt's surgery in this case has been even more radical, but there is no more heat in evidence here than that shared by Watt and Mrs. Gorman.

A mood of calm and cool stasis predominates in this and the other plates in the series. In each a clear relationship to the text may be established, and in most cases it is possible to identify a particular corresponding passage from the novel. Moreover, Erhardt has framed his series, as the novel itself is framed, with Watt's arrival and departure. This gives a sense of closure to the illustrations, while a precisely constructed visual balance between the two plates, the first bathed in light and the second set in darkness, implies the endless circularity articulated in Arsene's speech to Watt: "For in truth the same things happen to us all, especially to men in our situation, whatever that is, if only we chose to know it. . . . But another evening shall come and the light die away out of the sky and the colour from the earth. . . . And then another night fall and another man come and Watt go, Watt who is now come, for the coming is in the shadow of the going and the going is in the shadow of the coming" (45, 56, 57). Erhardt's suite of etchings for *Watt* is, by implication, itself "a term in a series, like the series of Mr Knott's dogs, or the series of Mr Knott's men, or like the centuries that fall, from the pod of eternity" (131).

Yet here, too, no story is told. The images of the series might be multiplied at will, but they would never result in a concatenation of events. In this sense Erhardt is still operating in a realm far removed from traditional illustration. He sees in *Watt* certain images, and he sees them in his own terms. His reading of *Watt* focuses on the question of sense perception, on thinking and talking, on coming and going. He plays Watt's world off against his own and tests the scope and variety of the artistic means by which he can come to grips with both.

At the same time, it is interesting to note, Erhardt's illustrations for *Watt* are completely compatible in style and tone with those works of art he creates independently of any text. The bare, open window of "Watt looks," for example, is clearly related to a later series of oil paintings of open windows entitled "Interior" and "Presumed View," as well as to the pastel, "Opening," of 1973 (Gallwitz, 1973). And this is true of his other series of illustrations as well. The spheres of *Come and Go* are closely paralleled, for example, in a lithograph from 1969 entitled "Two Fruits," in which the "fruits" are two perfect circles given volume by color. It thus appears that Erhardt pulls Beckett's texts as much into his own world as the texts pull him into theirs.

I began with the observation that both semiotics and reader-response theory offer new perspectives on the contemporary *livre d'artiste*. The artist's reading of a text results in a series of visual signs which, to be fully understood, must be read both in their own terms and as commentary. We hope for a mutual illumination: a deeper insight into the text provided by a sensitive, if necessarily partial, visual reading, and a more perceptive grasp of a series of images in terms of the text they accompany. H. M. Erhardt's illustrations of Beckett serve as salient examples of this process. Varying widely in approach, emphasis, and style, they enlarge our sense of the possibilities of meaning inherent in both image and text.

During his stay at Mr. Knott's house, Watt was obsessed by a desire to understand a series of everyday incidents "of great formal brilliance and indeterminable purport" (74). Indeed he felt "obliged, because of his peculiar character, to enquire into what they meant, oh not into what they really meant, his character was not so peculiar as all that, but into what they might be induced to mean, with the help of a little patience, a little ingenuity" (75). Faced with problematic modern texts, contemporary artists, with the help of a little patience and ingenuity, aid us in constructing the meaning of what we see and read. In spite of a recurrent longing for final answers, we must not be so peculiar as to expect more.

Notes

1. I speak here of the simplest case, in which a previously existing text is illustrated by an artist. A whole gamut of other relationships might be cited, from texts written for previously existing works of art, through collaborative efforts of artists and writers, to the numerous well-known examples of *Doppelbegabung*. Each of these relationships would require its own set of questions.

2. They are:

> 1. *Akt ohne Worte I. Akt ohne Worte II. (Act Without Words I and II)*. Stuttgart: Manus Presse, 1965, with 18 original linocuts and reproductions of 16 line drawings in an edition of 200 numbered copies.
>
> 2. *Kommen und Gehen. (Come and Go)*. Stuttgart: Manus Presse, 1968, with 7 original etchings in an edition of 45 numbered copies.
>
> 3. *Bing. (Ping)*. Stuttgart: Manus Presse, 1970, with 8 original blind-relief impressions in an edition of 50 numbered copies.
>
> 4. *Watt.* Stuttgart: Manus Presse, 1971, with 8 original etchings in an edition of 45 numbered copies.

Erhardt has also illustrated a short, untitled text by Franz Kafka and poems by Severo Sarduy.

3. Or was brought to see. A 1973 catalogue from the Manus Presse hints that Erhardt may have changed his original ideas for the illustrations after discussing them with Beckett in Paris.

4. Watt's perceptions, on the other hand, shift in the opposite direction. The Gall's visit, for example, soon "developed a purely plastic content, and gradually lost, in the nice processes of its light, its sound, its impacts and its rhythm, all meaning, even the most literal" (72–73).

5. An equally striking example may be found in the smooth and rounded forms which occupy the upper-right-hand corner of "Watt hears." Only our knowledge of the text has the power to transform this abstract assemblage into a pillow, a smooth head, and a listening ear.

Afterword

RUBY COHN

Inexhaustible Alan

Alan Schneider runs up the steps in Billie Whitelaw's London house. At age sixty-three it is like a boy that he runs in an early scene of the Pennebaker-Hegedus film about *Rockaby*. He runs as, so often in rehearsals in New York, London, Paris, Columbus, Buffalo, he ran back and forth to the stage, his lodestone. His energy was energizing, and the upward movement is endearing in this film that first seemed to show too much of Alan but will now be cherished for precious glimpses of him. To those of us blessed with Alan's friendship, another film scene is now wrenching. Looking Billie Whitelaw full in the face, Alan tells her that *Rockaby* is not about dying but about accepting death. And his death by cruel accident seems all the more unacceptable.

"He was at his peak," wrote Harold Pinter, the last playwright to work with him, and it was a peak that Alan scaled determinedly, whether one assumes ground level to be his 1941 premiere of Saroyan's *Jim Dandy*, or his first Broadway production, the 1953 *Remarkable Mr. Pennypacker*, or the 1956 Miami *Godot*. Despite my Beckett serendipity, I wasn't in Miami (does anyone admit to being there?), but Alan himself has recalled a few of the lowlights of that fiasco:

"Very simply, Bert Lahr wanted to relegate the role of Vladimir to that of straight man. In the instance of Lucky's speech, he wanted to cut it out entirely 'since nobody understood it anyway.' At the very least, since I would neither cut it nor let him go off-stage during the speech, he insisted on doing lots of comic business all through it, so that no one would have to listen and be bored. After all they had come to see Bert and not the actor playing Lucky, whoever he was. And to hear Bert repeat his familiar 'gnong-gnong' in response to the recurrent realisation of his fate, instead of Mr. Beckett's simpler and very ordinary (but how extraordinary!) 'Ahh.' The fact that Bert was superbly eloquent in many of his own manifestations of Estragon's character didn't make my choices easier. Eventually, another director more willing to accept and deal with Bert's insecurities, took the play to New York—and away from Beckett" (*Theatre Quarterly*, 19).

During forty years in the theater Alan Schneider directed well over a hundred productions, and it is too tantalizingly symbolic that there were thirty-three Beckett productions. I date back to his second—the 1958 *Endgame* at New York's Cherry Lane Theater. Still vivid in my mind's eye is the undraped back wall of brick; and still resonant in my mind's ear, as Clov/Epstein (who, with Alan's encouragement, played Hamm in 1984) rammed the wheelchair into that wall, Hamm/Rawlins's basso profundo: "Do you hear? Hollow bricks! . . . All that's hollow!" It seems to me now that Alan was directing for sonic variety in hollow men: Rawlins and Epstein were baritone and tenor; Nagg/Kelly was a lighter Irish tenor, and Nell/Westman his contralto echo; each pair with its irritable ping-pong beats. I recall none of Beckett's metronomic rhythms, at which Alan later became adept. Instead, there was a pervasive credibility in different voice timbres. Years later Alan would write: "Nagg and Nell are elderly, cold, hungry, sleepy, somewhat deaf, not so good at seeing, without legs, and feeling a certain way about their son Hamm keeping them cooped up in those ashcans. These qualities can be acted, while the concept of the 'older generation discarded' or the 'dead past put onto the garbage heap' or 'the flower of French civilization' cannot." Replete with his baseball cap and tennis shoes, Alan was assuming an anti-intellectual role, and yet there was a rigorous intellectual quality in his fidelity to texts, and in his outrage at infidelity: "Interpretation is one thing—like *Hamlet, Godot* will always be different when filtered through a director's temperament and the imponderables of casting—but interpolation is quite another thing, not to mention extrapolation, and the intrusion of a subtext that clearly distorts instead of illuminating its text" (*Theatre Quarterly*, 19). Of such liberties in *Endgame* he said scathingly: "When the author specifically says about a given character, Clov, 'I can't sit' and the director makes him sit, I find there's no point to that. I think the director has every right to find out why he can't sit and how many ways he can't sit, how interestingly he can't sit, or to make the audience understand why he can't sit. But to simply turn around because the author has said, 'I can't sit' about this character and then have him sit down, seems to me to be turning it inside out" (*New York Theatre Review*, November 1978).

In 1959 Alan returned to *Godot*—in Texas. I missed that happier occasion, as well as the American premiere of *Krapp's Last Tape* in 1960 and the world premiere of *Happy Days* in 1961, both in New York City. Alan resembled his friend Sam Beckett in his partiality to women, especially actresses, and I have the impression that Ruth White's Winnie was perhaps the Beckett performance he most treasured. He sometimes recalled her courage, and I was never quite sure whether he meant White's or Winnie's. In an article on directing (*New York Theatre Review*, Spring 1977), he would recall: "The first thing I write on the blank pages of my production notebook is not where someone is sitting or moving, but what the play is 'about', as well as what its tone or texture should be. . . . Winnie's absolute necessity as she sank further and further into the sands of *Happy Days* was 'to live.' "

In 1962 he directed new versions of *Endgame* and *Krapp* before Albee's *Virginia Woolf* made him famous. Famous but never imprisoned by Broadway, as he made clear in a program note of the Harold Clurman Theatre: "I don't just sit around and wait for the next Broadway show. I think of myself as being an American director, not a Broadway or Off-Broadway or avant-garde director. Besides, I think the American theatre's changing. It's no longer possible to confine yourself to one kind of writer or locale. Also, it's impossible to make a living on Broadway. . . . You can make a killing, but you can't make a living."

I choose to extrapolate: *Virginia Woolf* was Alan's killing and the whole Beckett canon was his living.

Alan himself viewed 1964 as a double-edged year in his relationship to Beckett. On the one edge was his only betrayal of Beckett's scenic directions—with Beckett's reluctant permission; in his English-language premiere of *Play* the lines were delivered more slowly than Beckett desired, and they were not repeated, as specified in the text. Looking back at *Play*, Alan felt that New York audiences were simply not ready for it, but I now think that Alan was not ready for it. At the time I was bewildered that Beckett should have succumbed to a lovers' triangle; the production seemed to me dank with stale pseudopsychology. Absent was any sense of the innate gameness of being; any awareness of the arbitrary nature of light; any appreciation of the trivial speed of emotional events. Old Testament family man that he was, Alan never quite mastered the theatrical counterpoint of that old adulterous play—even in recent productions.

But 1964 also brought Alan the joy of Beckett's presence while he worked—on *Film*. Since that film has circulated widely, and Grove Press has published a delightful volume, with many photographs and a long essay by Alan, I won't labor my disappointment.

For the remainder of the swinging sixties, Alan continued to direct in small and large theaters, in and out of New York, seeking new scripts, even while enthusiastically directing new productions of what were becoming contemporary classics. He was devoted to all kinds of theater—amateur and professional, New York and regional, and always educational. He has been affiliated with several universities and several professional training programs. Indefatigable, he wrote, lectured, directed.

By the mid-seventies, Alan Schneider was internationally known as The Beckett Director, and he described his approach (*Theatre Quarterly*, 19): "The key to my directing of Beckett, then, may be described as that of dealing simultaneously with what I have come to call 'the local situation' (in contrast to that other more cosmic one) and his rhythmical and tonal structure, his specific style or 'texture'. . . . It is only through constant attention to both

Beckettian 'texture' and the 'local situation' that his plays can be presented faithfully. . . . Helped by Beckett's own pauses, I have always worked out the 'beats' in the text—with the proper intentions, adjustments, circumstances, and other standard underpinnings. Most of all, I have tried to cast only those actors whom I felt to be suitable and agreeable to Beckett's world—and not cast those who would destroy or deny that world."

With many of those actors now grieving for Alan, I do not want to make invidious comparisons of performances, but to dwell tenderly on the last decade. It was in 1975 at a Beckett summer at Stanford University that I came to know and love this funny, feisty, loyal, and indefatigable director. Directing *Godot* for perhaps the fifth time, Alan nevertheless gave it his scrupulous attention, from casting to combing the California landscape for the perfect tree; with one professional in the student cast, Alan treated all the actors as individuals, catering to their particular temperaments, but with special gentleness toward Godot's Boy. He was, however, inexorably demanding of the technical staff, who were all terrified of him. In short, he paid them the unappreciated compliment of professional exigency. And in a poorly equipped theater, after days and often mealless days of rehearsal, Alan labored to bring forth a coordinated ensemble from a professorial Vladimir, a childishly petulant Estragon, a weary Pozzo, and a manic Lucky played by a student who had never before set foot on stage. It was an education for educators like me.

As was *Rockaby*. Contrary to what has appeared in print, the play was not written for Billie Whitelaw but offered to Dan Labeille in connection with a creative film project. When the originally cast actress withdrew, I suggested Billie to Dan. From inception Alan was the director, and he stood by at the ready while Dan negotiated the complicated transatlantic logistics of the enterprise. The Pennebaker-Hegedus film conveys the tender esteem in which Billie and Alan held one another from their very first meeting. Billie is an actress who likes a strong director, and Alan was a strong director. The film provides some telling insights into Alan's rehearsal habits, but it fails to mention that Alan introduced Dan to Beckett, that Alan and Billie both consulted Beckett by telephone from London, that ten grueling hours were required to make the tape and another day to edit it.

Once in Buffalo, Alan struck customary terror into the student technicians even while he protected Billie from photographers and stage lights, which irritate her sensitive eyes. While ordering Billie to rest, he drafted anyone and everyone to sit in that carefully selected and burnished rocking chair while the lights were adjusted, the creak was greased out, and the manual rocker controlled the chair's movements to a hair's breadth. Everyone fell in love with Billie during rehearsals, but Alan's irascible demands achieved the flawless whole that no film can capture. His wife, Jean—his island, as he called her—found an exquisite miniature rocking chair, which he gave Billie after their opening. The two women would mourn Alan together in April 1984, in

London, but at the Buffalo opening all was radiance and joy. Publisher Barney Rosset hosted a supper, and alcohol lubricated transatlantic theater stories, with Alan mercilessly funny about his own rehearsal irascibility. He inscribed my copy of *Rockaby* not only in his native Russian but in his non-French: "Pour Ruby Avec Amour Alain Schneydaire." Only momentarily did he relinquish the thirteen letters of the more usual spelling—infallible sign that he was attuned to Beckett.

In that same year, 1981, in my native Columbus, Ohio, there was no time for "amour." At this mammoth university, humanities and theater departments did not communicate; on the same weekend the former hosted a Beckett Symposium and the latter a conference on post-Beckett theater. For the former occasion Beckett had sent *Ohio Impromptu*, to be directed by Alan. I no longer recall whether casting David Warrilow was his idea or Beckett's suggestion. What I do recall is my surprise at how beautifully they worked together. Warrilow's noncharacter approach to acting would seem to be at the antipode of Alan's Method-grounded psychology, and yet the two of them subordinated theory to the scrupulous and meticulous practice of perhaps Beckett's most elegiac text. Alan had worked previously with Rand Mitchell, whom he cast as the Listener; that thankless role demanded extreme concentration, flawless timing, and ego subordination, as well as some minimal resemblance to the Reader. When Alan earlier wrote about casting "only those actors whom I felt to be suitable and agreeable to Beckett's world," he could scarcely have predicted Mitchell's selfless contribution to a black-and-white image that will remain indelibly etched in memory.

Before arrival in Columbus, Alan worked in happy harmony with the two actors of *Ohio Impromptu*, but technical problems in the Columbus theater—ugly and unsuitable—were almost insurmountable. Alan never minimized the technical difficulties in Beckett's seemingly simple plays: ". . . all those complications that those simple little Beckett plays with one or two characters and hardly any scenery, manage to be loaded with: undersized ashcans and oversized urns, parasols that burn up on cue, but not before, carafes that fly without twisting slowly, slowly in the wind, a Mouth that floats unsupported in space, and a Figure with head and arms lit up, but feet invisible" (*TQ*, 19). To these he might have added a table that dwarfed its human companions, a hat that got lost on its broad expanse, a book too large for its function, and a general scarcity of technical support, which was perhaps attending the Theater Conference in another corner of the vast campus. Were it not for the unsung troubleshooting of Marty Fehsenfeld, there might have been no *Ohio Impromptu* in Ohio.

1981 seems to me Alan's most triumphant Beckett year. Working with profound Beckett texts—"profounds of mind"—working with "suitable and agreeable" and precisely gifted actors, working against and overcoming irritating obstacles, Alan created memorable Beckett events. As the plays continued to run, he continued to hone the productions—new sequins on the gown of the rocking woman in "best black," two distinct tones for the knocks of the Listener, a raked table—and of course he also turned his inexhaustible energies to *Catastrophe* and *What Where*.

At the peak of his career in 1984, Alan Schneider had six Beckett productions running in New York in two different theaters. They were short dramas in small theaters (which toured greedily in larger theaters), but the actors were devoted to the texts, and the audiences were appreciative of the striking precision of this late work of Beckett and Schneider. Alan remarked buoyantly: "Beckett has come into the mainstream of playwriting; he's no longer considered an aberration. I see the shows about once a week, and it's a general audience, with people of every age group." And yet, Alan could also view his work with humor. In an article in *American Theatre*, published in April 1984, the month of his death, he jokingly predicted: "In Samuel Beckett's newest and most minimal masterpiece, titled *Untitled*, the first act will open on an empty stage, no actors visible. The play will be composed of simple forms and fundamental sounds (in the words of the author, 'no pun intended'). It will run approximately 7 to 11 minutes, depending on the director's interpretation of the pauses. In the second act, the curtain will not rise at all. It will be a very short act. Actors' Equity—ever vigilant and alert—will react by passing a new rule requiring a minimum of roles for its members per act, properly proportioned by sex, race and national origin."

Alan might have added: "Schneider will be accused of taking liberties," as when he added a vertical light to the end of *Footfalls*, in accordance with Beckett's wishes subsequent to publication; or: "Schneider will be accused of slavish subservience," as when he turned on me for calling him "traditional" in contrast to Lee Breuer and Joe Dunn; or, perhaps most damning of all: "Schneider will be accorded respect" when what he achieved at his peak is an exhilaration and radiance in that ephemeral phenomenon that is theater.

By the time Alan Schneider befriended me in 1975, he used to chuckle: "I'm the only director who's been shoved from the avant-garde to the old-garde, without ever passing through the Establishment." His death robs us all—avant-garde, old-garde, and mere Beckett lovers.

Bibliography

Abbott, H. Porter. "A Poetics of Radical Displacement: Samuel Beckett Coming up to Seventy." *Texas Studies in Literature and Language* 17 (1975): 232–38.

———. "The Writer's Laboratory: Samuel Beckett and the Death of the Book." In *Diary Fiction: Writing as Action*. Ithaca: Cornell University Press, 1984, 183–206.

Acheson, James. "Chess with the Audience: Samuel Beckett's *Endgame*." *Critical Quarterly* 22 (1980): 33–45.

Alvarez, A. *Samuel Beckett*. New York: Viking Press, 1973.

Anders, Günther. "Being without Time: On Beckett's Play *Waiting for Godot*." In *Samuel Beckett: A Collection of Critical Essays*. Ed. Martin Esslin. Englewood Cliffs, N.J.: Prentice-Hall, 1965, 140–51.

Antin, David. "Duchamp and Language: Notation of an Improvised Talk," 12 April 1972. *Marcel Duchamp*. Ed. Anne D'Harnoncourt and Kynaston McShine. New York: Museum of Modern Art, 1973, 100–115.

Arthos, John. *The Language of Natural Description in Eighteenth-Century Poetry*. 1949; New York: Octagon Books, 1966.

Asmus, Walter. "Beckett Directs Godot." *Theatre Quarterly* 5 (1975): 19–26.

Bair, Deirdre. *Samuel Beckett: A Biography*. New York: Harcourt Brace Jovanovich, 1978.

Barth, John. "The Literature of Exhaustion." *The Atlantic*, August 1967, 29–34.

Barthes, Roland. *Leçon*. Paris: Seuil, 1978.

Battestin, Martin. *The Providence of Wit: Aspects of Form in Augustan Literature*. Oxford: Clarendon Press, 1974.

Beaujour, Michel. *Miroirs d'encre: Rhétorique de l'autoportrait*. Paris: Seuil, 1980.

Beckett, Samuel. *All Strange Away*. New York: Grove Press, 1974.

———. *All That Falls* (in *Krapp's Last Tape and Other Pieces*). New York: Grove Press, 1960.

———. "Assez." In *Têtes-mortes*. Paris: Les Editions de Minuit, 1967, 44.

———. "Berceuse." In *Catastrophe et autres dramaticules*. Paris: Les Editions de Minuit, 1982, 52.

———. *Bing*. Paris: Les Editions de Minuit, 1966.

———. *Cascando and Other Short Dramatic Pieces*. New York: Grove Press, 1970.

———. *Collected Poems in English and French*. New York: Grove Press, 1977.

———. *Collected Shorter Plays of Samuel Beckett*. London and Boston: Faber and Faber, 1984; New York: Grove Press, 1984.

———. *Comment c'est*. Paris: Les Editions de Minuit, 1961.

———. *Compagnie*. Paris: Les Editions de Minuit, 1980.

———. *Company*. New York: Grove Press; London: John Calder, 1980.

———. "Dante . . . Bruno . Vico . . Joyce." In *transition* 16–17 (1929): 242–53.

————. *Disjecta: Miscellaneous Writings and a Dramatic Fragment.* Ed. Ruby Cohn. New York: Grove Press, 1984.

————. *Endgame.* New York: Grove Press, 1958; London: Faber and Faber, 1976.

————. *Ends and Odds: Eight New Dramatic Pieces.* New York: Grove Press, 1976.

————. *Ends and Odds: Plays and Sketches.* London: Faber and Faber, 1977.

————. "The Expelled." In *I Can't Go On, I'll Go On.* Ed. Richard W. Seaver. New York: Grove Press, 1976, 197–98.

————. *Film.* New York: Grove Press, 1972.

————. *First Love and Other Shorts.* New York: Grove Press, 1974.

————. *Fizzles.* New York: Grove Press, 1976.

————. *From an Abandoned Work.* Stuttgart: Manus Presse, 1967.

————. *Happy Days.* New York: Grove Press, 1961.

————. *How It Is.* New York: Grove Press, 1964.

————. *Ill Seen Ill Said.* New York: Grove Press, 1981.

————. *L'Innommable.* Paris: Les Editions de Minuit, 1953.

————. *Krapp's Last Tape.* New York: Grove Press, 1958.

————. "Lessness," *New Statesman* 79 (1 May 1970): 635.

————. *The Lost Ones.* New York: Grove Press, 1972.

————. *Mal vu mal dit.* Paris: Les Editions de Minuit, 1981.

————. *Mercier and Camier.* New York: Grove Press, 1974.

————. *More Pricks Than Kicks.* 1934; New York: Grove Press, 1970.

————. *Murphy.* New York: Grove Press, 1957.

————. *Not I.* In *Ends and Odds.* New York: Grove Press, 1976, 13–23.

————. *Oh les beaux jours.* Paris: Les Editions de Minuit, 1963.

————. *Ohio Impromptu/Catastrophe/What Where.* New York: Grove Press, 1984.

————. *Poems in English.* New York: Grove Press, 1961.

————. *Proust.* 1931; New York: Grove Press, 1970.

————. *Quad.* In *Collected Shorter Plays by Samuel Beckett.* New York: Grove Press, 1984, 289–94.

————. *Radio II.* In *Ends and Odds.* New York: Grove Press, 1976, 115–28.

————. *Rockaby and Other Short Pieces.* New York: Grove Press, 1981.

————. *Stories and Texts for Nothing.* New York: Grove Press, 1967.

————. *Texts for Nothing.* In *No's Knife: Collected Shorter Prose, 1945–1966.* London: Calder and Boyars, 1967.

————. "Three Dialogues by Samuel Beckett and Georges Duthuit." In *Samuel Beckett: A Collection of Critical Essays.* Ed. Martin Esslin. Englewood Cliffs, N.J.: Prentice-Hall, 1965, 16–22.

————. *Three Novels (Molloy/Malone Dies/The Unnamable).* New York: Grove Press, 1965.

————. *Waiting for Godot.* New York: Grove Press, 1954.

————. *Watt.* New York: Grove Press, 1959.

————. *Worstward Ho.* London: John Calder; New York: Grove Press, 1983.

————, and Jasper Johns. *Foirades/Fizzles.* New York: Petersburg Press, 1976.

———— et al. *Our Exagmination Round his Factification for Incamination of Work in Progress.* 1929; reprint, London: Faber and Faber, 1972.

Ben-Zvi, Linda. "Fritz Mauthner for Company." *Journal of Beckett Studies* 9 (1984): 65–88.

————. "Samuel Beckett, Fritz Mauthner, and the Limits of Language." *PMLA* 95 (1980): 183–200.

————. "The Schismatic Self in *A Piece of Monologue.*" *Journal of Beckett Studies* 7 (Spring 1982): 9–17.

Bergler, Edmund. "A Clinical Contribution to the Psychogenesis of Humor." *Psychoanalytical Review* 24 (1937): 34–53.

Bergson, Henri. *Laughter*. Trans. Claudesley Brereton and Fred Rothwell. New York: Macmillan, 1921.

Bernal, Olga. *Langage et fiction dans le roman de Beckett*. Paris: Gallimard, 1969.

Brater, Enoch. "The *Company* Beckett Keeps: The Shape of Memory and One Fablist's Decay of Lying." In *Samuel Beckett: Humanistic Perspectives*. Ed. Morris Beja, S. E. Gontarski, and Pierre Astier. Columbus: Ohio State University Press, 1983, 157–71.

———. "Dada, Surrealism and the Genesis of *Not I*." *Modern Drama* 18 (1975): 49–59.

———. "Light, Sound, Movement, and Action in Beckett's *Rockaby*." *Modern Drama* 25, no. 3 (September 1982): 342–48.

———. "Still/Beckett: The Essential and the Incidental." *Journal of Modern Literature* 3 (1977): 3–16.

Brooks, Curtis M. "The Mythic Pattern in *Waiting for Godot*." *Modern Drama* 9 (December 1966): 292–99.

Bruss, Elizabeth. *Autobiographical Acts: The Changing Situation of a Literary Genre*. Baltimore: Johns Hopkins University Press, 1976.

Buffet, Gabrielle. "Magic Circles." *View* 5 (1945): 14–23.

Burke, Kenneth. *Attitudes Toward History*. New York: New Republic Press, 1937.

Busi, Frederick. *The Transformations of Godot*. Lexington: University Press of Kentucky, 1980.

Butler, Alban. *Lives of the Saints*, vol. 8. London: Burns Oates & Washbourn, 1933.

Cabanne, Pierre. *Dialogues with Marcel Duchamp*. Trans. Ron Padgett. New York: Viking Press, 1971.

Canaris, Volker, ed. *Samuel Beckett "Das letzte Band." Regiebuch der Berliner Inszenierung*. Frankfurt: Suhrkamp, 1970.

Carey, Elaine. "Donald Davis Brings Beckett Back Home." *Toronto Star*, 10 March 1984, sec. H, 1.

Carroll, Lewis. *Logique sans peine*. Illustrations de Max Ernst. Paris: Hermann, 1966.

Cary, Langlede, and Taburet Missoffe. *Dictionnaire des Saints*. Paris: Editions François Beauval, 1969.

Chubb, Kenneth. "Metaphors, Mad Dogs and Old Time Cowboys." An interview with Sam Shepard. *Theatre Quarterly* 4 (August–October 1974): 3–16.

Cixous, Hélène, and Catherine Clément. *La Jeune Née*. Paris: Union Générale d'Editions, 1975.

Cockerham, Harry. "Bilingual Playwright." In *Beckett the Shape Changer*. Ed. Katharine Worth. London and Boston: Routledge and Kegan Paul, 1975, 139–59.

Cody, Richard. *The Landscape of the Mind: Pastoralism and Platonic Theory in Tasso's "Aminta" and Shakespeare's Early Comedies*. Oxford: Clarendon Press, 1969.

Coe, Richard. *Samuel Beckett*. New York: Grove Press, 1969.

Cohn, Ruby. *Back to Beckett*. Princeton: Princeton University Press, 1973.

———. *Just Play: Beckett's Theater*. Princeton: Princeton University Press, 1980.

———. "The Laughter of Sad Sam Beckett." In *Samuel Beckett Now: Critical Approaches to His Novels, Poetry, and Plays*. Ed. Melvin J. Friedman. Chicago: University of Chicago Press, 1970, 185–97.

———. *New American Dramatists: 1960–1980*. New York: Grove Press, 1984.

———. "Philosophical Fragments in the Works of Samuel Beckett." *Criticism* 6 (1964): 33–43.

———. *Samuel Beckett: The Comic Gamut*. New Brunswick: Rutgers University Press, 1962.

———. "Samuel Beckett, Self-Translator." *PMLA* 76 (December 1961): 613–21.

———, ed. *Disjecta: Miscellaneous Writings and a Dramatic Fragment*. New York: Grove Press, 1984.

Conrad, Joseph. *Heart of Darkness*. Ed. Robert Kimbraugh. New York: W. W. Norton, 1971.

Cooley, Thomas. *Educated Lives: The Rise of Modern Autobiography in America*. Columbus: Ohio State University Press, 1976.

Copeland, Hannah C. *Art and the Artist in the Works of Samuel Beckett*. The Hague: Mouton, 1975.

Craig, George. "The Voice of Childhood and Great Age." In *Times Literary Supplement*, 27 August 1982, p. 921.

Crystal, David. *A First Dictionary of Linguistics and Phonetics*. Boulder, Colo.: Westview Press, 1980.

Dante Alighieri. *The Divine Comedy*. Trans. John D. Sinclair. 3 vols. Reprint, 1939. New York: Oxford University Press, 1968–70.

Dearlove, Judith E. *Accommodating the Chaos: Samuel Beckett's Nonrelational Art*. Durham, N.C.: Duke University Press, 1982.

Deleuze, Gilles. *Différence et répétition*. Paris: Presses universitaires de France, 1968.

de Man, Paul. "Autobiography as De-facement." *Modern Language Notes* 94 (1979): 919–30.

Denes, Peter B., and Elliot N. Pinson. *The Speech Chain: The Physics and Biology of Spoken Language*. New York: Anchor Books, 1973.

Donne, John. *Poetical Works*. Ed. Herbert J. C. Grierson. Oxford University Press, 1971.

Duchamp, Marcel. *The Bride Stripped Bare by Her Bachelors, Even*. Ed. Richard Hamilton. Trans. George Heard Hamilton. London: Lund Humphries, 1960.

———. *Notes and Projects for the Large Glass*. Ed. Arturo Schwarz. New York: Harry N. Abrams, 1969.

———. *Salt Seller*. Ed. Michel Sanouille and Elmer Peterson. New York: Oxford University Press, 1973.

Eastman, Max. *The Sense of Humor*. New York: Charles Scribner's Sons, 1921.

Erhardt, H. M. *Akt ohne Worte I. Akt ohne Worte II [Act Without Words I and II]*. Stuttgart: Manus Presse, 1965. (linocuts)

———. *Bing [Ping]*. Stuttgart: Manus Presse, 1970. (drawings)

———. *Kommen und Gehen [Come and Go]*. Stuttgart: Manus Presse, 1968. (etchings)

———. *Watt*. Stuttgart. Manus Presse, 1971. (etchings)

Ernst, Max. *Les malheurs des immortels*. Paris: Editions de la Fontaine, 1922.

———. *Maximiliana ou l'exercice illégal de l'astronomie*. Paris: Iliazd, 1964.

Esslin, Martin. "Introduction." In *Samuel Beckett: A Collection of Critical Essays*. Ed. Martin Esslin. Englewood Cliffs, N.J.: Prentice-Hall, 1965, 1–15.

———. *Mediations*. Baton Rouge: Louisiana State University Press, 1980.

———. *The Theatre of the Absurd*. New York: Doubleday, Anchor Books, 1961.

Falk, Florence. "The Role of Performance in Sam Shepard's Plays." *Theatre Journal* 33, no. 2 (May 1981): 182–98.

Federman, Raymond. "The Impossibility of Saying the Same Old Thing in the Same Old Way: Samuel Beckett's *Comment c'est*." *L'esprit créateur* 11 (Fall 1971): 21–43.

———. *Journey to Chaos: Samuel Beckett's Early Fiction*. Berkeley: University of California Press, 1970.

Fitch, Brian T. "L'Intra-intertextualité interlinguistique de Beckett: La problématique de la traduction de soi." *Texte* 2 (1983): 85–100.

———. "La Problématique de l'étude de l'oeuvre bilingue de Beckett." *Symposium* 38 (Summer 1984): 91–112.

———. "The Status of Self-Translation." *Texte* 4 (1985): 111–25.

———. "Textualité." In *Dimensions, structures et textualité dans la trilogie romanesque de Beckett*. Paris: Lettres Modernes, 1977, 127–83.

Fleishman, Avrom. *Figures of Autobiography: The Language of Self-Writing in Victorian and Modern England*. Berkeley: University of California Press, 1983.

Fletcher, John. "Ecrivain bilingue." In *Samuel Beckett*, special issue of *Cahier de l'Herne*. Ed. Tom Bishop and Raymond Federman. Paris: Editions de l'Herne, 1976, 212–18.

———. *The Novels of Samuel Beckett*. London: Chatto and Windus, 1972.

———. *Samuel Beckett's Art*. London: Chatto and Windus, 1967.

Frankl, Victor. *Man's Search for Meaning: An Introduction to Logotherapy.* New York: Pocket Books, 1959; reprint, 1963.

Frazer, Sir James G. *The Golden Bough,* vol. 1, pt. 4. 3d ed., 1914; reprint, London: Macmillan, 1966.

Freud, Sigmund. "Humour." In *The Complete Psychological Works of Sigmund Freud.* Trans. James Strachey. London: Hogarth Press, 1961, 160–66.

———. "The Uncanny." In *The Complete Psychological Works of Sigmund Freud.* Trans. James Strachey. London: Hogarth Press, 1961, 219–52.

———. *Jokes and Their Relation to the Unconscious.* Trans. James Strachey. New York: W. W. Norton, 1960.

Friedman, Melvin J. "The Creative Writer as Polyglot: Valery Larbaud and Samuel Beckett." *Transactions of the Wisconsin Academy of Sciences, Art and Letters* 49 (1960): 229–36.

Frye, Northrop. *The Anatomy of Criticism.* Princeton: Princeton University Press, 1957.

Gallwitz, Klaus. *HM Erhardt* (publisher's catalogue). Stuttgart: Manus Presse, 1973.

Gelber, Jack. "Sam Shepard: The Playwright as Shaman." Introduction to *Angel City,* by Sam Shepard. New York: Urizen Books, 1981, 1–4.

Golding, William. *A Moving Target.* London: Faber and Faber, 1982.

Gontarski, S. E. "Film and Formal Integrity." In *Samuel Beckett: Humanistic Perspectives.* Eds. Morris Beja, S. E. Gontarski, and Pierre Astier. Columbus: Ohio State University Press, 1983, 129–36.

———. *The Intent of Undoing in Samuel Beckett's Dramatic Texts.* Bloomington: Indiana University Press, 1985.

Graver, Lawrence, and Raymond Federman, eds. *Samuel Beckett: The Critical Heritage.* London and Boston: Routledge and Kegan Paul, 1979.

Grice, Paul. "Logic and Conversation." Unpublished manuscript of the William James Lectures, Harvard University.

Gunn, Janet Varner. *Autobiography: Toward a Poetics of Experience.* Philadelphia: University of Pennsylvania Press, 1982.

Gussow, Mel. "Billie Whitelaw's Guide to Performing Beckett." *New York Times,* 14 February 1984, 21.

Haerdter, Michael. "Samuel Beckett inszeniert das 'Endspiel.' " In *Materialen zu Beckett's 'Endspiel.'* Frankfurt: Suhrkamp, 1968, 54–59.

Hardwick, Elizabeth. "An Introduction: *La Turista.*" In *American Dreams: The Imagination of Sam Shepard.* Ed. Bonnie Marranca. New York: Performing Arts Journal Publications, 1981, 67–73.

Harvey, Lawrence. "Samuel Beckett on Life, Art, and Criticism." *Modern Language Notes* 80 (December 1965): 545–62.

———. *Samuel Beckett: Poet and Critic.* Princeton: Princeton University Press, 1970.

Hayman, David. "Joyce/Beckett/Joyce." In *The Seventh of Joyce.* Ed. Bernard Benstock. Bloomington: Indiana University Press, 1982, 38–40.

———. "A Meeting in the Park and a Meeting on the Bridge: Joyce and Beckett." *The James Joyce Quarterly* 8, no. 4 (Summer 1971): 372–84.

———. "Quest for Meaninglessness: The Boundless Poverty of *Molloy.*" In *Beckett Now.* Ed. Melvin Friedman. Chicago: University of Chicago Press, 1970, 140–45.

Hayman, Ronald. *Theatre and Anti-Theatre: New Movements Since Beckett.* New York: Oxford University Press, 1979.

———. *Tom Stoppard.* London: Heinemann, 1977.

Heaney, Seamus. "An Interview with Frank Kinahan." *Critical Inquiry* 8 (1982): 405–14.

Henry, Parrish Dice. "Got It at Last, My Legend: Homage to Samuel Beckett." *Georgia Review* 36 (Summer 1982): 429–34.

Hobsen, Harold. "Samuel Beckett: Dramatist of the Year." *International Theatre Annual.* London, 1956, 153–55.

Hoeffer, Jacqueline. "Watt." *Perspective* 11 (1959): 166–82.

Hoffman, Samuel. *Samuel Beckett: The Language of Self.* Carbondale and Edwardsville: Southern Illinois University Press, 1962.

Homan, Sidney. *Beckett's Theatres: Interpretations for Performance.* Lewisburg, Pa.: Bucknell University Press, 1984.

House, Juliane. "Of the Limits of Translatability." *Babel* 19, no. 4 (1973): 166–67.

Hübner, Alfred. *Samuel Beckett inszeniert 'Glückliche Tage,'* Probenprotokoll von Alfred Hübner, Fotos von Horst Güldemeister. Frankfurt: Suhrkamp, 1976.

Hunt, John Dixon. *The Figure in the Landscape: Poetry, Painting, and Gardening in the Eighteenth Century.* Baltimore: Johns Hopkins University Press, 1976.

Jacobsen, Josephine, and William Mueller. *The Testament of Samuel Beckett.* New York: Hill and Wang, 1964.

Jakobson, Roman. "Poetry of Grammar and Grammar of Poetry." *Lingua* 21 (1968): 597–609.

James, E. O. *The Cult of the Mother-Goddess.* New York: Barnes and Noble, 1959.

Janvier, Ludovic. *Pour Samuel Beckett.* Paris: Les Editions de Minuit, 1966.

———. "Lieu Dire." In *Samuel Beckett,* special issue of *Cahier de l'Herne.* Ed. Tom Bishop and Raymond Federman. Paris: Editions de l'Herne, 1976, 193–205.

Jonas, Hans. *The Gnostic Religion.* Boston: Beacon Press, 1958.

Joyce, James. *Finnegans Wake.* New York: Viking Press, 1966.

———. *A Portrait of the Artist as a Young Man.* 1916; reprint, New York: Viking Press, 1964.

Jung, Carl G. *Symbols of Transformation,* 2d ed. Princeton: Princeton University Press, 1967.

Kafka, Franz. "In the Penal Colony." In *The Penal Colony: Stories and Short Pieces.* New York: Schocken Books, 1948.

Kennedy, Sighle. *Murphy's Bed.* Lewisburg, Pa.: Bucknell University Press, 1971.

Kenner, Hugh. "Beckett Translating Beckett: *Comment c'est.*" *Delos* 5 (1970): 194–210.

———. *Flaubert, Joyce, and Beckett: The Stoic Comedians.* Boston: Beacon Press, 1962.

———. *Samuel Beckett: A Critical Study.* Berkeley and Los Angeles: University of California Press; London: John Calder, 1961. Revised edition, 1968.

Kermode, Frank. *English Pastoral Poetry.* London: G. C. Harrap, 1952.

Kern, Edith. "Beckett and the Spirit of the Commedia dell'arte." *Modern Drama* 9 (1966): 260–67.

Knott, John R., Jr. *Milton's Pastoral Vision: An Approach to Paradise Lost.* Chicago: University of Chicago Press, 1971.

Knowlson, James. "Beckett's 'Bits of Pipe.' " In *Samuel Beckett: Humanistic Perspectives.* Ed. Morris Beja, S. E. Gontarski, and Pierre Astier. Columbus: Ohio State University Press, 1983, 16–25.

———. " 'Krapp's Last Tape': The Evolution of a Play, 1958–1975." *Journal of Beckett Studies* 1 (Winter 1976): 54–56, 59–65.

———. *Light and Darkness in the Theatre of Samuel Beckett.* London: Turret Books, 1972.

———, ed. *Samuel Beckett: Krapp's Last Tape. Theatre Workbook No. 1.* London: Brutus Books, 1980.

———, and John Pilling. *Frescoes of the Skull: The Later Prose and Drama of Samuel Beckett.* London: John Calder, 1979.

Kott, Jan. *Shakespeare Our Contemporary.* Trans. Boleslaw Taborski. New York: W. W. Norton, 1974.

Kris, Ernest. *Psychoanalytic Explorations in Art.* New York: Schocken Books, 1952; reprint 1964.

Kristeva, Julia. "La Père, l'amour, l'exil." In *Cahier de l'Herne.* Ed. Tom Bishop and Raymond Federman. Paris: Editions de l'Herne, 1976, 246–52.

Lacan, Jacques. *Ecrits.* Paris: Seuil, 1966.

Lamont, Rosette. "The Metaphysical Farce: Beckett and Ionesco." *French Review* 32 (1969): 319–28.

Langdon, Stephen. *Tammuz and Ishtar.* Oxford: Clarendon Press, 1914.

Lebel, Robert. *Marcel Duchamp.* Trans. George Heard Hamilton. New York: Grove Press, 1959.

Lejeune, Philippe. *Le Pacte autobiographique.* Paris: Seuil, 1975.

Levy, Jacques. "Notes on *Red Cross.*" In *Chicago and Other Plays, by Sam Shepard.* New York: Urizen Books, 1967.

Lewis, Wyndham. "Studies in the Art of Laughter." In *Enemy Salvoes: Selected Literary Criticism.* Ed. C. J. Fox. New York: Barnes and Noble, 1976, 41–49.

Ludovici, Anthony. *The Secret of Laughter.* New York: Viking Press, 1933.

Marks, Elaine, and Isabelle de Courtivron, eds. *New French Feminism: An Anthology.* Amherst: University of Massachusetts Press, 1980.

Marranca, Bonnie, ed. *American Dreams: The Imagination of Sam Shepard.* New York: Performing Arts Journal Publications, 1981.

Marvell, Andrew. *The Poems of Andrew Marvell.* Ed. H. M. Margoliouth. Oxford: Clarendon Press, 1927.

McCarthy, Gerry. " 'Acting It Out': Sam Shepard's *Action.*" *Modern Drama* 24 (March 1981): 1–12.

McMillan, Dougald. "Samuel Beckett and the Visual Arts: The Embarrassment of Allegory." In *Samuel Beckett: A Collection of Criticism.* Ed. Ruby Cohn. New York: McGraw-Hill, 1975, 121–36.

Mercier, Vivian. *Beckett/Beckett.* New York: Oxford University Press, 1977.

———. "How to Read 'Endgame.' " *The Griffin* 8 (1959): 10–14.

———. *The Irish Comic Tradition.* London: Oxford University Press, 1962.

Meschonnic, Henri. *Pour la poétique.* Paris: Gallimard, 1970.

Meumann, Erich. *The Great Mother,* 2d ed. Princeton: Princeton University Press, 1963.

Mikes, George. *Laughing Matter: Towards a Personal Philosophy of Wit and Humor.* New York: Library Press, 1971.

Miller, J. Hillis. "Ariadne's Thread, Repetition and Narrative Line." *Critical Inquiry* 3 (1976): 57–77.

Milton, John. *Complete Poems and Major Prose.* Ed. Merritt Y. Hughes. New York: Odyssey Press, 1957.

Moorjani, Angela B. *Abysmal Games in the Novels of Samuel Beckett.* Chapel Hill: University of North Carolina Studies in the Romance Languages and Literatures, 1982.

Morot-Sir, Edouard. "Samuel Beckett and Cartesian Emblems." In *Samuel Beckett: The Art of Rhetoric.* Ed. E. Morot-Sir. Chapel Hill: University of North Carolina Studies in the Romance Languages and Literatures, 1976, 25–104.

Morrison, Kristin. *Canters and Chronicles: The Use of Narrative in the Plays of Samuel Beckett and Harold Pinter.* Chicago: University of Chicago Press, 1983.

Morton, Henry C. V. *In Search of London.* New York: Dodd, Mead, 1951.

Myrdal, Gunnar. *An American Dilemma: The Negro Problem and Modern Democracy.* New York: Harper and Brothers, 1944.

Nadeau, Maurice. "Samuel Beckett: Humor and the Void." In *Samuel Beckett: A Collection of Critical Essays.* Ed. Martin Esslin. Englewood Cliffs, N.J.: Prentice-Hall, 1965, 33–36.

Niebuhr, Reinhold. "Humor and Faith." In *Holy Laughter.* Ed. M. Conrad Hyers. New York: Seabury Press, 1969, 134–49.

Obrdlik, Anton. " 'Gallows Humor': A Sociological Phenomenon." *American Journal of Sociology* 47 (1942): 709–16.

Onimus, Jean. *Beckett.* Paris: Desclée de Brouwer, 1968.

Pagels, Elaine. *The Gnostic Gospels.* New York: Random House, Vintage, 1981.

Panofsky, Erwin. "*Et in Arcadia ego:* Poussin and the Elegiac Tradition." In *Meaning in the Visual Arts.* Garden City, N.Y.: Doubleday, Anchor, 1955.

Pearce, Richard. *The Novel of Motion*. Columbus: Ohio State University Press, 1983.

Perloff, Marjorie. "Between Verse and Prose: Beckett and the New Poetry." *Critical Inquiry* 9 (1982): 415–33.

Philips, Ambrose. *Pastorals, Epistles, and Other Original Poems*. Facsimile ed. Menston, England: Scolar Press, 1973.

Pilling, John. *Samuel Beckett*. London: Routledge and Kegan Paul, 1976.

Plyusch, Leonid. *History's Carnival: A Dissident's Autobiography*. Ed. and trans. Marco Carynnyk. New York and London: Harcourt Brace Jovanovich, 1979.

Pope, Alexander. *The Poems of Alexander Pope*. Ed. John Butt. New Haven: Yale University Press, 1963.

Prinz, Jessica. "Foirades/Fizzles/Beckett/Johns." *Contemporary Literature* 9 (Summer 1980): 480–510.

Pynchon, Thomas. *The Crying of Lot 49*. New York: Bantam, 1982.

Rabinovitz, Rubin. *The Development of Samuel Beckett's Fiction*. Champaign: University of Illinois Press, 1984.

Read, David. "Beckett's Search for Unseeable and Unmakeable: *Company* and *Ill Seen Ill Said*." *Modern Fiction Studies* 29 (Summer 1983): 111–26.

Reik, Theodor. *Lust und Leid im Witz*. Vienna: Internationaler Psychoanalytischer Verlag, 1929.

Renza, Louis A. "The Veto of the Imagination: A Theory of Autobiography." *New Literary History* 9 (1977): 5–22. Reprinted in *Autobiography: Essays Theoretical and Critical*. Ed. James Olney. Princeton: Princeton University Press, 1980, 268–95.

Robbe-Grillet, Alain. *For a New Novel: Essays on Fiction*. Trans. Richard Howard. New York: Grove Press, 1966.

Robinson, James M., ed. *The Nag Hammadi Library in English*. San Francisco: Harper and Row, 1981.

Robinson, Michael. "From Purgatory to the Inferno: Beckett and Dante Revisited." In *Journal of Beckett Studies* 5 (Autumn 1979): 60–83.

———. *The Long Sonata of the Dead*. New York: Grove Press, 1969.

Rosen, Stephen J. *Samuel Beckett and the Pessimistic Tradition*. New Brunswick: Rutgers University Press, 1976.

Rudolph, Kurt. *Gnosis*. Ed. and trans. Robert McLachlan Wilson. San Francisco: Harper and Row, 1983.

Rusinko, Elaine. "Intertextuality: The Soviet Approach to Subtext." *Dispositio* 4 (1979): 212–35.

Sapir, Edward. *Language*. New York: Harcourt, Brace, 1949.

Sartre, Jean-Paul. "Foreward: Rats and Men." In André Gorz, *The Traitor*. Trans. Richard Howard. New York: Simon and Schuster, 1959, 1–36.

Schneider, Alan. "Waiting for Beckett." *Chelsea Review* 2 (1958): 3–20.

———. "Working with Beckett." In *Samuel Beckett: The Art of Rhetoric*. Ed. Edouard Morot-Sir. Chapel Hill: University of North Carolina Studies in the Romance Languages and Literatures, No. 5 (1976): 271–89.

Scott, Nathan. *Samuel Beckett*. London: Bowes and Bowes, 1965.

Sheedy, John J. "The Comic Apocalypse of King Hamm." *Modern Drama* 9 (1966): 310–18.

Shenker, Israel. "Moody Man of Letters: A Portrait of Samuel Beckett, Author of the Puzzling *Waiting for Godot*." *New York Times*, 6 May 1956, sec. 2, 1–3.

Shepard, Sam. *Angel City, Curse of the Starving Class and Other Plays*. New York: Urizen Books, 1981.

———. *Fool for Love and Other Plays*. New York: Bantam Books, 1984.

———. "Metaphors, Mad Dogs, and Old Time Cowboys." *Theatre Quarterly* 4 (August–October 1974): 3–16.

———. "Underground Landscapes" (an interview). *The Guardian*, 20 February 1974, 8.

———. "Visualization, Language and the Inner Library." *Drama Review* 21 (1977): 49–58.

Sheppard, Richard. "The Crises of Language." In *Modernism: 1890–1930*. Ed. Malcolm Bradbury and James MacFarlane. New York: Penguin Books, 1978, 323–26.

Sherzer, Dina. *Structure de la trilogie de Beckett*. The Hague: Mouton, 1976.

———. "Saying Is Inventing: Gnomic Expressions in *Molloy*." In *Speech Play*. Ed. Barbara Kirshenblatt-Gimblett. Philadelphia: University of Pennsylvania Press, 1976, 163–71.

———. "Dialogic Incongruities in the Theater of the Absurd." *Semiotica* 22, no. 2/6 (1978): 271–85.

———. "Endgame, or what talk can do," *Modern Drama* 5 (1979): 291–303.

———. "Didi, Gogo, Pozzo, Lucky: Linguistes déconstructeurs." *Etudes littéraires* 3 (December 1980): 539–58.

Simon, Alfred. *Beckett*. Paris: Pierre Belfond, 1983.

Simon, John. "Theater: Underwriting." *New York*, 12 March 1984, 96–97.

Simpson, Ekundayo. *Samuel Beckett: Traducteur de lui-même: Aspects de bilingualisme littéraire*. Quebec: International Center for Research on Bilingualism, 1978.

Skerl, Jennie. "Fritz Mauthner's Critique of Language in Samuel Beckett's *Watt*." *Contemporary Literature* 15 (1974): 474–87.

Smith, Hallett. *Elizabethan Poetry: A Study in Conventions, Meaning, and Expression*. Cambridge: Harvard University Press, 1966.

Solomon, Philip H. *The Life After Birth: Imagery in Samuel Beckett's Trilogy*. University of Mississippi: Romance Monographs, 1975.

Spenser, Edmund. *The Works of Edmund Spenser: A Variorum Edition*. Ed. Edwin Greenlaw et al. Baltimore: Johns Hopkins University Press, 1943.

Spies, Werner. *Max Ernst, Loplop, the Artist in the Third Person*. New York: Braziller, 1983.

Spretnak, Charlene. *Lost Goddesses of Early Greece*. Boston: Beacon Press, 1981.

Stephan, Jude. *Nouvelle Revue Française* 344 (1981): 126.

Stewart, Philip. *Imitation and Illusion in the French Memoir-Novel, 1700–1750: The Art of Make-Believe*. New Haven: Yale University Press, 1969.

Strauss, Walter. "Dante's Belacqua and Beckett's Tramps." *Comparative Literature* 11 (Summer 1959): 250–61.

Tagliaferri, Aldo. *Beckett et la surdétermination littéraire*. Paris: Payot, 1977.

Takahashi, Yasunari. "Fool's Progress." In *Samuel Beckett: A Collection of Criticism*. Ed. Ruby Cohn. New York: McGraw-Hill, 1975, 33–40.

Taranovsky, Kiril. *Essays on Mandel'štam*. Cambridge: Harvard University Press, 1976.

Taubman, Robert. "Beckett's Buttonhook." *London Review of Books*, 21 October–3 November 1982, 16.

Tayler, Edward William. *Nature and Art in Renaissance Literature*. New York: Columbia University Press, 1964.

Theocritus. Trans. H. Rushton Fairclough. Cambridge: Harvard University Press, 1928.

Thomas, Dylan. *The Collected Poems of Dylan Thomas*. New York: New Directions, 1957.

Thomson, James. *The Seasons*. Ed. James Sambrook. Oxford: Clarendon Press, 1972.

Tillotson, Geoffrey. *Augustan Poetic Diction*. London: Athlone Press, 1964.

Todorov, Tzvetan. *Mikhaïl Bakhtine: Le Principe dialogique, suivi de[s] Ecrits du Cercle de Bakhtine*. Paris: Seuil, "Poétique," 1981.

Tomkins, Calvin. *The Bride and the Bachelors: Five Masters of the Avant-Garde*. New York: Viking Press, 1965.

Virgil. Trans. H. Rushton Fairclough. Loeb Classical Library. Revised edition. Cambridge: Harvard University Press, 1935.

Walker, Barbara G. *The Woman's Encyclopedia of Myths and Secrets*. San Francisco: Harper and Row, 1983.

Watts, Ann Chalmers. "*Pearl*, Inexpressibility and Poems of Human Loss." *PMLA* 99 (1984): 26–44.

Webb, Eugene. *The Plays of Samuel Beckett.* Seattle: University of Washington Press; London: Peter Owen, 1972.

———. *Samuel Beckett: A Study of the Novels.* Seattle: University of Washington Press, 1973.

Weiler, Gershon. *Mauthner's Critique of Language.* Cambridge: Cambridge University Press, 1970.

White, James, ed. *Jack B. Yeats: A Centenary Exhibition.* Dublin, September to December 1971.

Wittgenstein, Ludwig. *Philosophical Investigations.* New York: Macmillan, 1968.

Wordsworth, William. *Selected Poems and Prefaces.* Ed. Jack Stillinger. Boston: Houghton Mifflin, 1965.

———, and Samuel Taylor Coleridge. *Lyrical Ballads.* Ed. R. L. Brett and A. R. Jones. London: Methuen, 1963.

Worth, Katharine, ed. *Beckett the Shape Changer.* London and Boston: Routledge and Kegan Paul, 1975.

Yeats, W. B. *The Collected Poems of W. B. Yeats.* New York: Macmillan, 1950.

Notes on the Editors and Contributors

H. PORTER ABBOTT is professor and chair of the department of English at the University of California, Santa Barbara. His publications include *The Fiction of Samuel Beckett* and *Diary Fiction: Writing as Action.*

LINDA BEN-ZVI is professor of English at Colorado State University. She is the author of *Samuel Beckett*, as well as of numerous articles on Beckett, James Joyce, Harold Pinter, Eugene O'Neill, and Susan Glaspell.

TOM BISHOP, Florence Gould Professor of French Literature and chair of the department of French and English at New York University, is the author of numerous works in French and English and the co-editor of *Cahier de l'Herne.*

SUSAN BRIENZA teaches twentieth-century literature at UCLA. She is an officer of the Samuel Beckett society, and past editor of the society's newsletter. She has written numerous articles on such writers as Beckett, Joyce, and E. L. Doctorow.

LORI CHAMBERLAIN, visiting lecturer in the department of literature at the University of California, San Diego, has published articles on contemporary poetry and fiction. She is at work on a book on the semiotics of translation.

RUBY COHN is professor of Comparative Literature at the University of California, Davis. She has written and edited numerous books on Beckett, including *Samuel Beckett: The Comic Gamut*, *Back to Beckett*, and *Just Play: Beckett's Theater.*

MARTIN ESSLIN teaches drama at Stanford University. Before that he was head of Radio Drama at the BBC and collaborated with Samuel Beckett on a number of broadcasts. He is the author of *The Theatre of the Absurd*, as well as books on Harold Pinter, Antonin Artaud, Bertolt Brecht, and others.

RAYMOND FEDERMAN teaches in the English department at SUNY–Buffalo. A bilingual writer, he is the author of two volumes of poetry, three books of criticism on Samuel Beckett, and six novels, including *Smiles on Washington Square*, which won the American Book Award for 1986.

BRIAN T. FITCH is Gerald Larkin Professor of French at Trinity College, University of Toronto. He is the author of books on Beckett, Camus, Malraux,

Green, Georges Bernanos, and Georges Bataille, as well as founding editor of the journal *Albert Camus* and founding co-editor of the journal *Texte*.

ALAN WARREN FRIEDMAN is professor of English at the University of Texas at Austin. He is the author or editor of six books, including recent books on Faulkner and Lawrence Durrell. His many essays treat such diverse subjects as Joseph Conrad, E. M. Forster, Virginia Woolf, Lawrence Durrell, and Shakespeare.

DAVID HAYMAN teaches Comparative Literature at the University of Wisconsin. Despite his numerous publications on Beckett, he does not think of himself as a "Beckettian." His most recent books are *In the Wake of the Wake* and *Vision a New York*. Several current projects involve James Joyce.

RENÉE RIESE HUBERT is professor of French and Comparative Literature at the University of California, Irvine. She has published widely on modern poetry and the relations of literature to the fine arts. She is the author of *Surrealism and the Book*.

ROSETTE LAMONT is professor of French and Comparative Literature at CUNY. She recently finished a year as visiting professor at the Université de Paris III. She is the author of numerous essays and reviews on a wide variety of topics.

BREON MITCHELL is professor of Comparative Literature and Germanic Studies at Indiana University. He compiled and wrote the catalogue for *Beyond Illustration: The Livre d'Artiste in the Twentieth Century*. He writes regularly on contemporary literature.

ANGELA B. MOORJANI is associate professor of French at the University of Maryland, Baltimore County. She is the author of *Abysmal Games in the Novels of Samuel Beckett* and has published a number of deconstructive readings of myth in Beckett's fiction.

MARJORIE PERLOFF is professor of English and Comparative Literature at Stanford. She is the author of numerous articles and several books. Her most recent book is *The Futurist Moment: Avant-Garde, Avant-Guerre, and the Language of Rupture*.

JESSICA PRINZ is assistant professor of English at Ohio State University. She has published articles on Milton, Pound, and Beckett and Jasper Johns. She is currently at work on a study of contemporary interdisciplinary art.

RUBIN RABINOVITZ is professor of English at the University of Colorado, Boulder. He is the author of three books, including *The Development of Samuel Beckett's Fiction*, as well as numerous essays and reviews. He also writes frequently about computers.

CHARLES ROSSMAN, associate professor of English at the University of Texas at Austin, has edited or co-edited previous collections of essays on Mario Vargas Llosa, Carlos Fuentes, and Gabriel García Márquez. His essays and reviews, chiefly on D. H. Lawrence and James Joyce, have appeared in a variety of journals.

RICHARD KELLER SIMON has taught at the University of California, San Diego, and at the University of Texas at Austin. He is the author of *The Labyrinth of the Comic: Theory and Practice from Fielding to Freud*, and of several essays.

DINA SHERZER is professor of French at the University of Texas at Austin. In addition to articles on Beckett's plays, she has published a book on Beckett's trilogy, *Structure de la trilogie de Beckett: Molloy, Malone meurt, L'Innommable*. Her recent book, *Contemporary French Fiction*, contains a section on Beckett.

FREDERIK N. SMITH is professor and chair of the department of English at the University of North Carolina, Charlotte. He has published a book and numerous articles on Jonathan Swift, as well as articles on modern fiction.

HERSH ZEIFMAN, associate professor of English at York University, Toronto, is on the executive board of the Samuel Beckett Society and the advisory board of *Modern Drama*. He has published many articles on Beckett, Stoppard, and Pinter.